POLAR COUSINS

BEYOND BOUNDARIES: CANADIAN DEFENCE AND STRATEGIC STUDIES SERIES

Rob Huebert, Series Editor
ISSN 1716-2645 (Print) ISSN 1925-2919 (Online)

Canada's role in international military and strategic studies ranges from peacebuilding and Arctic sovereignty to unconventional warfare and domestic security. This series provides narratives and analyses of the Canadian military from both an historical and a contemporary perspective.

UNIVERSITY OF CALGARY
Press

POLAR COUSINS

Comparing Antarctic and Arctic Geostrategic Futures

Edited by

CHRISTIAN LEUPRECHT

with

DOUGLAS CAUSEY

Beyond Boundaries:
Canadian Defence and Strategic Studies Series
ISSN 1716-2645 (Print) ISSN 1925-2919 (Online)

University of Calgary Press
2500 University Drive NW
Calgary, Alberta
Canada T2N 1N4
press.ucalgary.ca

LIBRARY AND ARCHIVES CANADA CATALOGUING IN PUBLICATION

Title: Polar cousins : comparing Antarctic and Arctic geostrategic futures / edited by Christian
    Leuprecht with Douglas Causey.
Names: Leuprecht, Christian, 1973- editor. | Causey, Douglas, editor.
Series: Beyond boundaries series ; no. 12.
Description: Series statement: Beyond boundaries : Canadian defence and strategic studies series,
    1716-2645 ; no. 12 | Includes bibliographical references and index.
Identifiers: Canadiana (print) 20220439559 | Canadiana (ebook) 20220439648 | ISBN
    9781773853888 (softcover) | ISBN 9781773854373 (hardcover) | ISBN 9781773853918 (EPUB) |
    ISBN 9781773853901 (PDF) | ISBN 9781773853895 (Open Access PDF)
Subjects: LCSH: Arctic regions—Strategic aspects. | LCSH: Antarctica—Strategic aspects. | LCSH:
    Security, International—Arctic regions. | LCSH: Security, International—Antarctica. | LCSH:
    Geopolitics—Arctic regions. | LCSH: Geopolitics—Antarctica. | LCSH: Climatic changes—
    Arctic regions. | LCSH: Climatic changes—Antarctica.
Classification: LCC UA880 .P65 2022 | DDC 355/.0335113—dc23

The University of Calgary Press acknowledges the support of the Government of Alberta through
the Alberta Media Fund for our publications. We acknowledge the financial support of the
Government of Canada. We acknowledge the financial support of the Canada Council for the Arts
for our publishing program.

Generous support for this book was provided by the Konrad Adenauer Stiftung.

Printed and bound in Canada by Marquis
♻ This book is printed on Enviro paper

Cover images front:
Daniel R. Strebe, "Azimuthal equidistant projection south SW," May 13, 2018,
https://commons.wikimedia.org/wiki/File:Azimuthal_equidistant_projection_south_SW.jpg
Daniel R. Strebe, "Azimuthal equidistant projection SW," August 15, 2011,
https://en.wikipedia.org/wiki/File:Azimuthal_equidistant_projection_SW.jpg
Cover image back: Colourbox 9097048
Copyediting by Ryan Perks
Cover design, page design, and typesetting by Melina Cusano

Dedicated to my daughter Anna,
who is always up for an adventure outdoors

We acknowledge that this book has been written by scholars living on traditional territory and lands that have belonged to Indigenous peoples since time immemorial.

Contents

Acknowledgements

By and large, geostrategic considerations seem to treat the two poles as distinct. Yet, when Christian spent a year in Australia, he realized the considerable and arguably growing geostrategic complementarity between the Arctic and Antarctic along with the Southern Ocean. At the same time, Douglas was increasingly drawn into resolving some of the complex interactions of sovereignty and environmental security in the Arctic through his establishment of the Arctic Domain Awareness Center at the University of Alaska. So, we orchestrated a dialogue among some clever strategic minds across the northern and southern hemispheres. Five years on, this open access book is the result. The time that has elapsed since this project was initially conceived has only reinforced concern about the deleterious impact of adversarial behaviour and climate change on both poles, the need to learn from complementary experiences, and opportunities for cross-polar collaboration among allies and partners to shape the geostrategic environment across both poles. Polar ice caps that used to be flyover country at the edge of the world have become central to geostrategic competition. How that competition plays out has serious ramifications for environmental, political, economic, and human security and stability around the globe.

Australian Defence underwrote the initial project with competitive funding from their Strategic Policy Grants Program, which, *inter alia*, enabled an author and practitioner workshop in Canberra. The Konrad Adenauer Foundation was so convinced of the project's novelty and broader importance that it agreed to facilitate open access publication of this volume through its fairly new office in Australia. We are especially grateful to the office's former director, Dr. Beatrice Gorawantschy, as well as her successor, Bertil Wenger.

Christian started this project while on a fellowship at Flinders University in Adelaide, South Australia, in collaboration with his local colleague Cassandra, who directs the Climate and Sustainability Policy Research (CASPR) group. She and her team organized and led the author and practitioner workshop leading to this publication in Canberra in December 2019. Regrettably, competing commitments did not allow her to join with us in seeing this publication through to completion. CASPR research associate Dr. Claire Nettle provided indispensable operational, editorial, and administrative support throughout the workshop and initial stages in preparing papers for publication. This project would not have come to fruition without them.

Douglas is most grateful for the assistance and support from his colleagues in the Arctic Initiative of the Harvard Kennedy School's Belfer Center for Science and International Affairs in helping bring this volume to completion. Often the most challenging part of completing a multi-authored volume as this one is left at the end, where all of the fine details of editing are resolved. Daniel Bicknell found time to help considerably in pulling these all together.

We would be equally remiss if we did not acknowledge the unequivocal support from Brian Scrivener, Helen Hajnoczky, and the board at the University of Calgary Press, as well as exceptional copy editing by Anne Holley-Hime, Ryan Perks in readying the manuscript for publication, and editorial assistance by Rhianna Hamilton and Mary Kennedy. I am also thankful to the two peer reviewers who endorsed the quality of the project and whose thoughtful comments greatly enriched the final version of each chapter.

And while we are delighted how the contributors and their chapters came together, a special shoutout goes to three of them: Dr. Heather Nicol, whose mentorship time and again provided us with superior input at critical times from inception through publication, MGen (ret'd) Randy "Church" Kee for this dedication to the polar cause and his friendship, and Dr. Jamie Ferrill, whose skillful intervention, adroit managerial skills, and unwavering and selfless commitment proved vital in leveraging Charles Sturt University and the fine people at their research office to get the project over the line.

Far from being the be all and end all on this topic, this volume instead intends to raise the geostrategic spectre of the two poles to enable a broader, more informed conversation. For too long this topic has flown under the radar; the intent here is to put the *Polar Cousins* on the radar to foster a more comprehensive and integrated approach to global geostrategy among the Five Eyes countries in particular, and polar allies and partners more generally. This volume's title is inspired by a book John Blaxland published some years ago on the way common interests yet divergent domestic circumstances encourage bilateral collaboration that manifests in different security strategies.

As Christian has written elsewhere, the Five Eyes,–the United States, the United Kingdom, Canada, Australia, and New Zealand–are the world's most powerful and long-standing foreign policy coordination mechanism, which sits at the apex of the international security pyramid. The Anglosphere security community of like-minded states is characterized by shared norms, values, and practices. This Anglo-American tradition in foreign affairs has traditionally perpetuated and staked its reputation on a common set of core national interests: sovereignty; security; prosperity; national, regional, international, and transnational security and stability, including the liberal international rules-based order as well as a democratic conception of the rule of law; and fundamental human rights. By virtue of their geostrategic proximity, these five countries have a disproportionate stake in the two polar regions.

What happens in the polar regions used to stay in the polar regions–not anymore.

Christian Leuprecht
Kingston, Ontario
August 2022

Cassandra Star
Adelaide, South Australia

Douglas Causey
Anchorage, Alaska

Introduction

Christian Leuprecht, Douglas Causey, Roger Bradbury,
and Heather Nicol

The world's polar regions are now central to geopolitical and strategic competition. Spillover effects from rapid political, social, and environmental change present unprecedented challenges for governance, environmental protection, and maritime operations in the Arctic and Antarctic regions. Both geographic areas can be distinguished by specific terms—namely, the "Arctic" and "Antarctica" (continental landmass)—and by more general descriptions that include adjacent waters and countries— the "circumpolar North" and "polar regions," for example. Climate change in the polar regions has a direct impact on the geopolitical dynamics of what were previously areas of relative predictability but are now areas of transformation—not only in the environment, but also in how the international community operates. Hitherto little-known regions of inaccessible and extreme conditions—the "white stuff at the top [or bottom] of the map"—the Arctic, the Antarctic, and their associated marine environments are emerging as regions for exploration, exploitation, and extraction. Accordingly, this book captures the complex, multi-factorial framework behind the interconnectivity that is inherent, and increasingly apparent, between the Arctic and Antarctic.

Geopolitics and climate change now have immediate consequences for national and international security interests across the Arctic and Antarctic regions (Heininen and Exner-Pirot 2019; McGee, Edmiston, and Haward

2021). This volume takes a comparative approach by harnessing insights from international research and policy to address geostrategic challenges in the polar regions: Antarctica and the Southern Ocean, as compared to the Arctic and the circumpolar North. Contributors to this volume include international defence experts, scientists, academics, policy-makers, and decision makers who assess the strategic, political, scientific, economic, and environmental challenges of managing the polar regions.

Our comparative approach, which entails identifying emerging patterns of commonality and divergence across the polar regions, is intended to inform evidence-based strategic policy options. To this end, the chapters enhance domain awareness, address challenges, and inform policy options by comparing the state of strategic thinking on Antarctica and the Southern Ocean with that of the Arctic and the circumpolar North. We discuss the strategic issues for policy-makers with the aim of shaping a new paradigm in geo-strategic thinking, strategic policy, and strategy development.

This book has a blunt and simple message: once an afterthought banished to the global periphery, the polar regions are now the subject of intense geopolitical interest (Dodds and Nuttal 2016). Few states previously engaged in the formation of diplomatic entities overseeing the polar regions, but the community of polar states has grown as the Arctic and Antarctic regions garner greater international attention. The Arctic Council's eight permanent members, comprising five Arctic Ocean littoral states as well as three countries with territory on or above the Arctic Circle (Axworthy, Koivurova, and Hasanat 2012, 127; Bloom 1999, 712), are now joined by thirteen observer states (Barry et al. 2020, 2; Graczyk and Koivurova 2014; Śmieszek and Koivurova 2017). Although, conventional defence and security issues are specifically precluded from this framework, in the aftermath of the Cold War the Arctic Military Environmental Cooperation project provided a forum for Russia, the United States, and Norway to address military-related environmental concerns.

At the time of writing, the work of the Arctic Council has been paused because of the current Chair's (Russia) invasion of Ukraine and general condemnation from all Arctic states. What the future holds for this cooperation is open to speculation, although hopes are then it will be sufficiently robust to survive or regroup in effective ways. This volume acknowledges this uncertainty, but it does not essentially change its message.

The original twelve signatories of the 1959 Antarctic Treaty are now complemented by seventeen additional states with the same consultative rights under the treaty and a further twenty-five states with observer status (Peterson 1988; Joyner 2021). This penumbra of associated states—a mixture of the earnest and the opportunistic—adds complexity to the emerging geopolitical competition and clash of ambitions among a growing number of state and non-state actors.

The important environmental and resource issues confronting, in their different ways, the Arctic (ACIA 2004; AMAP 2010) and Antarctic (Chown et al. 2022; Gutt et al. n.d.) should not deflect from looming security challenges in the polar regions. Indeed, environmental and resource issues amplify growing competition and will require policy-makers, for whom the polar regions are not usually top of mind and who often possess an inchoate understanding of these regions, to develop comprehensive strategies that address geopolitical, environmental, and resource issues in a holistic way (McGee, Edmiston, and Haward 2021).

Why and how have the polar regions become an active arena of national self-interest? This book applies lessons learned to date in the Arctic, where strategic competition is entering an acute phase, to sharpen our strategic thinking about the Antarctic, which has thus far played something of a sleepy polar cousin—and vice versa. Both the Arctic Council and the Antarctic Treaty have their origins in the Cold War, although significant diplomatic efforts have been made to minimize those problematic roots and construct a narrative that rewrites the history of these organizations as soft, inclusive international initiatives focused on scientific co-operation and environmental protection.

The Arctic Council, with its eight member states, each possessing Arctic territory—Canada, Denmark (representing Greenland), Finland, Iceland, Norway, Russia, Sweden, and the United States—and precursors such as the Arctic Environmental Protection Strategy, articulates concerns for sustainable development, environmental protection, and the needs of Arctic Indigenous communities. In contrast to the Antarctic, in the Arctic the presence of local Indigenous residents with legitimate claims to land and maritime resources is a key aspect of governance dynamics. The Arctic Council admits non-Arctic observer states—there are currently thirteen—provided they recognize the eight Arctic states' sovereignty, sovereign rights, and jurisdiction in the region, and, particularly, the application of the United Nations Convention on the Law of the Sea to the Arctic Ocean.

That said, China's and Russia's designs on both poles present an extremely problematic new strategic context insofar as both countries have demonstrated a realist proclivity for subjugating international law to their pursuit of strategic objectives (Sheikh, Vaughn, and Procita 2021, 2–3). In the maritime domain in particular, China has a proven track record of flouting—if not ignoring altogether—its international obligations under the Law of the Sea Treaty, instrumentalizing them as "lawfare" (a major component of its strategic doctrine), and using tactics designed to gain advantage from the greater compliance leverage that international law and its processes exert over China's rivals (Kittrie 2016, 166). Ergo, China's recent ascent to observer status within the council as a "near Arctic" state is a particular cause for concern for all eight original members, including Russia (Lanteigne 2022). Attempts by China and Russia to game the international rules-based order bode poorly for the poles' international governance regimes and the prevailing narrative that characterizes these regions as zones of peace and stability (Hoogensen Gjørv, Lanteigne, and Sam-Aggrey 2020). Although both areas have remained peaceful to date, Russian activities in the Ukraine have nevertheless resulted in the suspension of Arctic Council meetings under Russia's chairmanship.

Yet, those engaged in polar science and policy-making remind us that problems tend to result from the simplification of geopolitical perspectives. Without meaningful observer participation from China, as well as other large and essentially non-polar observer states, the Arctic Council is rendered ineffective and indeed irrelevant: "The core issue here goes well beyond the rules governing permanent observer status in the AC. Given the economic and political shifts occurring at the global level today, there is no way to address Arctic issues successfully without recognizing the heightened connectivity between the Arctic and the global system" (Kankaanpa and Young 2012, 12). In other words, Arctic security must be understood in a larger context, including with reference to existing frameworks for managing conflict.

The same is true of the Antarctic. Indeed, as comprehensive studies of geopolitical futures (e.g., McGee, Edmiston, and Haward 2021) and historical pasts (e.g., Antonello 2019) in the Antarctic show, the intersection between geopolitics, security, and changing environmental conditions have been shaped by the definition and use of existing structures. Over time, diplomats and scientists thought about the Antarctic environment and Antarctic space, and how they attempted to use it for geopolitical and institutional advantage. That said, the extent to which climate change is likely to further exacerbate geopolitical tensions across both poles and their adjoining oceans is staggering (Borgerson 2008; Dodds 2012; Young 2009). In the Arctic, climate change has the potential to open the region to resource exploitation and shipping in ways that were inconceivable only a few years ago (PAME 2009, 2020; Lasserre and Faury 2019). Thanks to modern technology, oil and gas are now potentially exploitable in the Arctic Ocean, and the prospect of year-round transit through the Russian-controlled Northern Sea Route is now within view (AMAP 2010, 12; Faury and Cariou 2016, 229).

In the southern polar region, geopolitical developments resulting from profound economic, political, and environmental change are also being forecasted (Press 2015). The original attributes of the Antarctic Treaty have now been overlaid by further treaties and conventions in what is known as the Antarctic Treaty System (ATS). These are nearly all to do with environmental protection and marine fisheries management. As such, they effectively detract from the initial objectives of banning military activity and Cold War rivalries on the southernmost continent. This has been so successful that the treaty system is today often considered, in international law, the exemplar of the "common heritage of mankind" principle. However, the use of that term with respect to Antarctica leads directly to the proposition of mining in the Antarctic, which like-minded states would rather avoid. Moreover, countries that have Antarctic claims—in addition to the United States and Russia, who assert a right to such claims—would never apply that term to Antarctica. We might say, then, that geopolitical issues never really went away, and the argument has been made that the treaty's structure facilitated the survival of national interests, albeit under the surface (Antonello 2019; Dodds 2012).

Both Russia and China are signatories to the Convention on the Conservation of Antarctic Marine Living Resources (CAMLR). The convention is the ATS's main tool for realizing its objectives of protecting the only currently exploitable resources of the region: marine life. The Commission for the Conservation of Antarctic Marine Living Resources, which created and monitors the CAMLR Convention, was established in 1982 because of concerns about Russia's exploitation of krill fishing, which had a direct effect on the populations of great whales. Meanwhile, Russia no longer fishes for krill or, as of late, in the CAMLR area for that matter. Although Norway currently dominates the Antarctic krill fishery, and the catch is an order of magnitude lower than the calculated sustainable yield of krill across the Antarctic, China is emerging as a major fishing country, and is particularly interested in krill to meet some of its requirements for protein.

Subsequently, toothfish, another easily accessible resource in Antarctic waters, has become a focus of the CAMLR Commission. At the height of illegal, unreported, and unregulated (IUU) fishing for toothfish, the fish were transferred directly to ports in Africa, Asia, and South America. IUU fishing for toothfish was one of the reasons China joined the Commission. After the introduction of the Catch Documentation Scheme for toothfish in the 2000s, the market for IUU fish changed as trade became more difficult, which coincided when transfers at sea became common practice. As a result, much of the toothfish catch was then mixed with the legal catch in transfers at sea and Indian Ocean ports where regulations are either looser or insufficiently enforced. Many intelligence analysts believe that most of this catch eventually finds its way to China. Over recent decades, the CAMLR Convention's supply-side controls have thus provided enabling cover for both Russia and China to strip marine resources from the region (Sovacool and Siman-Sovacool 2008). This will have deleterious ramifications for fragile ecosystems: China is bound to try to shape the Antarctic fishery into its own image as its demand for aquaculture protein increases.

While there are many similarities in the geopolitical tensions shaping both polar regions, in some areas there are real differences. These are equally important in understanding the relationship between the "polar cousins." Unlike the Arctic, where mining and oil drilling present great technical difficulties, in Antarctica they are prohibited indefinitely by the Protocol on Environmental Protection to the Antarctic Treaty. Yet, like its well-endowed Gondwana siblings—Australasia, South America, and Africa—the continent is thought to have a full complement of mineral resources, possibly including (though as yet unverified) coal measures and hydrocarbons.

China has been playing the long game ever since first establishing an Antarctic base in 1984, and the nature of that game is indicative of the geopolitical future of the Antarctic (Brady 2017). China now has permanent stations in both East and West Antarctica. And it has been adamant about the need to strike a balance between protection and use of Antarctic resources. China's position is that environmental protection should serve the purpose of "reasonable and sustainable use." Chinese diplomat Wu Yulin (2009) has even argued that "the protection of Antarctica should not be simply interpreted as no use, rather environment protection should serve the purpose of reasonable and sustainable use. . . . The mining ban has won preparation time for China's peaceful use of Antarctic resources" (2009).

A simple reading of the situation might put the Arctic, say, a decade ahead of the Antarctic in terms of geopolitical competition. A more nuanced reading suggests that circumstances in the two regions differ—but that they are converging generally as a result of broader impacts of climate change and the global economy. Territorial issues, and military threats to, in, and through the Arctic remain prevalent as manifest in attention to renewing the North American Aerospace Defense Command's capabilities and to the strategic significance of the "High North" in the eyes of the North Atlantic Treaty Organization—but resource exploitation is rising in prominence. Geopolitical tension is, nonetheless, highly mediated by regional interests (Østhagen 2020), and these differ between Nordic/European, North American, and Russian contexts (Sheng 2022). Marine living resources are exploited in both the Arctic and the Southern Ocean. Climate change and global over-exploitation of marine living resources are likely to increase pressures to expand fisheries in the Southern Ocean in coming years. In contrast to the Arctic, exploitation in the Antarctic region is likely set to shift from the sea back to the land (Nicol 2002). Yet, as this volume shows, there is also a highly regional dimension to Antarctic geopolitics among Antarctic states, which are members of the ATS, much as there is in the Arctic, where interest in land-based endeavours has driven scientific exploration and investigation (Dodds 2012; National Research Council 1993, 14).

Given the complexity and transformation that is well underway, it takes a broad approach to inform multidisciplinary, comparative, and evidence-based strategic policy in the constituent arenas of geopolitics, environmental security, human resilience, sovereignty, and diplomatic discourse for the polar regions. Contributors to this volume review the state of strategic thinking and action on Antarctica and the Southern Ocean as well as the circumpolar North. They discuss the experience of participant nations and non-governmental organizations on geostrategic issues and focus on the awareness, understanding, and lessons learned so far. This complexity has not received widespread attention and is thus at high risk of leading to misinformed decision making. To inform underlying complex decision making, the contributions to this volume leverage insights from diverse disciplines, including political science, policy studies, strategic studies, geography, law, history, and environmental science, using a range of methodological approaches.

The book is organized into two main sections: one on circumpolar geopolitics and security in the polar North, and the other on the same topics as they relate to the Arctic's polar cousin, the Antarctic region, including Antarctica and the Southern Ocean. Each section begins with a prologue addressing the similarities and differences between the subjects of the different chapters as regards security, sovereignty and governance, and strategic planning and action, and these set the stage for the focused comparative discussion that follows.

The circumpolar North is distinguished by a long history of co-operation and collaboration among participant states, each with their own security self-interests and history. In the prologue to part 1, Randy Kee focuses on the nature of Arctic "exceptionalism" as it relates to the size, breadth, and depth of collaboration in diverse activities related to scientific research, economic endeavours, and governance. The region already hosts national military forces, and so alliances and partnerships are considered key attributes for the maintenance of sovereign rights.

The remainder of part 1 focuses on the polar North, but each of the four chapters seek to compare and contrast the Arctic region with its Antarctic counterpart. In the first chapter of this section, Douglas Causey, Randy Kee, and Brenda Dunkle explore the interactions among the environment, human resilience, and defence/sovereignty—components that together comprise a tripartite environmental security complex. They discuss the dynamics of change in each of these components, the attendant geopolitical effects on the Arctic, and what to anticipate for the Antarctic region.

Owing to different histories, events, and geopolitical developments, the idea that there could be a singular "polar geopolitics" is misleading. Heather Nicol and Lassi Heininen explore how the geopolitics of the polar regions, over the past one hundred years in particular, has reflected a degree of convergence in terms of their mapping and exploration, environmental destabilization and rapid climate change, the rising importance of polar research (with its "focus on science") as a strategic interest, and the role of non-polar states in regional governance.

Ilan Kelman discusses the concept of disaster diplomacy and its relationship with polar politics. Using Norway as a focus, he examines how multi-national collaborations for dealing with disasters are rarely successful for conflict resolution, including in the Arctic and the Antarctic. Instead, for Norway in the polar regions, science-related collaboration tends to be the most prominent interstate outcome of disaster diplomacy, with other co-operative disaster-related activities occurring, but not demonstrably leading to wider collaboration.

Greenland has come to occupy an increasingly prominent place in the public's awareness of geostrategic decision making—particularly after a former US president suggested that it should be purchased. Dwayne Ryan Menezes explores why Greenland matters just as much to Denmark, Europe, and other northern allies as it should to the constituent partner states of both polar regions.

Part 2 of the book deals with the geopolitics, the security, and the changing environment of the southern polar region, and because relatively little is understood about these topics in an Antarctic compared to an Arctic context, the four chapters that comprise this section focus predominantly on the approaches of the two closest and most important regional allies: Australia and New Zealand.

In his prologue to this section, Tony Press identifies the considerable differences between the two polar regions, not only in terms of geography and history, but also the extent to which their unique governance structures are consequential. In contrast to the Arctic, where a system of layered governance prevails, the ATS provides a common, consensus-based mechanism for the pursuit of national interests and aspirations. Press discusses which aspects of the ATS are working well, which aspects are increasingly being tested by Russia, China, and others, and which are not—either through active disregard or a failure of consensus.

In the next chapter, Joanna Vince explores the governance and sovereignty issues that Australia experiences with its Antarctic Territory and adjacent exclusive economic zone, which are not recognized by all the states active in the region. These governance issues have resulted in political tensions for claimant states over maritime boundaries, use of marine resources, and environmental protection.

Peter Layton begins his chapter by examining the current situation as regards geopolitical and environmental security in the East Antarctic regions that Australia claims; he then uses this as a basis from which to project the area's future course over the next twenty years. He offers four plausible geopolitical scenarios as examples of the possible consequences and realities that may play out based on today's reality.

The current laws and policy framework that enable environmental protection for Antarctica are strongly associated with the ATS. Robin Warner discusses key principles in global environmental law and their application to the southern polar region: namely, sustainable development, ecosystem-based management, the precautionary principle, and scientific environmental assessment. She analyzes how these principles and approaches have been incorporated, and how they may pose future challenges to the Antarctic environmental protection scheme.

Joe Burton then reviews the current direction of New Zealand's Antarctic policy, which he finds fraught with risk and contention as China and other powers become more assertive in the region. He explores hot spots and flashpoints that could precipitate conflict, summarizes key issues that small states such as New Zealand face, and discusses how small states can be pivotal advocates for rule-based actions by all participating countries.

The volume closes with a coda by Heather Nicol, Timo Koivurova, and Douglas Causey. They review the findings of the preceding chapters and examine the geostrategic importance of environmental governance in the northern and southern polar regions. While there is a deeper and more complete structure for collaboration and consensus among the participant states in the Arctic, and an active non-parliamentary organization for oversight in the Arctic Council, the evolving situation in the Antarctic region is equally informative to its polar cousin.

More broadly, the book posits the world's polar regions as central to geopolitical competition in the future. It makes the case for a strategic approach that is, on the one hand, comprehensive and forward-looking and, on the other, given the similarities and comparisons described in the different chapters, treats the polar regions and their adjacent oceans as complementary polar cousins. Both premises amount to a paradigmatic change in how allies and partners discuss the two regions and broach the prospect of considerable benefits from more systematic and comparative learning experiences across the two poles. In the process, this edited collection aims to provide a baseline for strategic decision making and planning so that allies and partners can regain the initiative in the two most rapidly changing regions of the world.

REFERENCES

ACIA (Arctic Climate Impact Assessment). 2004. *Impacts of a Warming Climate.* Cambridge: Cambridge University Press. https://www.amap.no/documents/download/1058/inline.

AMAP (Arctic Monitoring and Assessment Programme). 2010. *Assessment 2007: Oil and Gas Activities in the Arctic—Effects and Potential Effects*, vol. 2. Oslo: Arctic Monitoring and Assessment Programme.https://www.amap.no/documents/download/1016/inline.

Antonello, Alessandro. 2019. *The Greening of Antarctica: Assembling an International Environment.* Oxford: Oxford University Press.

Axworthy, T. S., T. Koivurova, and W. Hasanat. 2012. *The Arctic Council: Its Place in the Future of Arctic Governance.* Rovaniemi, FI: Arctic Centre.

Barry, Tom, Brynhildur Davíðsdóttira, Níels Einarsson, and Oran R. Young. 2020. "The Arctic Council: An Agent of Change?" *Global Environmental Change* 63 (July 2020): 102099.

Bloom, E. 1999. "Establishment of the Arctic Council." *American Journal of International Law* 93 (3): 712–22.

Borgerson, Scott G. 2008. "Arctic Meltdown: The Economic and Security Implications of Global Warming." *Foreign Affairs* 87 (2): 65–77.

Brady, Anne-Marie. 2017. *China as a Great Polar Power.* Cambridge: Cambridge University Press.

Chown, Steven, Rachel I. Leihy, Tim R. Naish, Cassandra M. Brooks, Peter Convey, Benjamin J. Henley, Andrew N. Mackintosh, Laura M. Phillips, Malon C. Kennicutt II, and Susie M. Grant. 2022. *Antarctic Climate Change and the Environment: A Decadal Synopsis and Recommendations for Action*. Cambridge: Scientific Committee on Antarctic Research, International Science Council. https://scar.org/library/scar-publications/occasional-publications/5758-acce-decadal-synopsis/file/.

Dodds, Klaus. 2012. *The Antarctic: A Very Short Introduction*. Oxford: Oxford University Press.

Dodds, Klaus, and Mark Nuttall. 2016. *The Scramble for the Poles: The Geopolitics of the Arctic and Antarctic*. Cambridge: Polity Press.

Faury, Olivier, and Pierre Cariou. 2016. "The Northern Sea Route Competitiveness for Oil Tankers." *Transportation Research Part A: Policy and Practice* 94 (December): 461–69.

Graczyk, Piotr, and Timo Koivurova. 2014. "A New Era in the Arctic Council's External Relations? Broader Consequences of the Nuuk Observer Rules for Arctic Governance." *Polar Record* 50 (3): 225–236.

Gutt, Julian, Enrique Isla, José C. Xavier, Byron J. Adams, In-Young Ahn, C.-H. Christina Cheng, Claudia Colesie, Vonda J. Cummings, Huw Griffiths, Ian Hogg, Trevor McIntyre, Klaus M. Meiners, David A. Pearce, Lloyd Peck, Dieter Piepenburg, Ryan R. Reisinger, Grace K. Saba, Irene R. Schloss, Camila N. Signori, Craig R. Smith, Marino Vacchi, Cinzia Verde, and Diana H. Wall. n.d. "Ten Scientific Messages on Risks and Opportunities for Life in the Antarctic." Scientific Committee on Antarctic, International Science Council, accessed 18 July 2022. https://environments.aq/wp-content/uploads/2022/02/Gutt_Ten_Messages_AntERA_EN.pdf.

Heininen, Lassi, and Heather Exner-Pirot. 2019. *Climate Change and Arctic Security: Searching for a Paradigm Shift*. Cham, CH: Palgrave Pivot.

Hoogensen Gjørv, Gunhild, Marc Lanteigne, and Horatio Sam-Aggrey. 2020. *Routledge Handbook of Arctic Security*. Abingdon, UK: Routledge.

Joyner, Christopher C. 2021. *Antarctica and the Law of the Sea*. Leiden, NL: Brill.

Kankaanpa, Paula, and Oran R. Young. 2012. "The Effectiveness of the Arctic Council." *Polar Research* 31 (1). https://doi.org/10.3402/polar.v31i0.17176.

Kittrie, Odre F. 2016. *Lawfare: Law as a Weapon of War*. Oxford: Oxford University Press.

Lanteigne, Marc. 2022. *China's Arctic Diplomacy*. Abingdon, UK: Routledge.

Lasserre, Frédéric, and Olivier Faury. 2019. *Arctic Shipping: Climate Change, Commercial Traffic and Port Development*. New York: Routledge.

McGee, Jeffrey, David Edmiston, and Marcus Haward. 2021. *The Future of Antarctica: Scenarios from Classical Geopolitics*. Singapore: Springer.

National Research Council. 1993. *Science and Stewardship in the Antarctic*. Washington, DC: National Academies Press.

Nicol, Stephen. 2002. "Resource Exploitation in the Antarctic." *Australian Antarctic Magazine* 3 (Autumn). https://www.antarctica.gov.au/magazine/issue-3-autumn-2002/feature/resource-exploitation-in-the-antarctic-region/.

Østhagen, Andreas. 2020. "The Nuances of Geopolitics in the Arctic." Arctic Institute, 7 January 2020. https://www.thearcticinstitute.org/nuances-geopolitics-arctic/.

PAME (Protection of the Arctic Marine Environment). 2009. *Arctic Marine Shipping Assessment 2009 Report.* Akureyri, IS: PAME, Arctic Centre. https://www.pame.is/images/03_Projects/AMSA/AMSA_2009_report/AMSA_2009_Report_2nd_print.pdf.

———. 2020. *The Increase in Arctic Shipping 2013–2019: Arctic Shipping Status Report (ASSR) #1.* Akureyri, IS: PAME, Arctic Centre. https://oaarchive.arctic-council.org/bitstream/handle/11374/2733/ASSR%201_final_.pdf?sequence=1.

Peterson, M. J. 1988. *Managing the Frozen South: The Creation and Evolution of the Antarctic Treaty System.* Berkeley: University of California Press.

Press, Tony A. 2015. "The Antarctic Treaty System: Future Mining Faces Many Mathematical Challenges." *Yearbook of Polar Law Online* 7 (1): 623–31. https://doi.org/10.1163/2211-6427_023.

Sheikh, Pervaze A., Bruce Vaughn, and Kezee Procita. 2021. *Overview of Geopolitical and Environmental Issues.* Congressional Research Service Report R46708. Washington, DC: Congressional Research Service. https://sgp.fas.org/crs/misc/R46708.pdf.

Sheng Li, Edmund. 2022. *Arctic Opportunities and Challenges: China, Russia and the US Cooperation and Competition.* New York: Palgrave Macmillan.

Śmieszek, Małgorzata (Gosia), and Timo Koivurova. 2017. "The Arctic Council: Between Continuity and Change." In *One Arctic: The Arctic Council and Circumpolar Governance*, edited by P. Whitney Lackenbauer, Heather Nicol, and Wilfrid Greaves, 1–26. Ottawa: Canadian Arctic Resources Committee.

Sovacool, Benjamin K., and Kelly E. Siman-Sovacool. 2008. "Creating Legal Teeth for Toothfish: Using the Market to Protect Fish Stocks in Antarctica." *Journal of Environmental Law* 20 (1): 15–33.

Wu Yulin. 2009. "Mineral Resources from the Evolution of the Antarctic Treaty System." *Journal of Ocean University of China* 5:11–13.

Young, Oran R. 2009. "Whither the Arctic? Conflict or Cooperation in the Circumpolar North." *Polar Record* 45 (1): 73–82.

PART I

Prologue: Arctic Polar Security

Randy "Church" Kee

The Arctic is a remarkable and dynamic place. It is much more than a geographic region that exists at or above 66 degrees and 33 minutes north latitude on the globe. What defines the Arctic of course depends on the given community vested with a particular definition. The Arctic Circle is a matter of geography. There are vegetation, temperatures, and political definitions as well. The pan-Arctic today remains an ocean space surrounded by lands that remain a part of each respective Arctic sovereign nations. The Arctic Basin is now largely claimed via these same national entities seeking sovereign ownership of ocean floors via the United Nations Convention on the Law of the Sea (UNCLOS), legal clauses referring to extended continental shelves. Accordingly (and in accordance with custom and usual terms), the Arctic is no longer a frontier.

In general and broad terms, the Arctic can be somewhat defined and described along three regional land aspects: the North American Arctic, which comprises the US state of Alaska, Canada's Yukon, Northwest, and Nunavut Territories, as well as Greenland (under the sovereign jurisdiction of the Kingdom of Denmark); the European Arctic, including the Nordic nations and the Russian Federation west of the Ural mountains; and the Asian Arctic, that region of modern-day Russia that extends east of the Urals to the Bering to the Chukchi Seas. While maritime access to the Arctic on the Atlantic side is thousands of miles wide (extending from Greenland to the Barents Sea), Arctic access on the Pacific side is limited to a narrow strait that is merely fifty-one nautical miles wide between the Chukchi and Seward Peninsulas.

The Arctic has been inhabited by groups of people who predate recorded history and who, in the modern era, have been made citizens of nations that have their origins in European historical organizational constructs (in particular, the Westphalian state model). The Arctic remains a region that is wild, remote, logistically challenging, and daunting to those who come from lower latitudes. It is the land of the midnight sun in summer, and it is also the place of weeks-long, seemingly perpetual darkness in winter.

The Arctic's physical environment is undergoing a remarkable series of changes that can be largely linked to sustained warming trends across the pan-Arctic. As written widely across the science community from the fall of 2020 and through mid-2021, the highlights are that the Arctic continues to warm at three to four times the rate of lower latitudes across the northern hemisphere (updating prior reports of the Arctic warming at two times the rate of these same latitudes).

Arctic warming is creating a growing number of cascading impacts that contribute to, among other things, a reduction in the volumes and area of Arctic sea ice, melting ice sheets in Greenland, and the thawing (and sometimes melting) of Arctic permafrost—all of which is affecting virtually every aspect of life in the region. The notion of a changing Arctic is certainly not new, nor are the implications surprising. The community of Arctic scientists have been expressing concern about a changing Arctic environment for decades, and this community continues to advance knowledge in characterizing the physical changes in the region at an increasingly fine scale. Media reports about activities of government and industry in the Arctic abound, indicating that the challenges of negotiating the geophysical elements of the region are diminishing due to warming. Accordingly, (acknowledging the vagueness of the remark) governments of Arctic nations are blending advocacy to encourage Arctic development with growing concerns about the activities and intentions of non-like-minded states and non-state actors within the region. Further, as Arctic warming forecasts indicate, this trend is poised to continue, and bring unique challenges that will strain all inhabitants' ability to resiliently adapt—flora, fauna, and people alike.

As the changing Arctic presents new economic and geopolitical threats, risks, and opportunities, environmental change imperils current economic systems and traditional lifestyles in the Arctic. Thawing permafrost is compromising the land that serves as the foundation for Arctic communities and the small number of connecting roads and ports. With less sea ice cover, weather systems are becoming more volatile, allowing for stronger storm systems that further exacerbate coastal erosion through storm surges, high winds, and coastal flooding. Environmental changes in the Bering Sea are now having an impact on traditional commercial and subsistence fisheries as fish stocks are starting to move north, risking, and in some instances already dislocating, traditional food sources for marine mammals and Alaskan Arctic residents alike. Collectively, these environmentally focused changes pose a significant threat to existing coastal communities, local economies, and associated infrastructure within the region.

Enabled by a changing environment, human activity across the Arctic is rising and includes increased commercial marine traffic, bolstered adventure tourism (albeit temporarily dampened due to the coronavirus pandemic), and expanded efforts to develop and conduct resource exploration and extraction methodologies. Newly opened pathways from the diminishing ice environment are a draw for nefarious influences in the region and can possibly contribute to unconventional marine safety and security threats, including increased illicit trafficking and criminal activity.

The opportunities to develop the Arctic are an incentive for both Arctic and non-Arctic nations to pursue easier access, extract mineral and petrochemical resources, pursue fish proteins (at present, outside of the Central Arctic Ocean), conduct maritime transport, advance tourism, and project sovereign influence through nationally flagged vessels. Transportation networks across the Arctic are principally limited to air and seasonal marine conveyance. Economic development remains limited due to the area's remoteness, lack of infrastructure, the high cost of extant modes of travel, and the difficulty of establishing new roads, ports, and facilities.

Reductions in sea ice have reduced the access barrier to maritime operations, and as a result, activity is increasing in the Bering, Chukchi, and Beaufort Sea regions. Of course, the same is true of the overall pan-Arctic, which includes the Northern Sea Route (NSR) along Russia's northern shore and the Northwest Passage across northern Canada. The

Arctic's diminishing sea ice environment is increasing accessibility to the vast hydrocarbon deposits within the region, which allows for Arctic nation-states like the Russian Federation to expand their resource-extraction efforts. It is also enabling sea lanes of the Arctic to open sooner and stay open longer through the summer months and increasingly into the fall. May 2020, for example, saw the earliest recorded springtime transit of the NSR, and January 2021 witnessed the route's latest wintertime transit, a record that is likely to be routinely broken in the seasons to come. The emerging economic potential of the NSR, and the possibility of a viable transpolar route within this century have incentivized nations and industry to consider leveraging these new and shorter routes for transporting maritime commerce as an economic advantage. Meanwhile, Canada's fabled Northwest Passage looms larger as a potential source of Canadian tourism in the post-COVID-19 world. Canada maintains the Northwest Passage as an internal waterway, not subject to the provisions of freedom-of-navigation principle as codified in the UNCLOS. The United States maintains the Northwest Passage is an international waterway and applies the same logic to Russia's NSR. This remains a source of disagreement between the United States and Canada, but both nations have continued to "agree to disagree" on the status and continue to find ways to accommodate their opposing views on an important Arctic waterway.

When the United States became an Arctic nation in 1867, it became responsible for facilitating domestic security and defending national sovereignty across a significant frontier, known to generations of Alaska Indigenous residents and a handful of explorers, miners, trappers, and settlers from the continental United States, Canada, Russia, or other places. Canada's Arctic shares similar geography, long-term resident human ancestry, and many elements of associated history with Alaska's Arctic regions. As well, the dynamics of environmental change, economic challenges, and the effects of influences from lower latitudes continue to complicate the overall North American Arctic, which is uniquely different in many aspects from either the European or Asian Arctic regions.

As trends indicate, human activity across the Arctic continues to increase in scope and magnitude. As new Arctic expansion and operations bring a more diverse and less experienced population to the region, and the rapidly changing Arctic environment confounds traditional understandings, the percentage of those truly prepared for the Arctic environment is in decline. This leads to risk-prone behaviours that stress resources and challenge security and defence forces' ability to conduct search and rescue; provide humanitarian assistance; protect fisheries, marine species, and wildlife; and lead disaster-response operations. Additionally, as more outsiders enter the Arctic, the reasons for their arrival become more diverse, resulting in increased need for vigilance when enforcing respective national laws and regulations.

The diminishing Arctic ice environment that is enabling rising competition is manifesting itself in a multi-faceted manner. It is well understood the Russian Federation has restored and refurbished several former Soviet bases across Russian Arctic, while creating new facilities and establishing forces at those stations capable of projecting power in and through the Arctic, well beyond national borders. If this were simply a matter establishing a safe and secure Russian Arctic by creating sound defence through a more than capable offence, then such activities may be reasonable and possibly even acceptable. However, Russian national decisions, and associated defence planning, are opaque at best, and the asymmetric Arctic military advantage created in the Russian Federation should be met with resolve and strength by the United States and Canada—as resolve and strength has historically been a successful method of stabilizing relations between Moscow, Washington, and Ottawa.

Russia's approach to managing the NSR potentially restricts well-established measures of maritime freedom of navigation outside of established territorial waters. The country's practices have the potential to obliquely, if not directly, restrict freedom of navigation and counter the NSR's status as an international waterway.

Russia is a considerable Arctic maritime power. With a dominant number of icebreakers, ranging from vessels suitable for riverine operations to nuclear-powered ocean-going ships and submarines, the Russian military can project sovereign influence throughout the pan-Arctic in multiple directions simultaneously. Indeed, Russia's ability to muster and project military forces in the Arctic are remarkable. The range and complexity of these activities have continued to grow substantially following the re-establishment of the Long-Range Aviation branch of the Russian Aerospace Forces back in January 2007.

The military exercises that Russia staged in the Bering Sea in late August 2020 are a deeply worrying example that demonstrates Moscow's lack of understanding, poor communication, and willingness to engage in provocation; this places not only military forces and response measures at risk, but citizens as well, as was the case with the US-flagged/owned/crewed commercial fishing vessels that were interrupted and alarmed by poorly understood and reportedly aggressive Russian military manoeuvres.

Since the routine establishment of extended economic zones (EEZ)—normally two hundred nautical miles from shore, as codified in the UNCLOS in 1982—foreign vessels are granted the right of innocent passage, which permits transit and freedom of navigation as long as these vessels are not conducting such prohibited activities as weapons testing, polluting, fishing, or scientific research.

As the Russian Federation is an Arctic nation that shares a critical waterways-management challenge with the United States, it is in both nations' interests to resolve conflicts, effectively communicate, and find solutions to prevent escalation of tension and a rise in military actions along shared and increasingly economically important waterways in the Chukchi and Bering Seas.

The Peoples Republic of China's efforts in the Arctic have thus far taken a different form than Russia's. China continues to maximize its influence through use of its economic power to create the potential for access to policy and governance forums such as the Arctic Council and uses its economic strength to potentially position itself to gain access to Arctic regional mineral wealth, fish proteins, and more. China's economic partnership with Russia for Arctic liquified natural gas (LNG) is one example of how China is using the Arctic to advance its so-called Belt and Road Initiative.

China continues to project its sovereign presence into and across the Arctic via *Xue Long I* and *Xue Long II* icebreaker cruises, with a third *Xue Long* ship to join these activities soon. There are media reports that China is seeking to follow Russia's examples by developing nuclear-powered icebreakers. In addition to investments in LNG on Russia's Arctic Yamal Peninsula, China's ability to leverage its influence to gain access to commercial ports in Iceland and its efforts to advance its commercial mining interests in Greenland signal that the country's strategic aims contain what is arguably a comprehensive pan-Arctic approach. Based on Beijing's actions in other regions, it is reasonable to conclude that China's need for raw resources, such as mineral and fish proteins, will continue to drive its aspirations and activities across the Arctic.

It is clear from its words and actions that the People's Republic of China sees the Arctic as an important aspect to its overall global ambitions. It is also fairly clear that China will continue its efforts to gain access to resources and deliver products to market while also establishing and exerting its influence among the community of Arctic nations, who may be tempted by promises of infrastructure investment and economic development through Chinese investment. To that end, it may prove wise for Arctic nations to look more closely at China's actions and the outcomes of its economic engagement in other regions around the planet. These countries would do well to ask: Is agreeing and accepting Chinese investment worth the risk?

Chinese icebreakers continue to ply Arctic waters, including in the Arctic Basin outside of the US Arctic EEZ in the Chukchi and Beaufort Seas. It is not inconceivable that such a presence could lead to mineral exploration and other extractive measures in the future—closer to the US Arctic maritime EEZ than we would likely prefer, particularly when we consider the insufficient measures Chinese industry has made toward environmental stewardship in other regions across the globe.

China's willingness to support infrastructure in developing regions provides many reasons for caution, and close examination of any promise or offer made by the Chinese government or government-supported industry is certainly warranted. Regrettably, there are several places where Beijing has yet to substantially deliver on such promises and, as is often the case, where profound disappointment has been the result. One need only look to Africa, South Asia, and Southeast Asia to get a full picture of the corresponding risks that await the Arctic. China is not an Arctic nation, of course, yet it is acting as though it has sovereign interests in the region, and its advocates have asserted that China seeks and should be granted a role in Arctic governance at a number of multi-national fora, such as the 2019 US Arctic Research Commission and the Woodrow Wilson Center, which hosted a conference on the "Impacts of a Diminishing Ice Arctic on Naval and Maritime Operations." In sum, China's effectiveness in leveraging its national economic strength as a means to gain political influence across the Arctic is competing and conflicting with corresponding US national interests.

To be sure, the Arctic is but one area in which China has chosen to pursue greater geostrategic competition with the United States and Canada, but the pace of Chinese advancement in and across the pan-Arctic region, including the country's increasing presence in Arctic waters, is outpacing efforts to deter and dissuade such actions, which potentially (and likely) challenge the respective national interests of the United States and Canada.

A similar intent may be discerned on Russia's part. However, while the strength and considerable reach of Russia's military forces across the Arctic—to say nothing of Europe and the Middle East—are of course cause for concern, these forces are dispatched by a nation whose economic ability to sustain such forces in the long term is subject to serious doubt. Russian economic shortfalls compromise Russian military strength, particularly when compared to the economic muscle of China, the world's second-largest economy. Accordingly, Russia's fellow Arctic nations should seek out ways to manage tensions with the Russian Federation. This is all the more feasible when one considers the mutual strength afforded by US, Canadian, and European membership in a multi-lateral security alliance like the North Atlantic Treaty Organization. Such measures should first and foremost seek to find a way to decouple joint approaches between Moscow and Beijing. This may be possible through a diplomatic rapprochement that does not condone or reward past and current malign actions by Russia but is nevertheless guided by the realization that Moscow, Washington, and Ottawa share several common interests in the Arctic. This approach may well be aligned with Canada-US interests and serve to better manage escalation of military tensions in the Arctic.

The above discussion provides a representative sample of the geostrategic challenges that face the United States and Canada as the two nations pursue their national interests in the Arctic. It is important to emphasize here that great power *competition* need not become great power *confrontation*, and measures to manage and de-escalate international tensions are important, if not critical. To be sure, escalation management requires the means and capabilities to back words with commensurate force. Such capabilities are the preserve of the US and Canadian security forces, and it will require vigilance in planning and strategizing to characterize existing risks and implement measures to mitigate associated threats.

The Arctic is an exceptional region. Indeed, its "exceptionalism" can be seen in the size, breadth, and depth of ongoing collaboration in such areas as Arctic science, economic activity, recognition of Indigenous peoples, and governance-related activities, including the mechanisms associated with the Arctic Council: these are the envy of many other regions across the globe. However, continuation of these aspects of Arctic exceptionalism is by no means assured, and investment in Arctic initiatives related to science, economics, and measures to ensure Canada-United States (CANUS) security and sovereignty are well within both countries' interests.

Responding to the drivers of concern, it will be important, if not critical, to provide sustained support to Canadian and US law-enforcement agencies with improvements and increased capabilities so that they can smartly project their respective nation's presence and power in the Arctic region. Possible measures range from providing the clenched fist of resolve through security missions to extending the hand of help in response to civil crises, as well as advancing science and research in a pan-Arctic context to support the public good.

Ultimately, the hoped-for result is the real and critical ability to field capable maritime and air platforms in the Arctic and enable US and Canadian security forces to secure and defend the maritime and air approaches to the North American Arctic. This also means providing these platforms with the ability to serve as fully capable instruments of national sovereignty, with the ability to deter, dissuade, and defend against risks and threats to US and Canadian national borders and receive and conduct command and control to establish situational awareness and overall domain understanding across remote and austere regions that have well-understood limitations in communications and logistics infrastructure.

As regards logistics: there should be consideration and deliberation when it comes to either developing or enhancing existing infrastructure in the North American Arctic, with the goal of serving an expeditionary/intermediary function of providing logistical support and an affordable level of repair function in support of security operations. Quite frankly, advancing expeditionary support/logistics activities in the Arctic region could prove the most helpful start in building the programmatic ramp that could result in a multi-year approach to smart civil/military solutions that enable security forces to better protect transportation, tourism, and other industry activities.

The North American Aerospace Defense Command (NORAD) is a binational keystone of defence from strategic attack, one that is oriented via the North Warning System to defend against attacks that would leverage air and space above the Arctic. A principal, day-to-day activity for CANUS defence and security forces in and across the Arctic region is to provide assistance to search-and-rescue and disaster responses. Both the Canadian and the US security forces conduct well-known and highly regarded search-and-rescue missions, in addition to providing pollution and other environmental responses. Oil spill response is costly, and proactive prevention is difficult and logistically straining. The scientific and spill response communities provide important support to these efforts, but, to be sure, advancing the science of spill response and improving inspection capabilities through the use of science and autonomous systems to better monitor storage facilities across vast and remote regions will grow more important as facilities age and become more compromised by thawing permafrost and other environmental changes underway across the Arctic.

Advancing the capability of CANUS security forces in the Arctic also means advancing trusted relationships. For example, the Arctic Coast Guard Forum provides an opportunity to advance needed co-operation among all eight Arctic coast guards. The Arctic Security Forces Roundtable provides a chance for seven of eight Arctic nations and several non-Arctic European nations to contribute Arctic-oriented defence support to civil authorities. The US Coast Guard maintains an important relationship with its Russian counterpart (for Bering and Chukchi Sea waterways management), and security and defence forces from the United States, Canada, and the Kingdom of Denmark work closely in Arctic military regional co-operation. Sustaining trusted relationships is a domestic matter as well. In the Alaskan Arctic, there exists good co-operation across federal- and state-level departments and agencies, Alaska Native communities, and academic partners. The same is true in Yukon, the Northwest Territories, and Nunavut, where federal and territorial authorities operate with respect and understanding vis-à-vis Arctic Indigenous communities. It remains critical to consult with and understand the challenges faced by Canadian and US citizens of the Arctic, who see first-hand the changes the region is undergoing and can provide uniquely important insights that are beneficial to safety and security responders. The adage that you can't surge trust or a trusted relationship applies in full measure to the Arctic.

While the region is increasingly impacted by the changing physical terrain and a rise in human activity, it also provides some of the best examples of international political, industrial, and academic co-operation on the planet. Highlights include the Arctic Council, led by eight nations and six internationally recognized Arctic Indigenous groups and supported by outstanding scientific research and focused working groups: namely, the International Maritime Organization (and its Polar Code), the International Arctic Science Committee, and the University of the Arctic.

The United States and Canada are fortunate to have each other as close Arctic defence and security partners and allies. This includes a shared defence commitment through the North Atlantic Treaty Organization, shared aerospace domains, and the maritime approaches to Canadian and US sovereign territory via NORAD and a complementary defence arrangement through United States Northern Command and Canada's Joint Operations Command. This binational defence co-operation is supported by the Canada-US Permanent Joint Board of Defence (PJBD), established in 1940 by joint declaration between the US president and the Canadian prime minister. PJBD today includes four CANUS departments: the US Department of Defense and Department of Homeland Security and the Canadian Department of National Defence and Department of Public Safety. As useful as the forum is in terms of advancing binational defence and security co-operation, it remains, perhaps, a bit episodically under-leveraged in both Washington and Ottawa.

National strategies for Canadian and US federal agencies drive policy and resource decisions that affect the security of both nations. The State of Alaska and the Canadian provinces drive regional governance, with local and tribal governance providing granular understanding of the developing threats, risks, and opportunities in the region. Looking to the future, it is important to understand, from the current baselines of security and defence, the policy, planning, and resourcing decisions needed in the near term, to better effect outcomes from the range of possible conditions that could emerge and dominate Canadian and US policy-makers, both nationally, regionally, and locally, in the years to come.

As the current crop of US and Canadian national leaders continue to evolve their strategic understanding of the Arctic region, knowledge-products, which capture insights and perspectives, and bi-national collaboration will provide a unique opportunity to inform planners and policy-makers alike as they revise and develop new federal strategies and policies in Ottawa and Washington. Such collaboration should extend to regional and local decision makers as well, to strengthen the fabric of CANUS co-operation in and across the North American Arctic.

In closing, it remains supremely important that Canada, the United States, and our respective allies and partners maintain a clear-eyed view of the Arctic's fast-approaching future. The region is already hosting an array of military forces. It is undergoing substantial physical change. Arctic environmental security is an integral part of the overall Arctic security equation, which in turn is vitally important to both Canadian and American national (and national security) interests. There is an opportunity for it to become a peaceful, protected, and integrated part of our respective nations, and while economic opportunity carries both a risk and a responsibility, it is important to see the Arctic as much more than a giant multi-national park—indeed, it is a region of many uses. However, we would do well to remember that such uses must be conducted with care, discernment, communication, and coordination, and ultimately with an eye to protecting a region that is fragile and still remote, wild, and remarkable.

Polar Environmental Security: Challenges, Threats, and Realities

Douglas Causey, Randy "Church" Kee, and Brenda Dunkle

The role of the environment in structuring the ecology of plants and animals has long been a focus of classical ecological research; however, recent developments in environmental security literature suggest that ecological conditions extend beyond flora and fauna to impact human security (Dalby 2018; Lee 2018), and potentially to defence and other areas of security. For example, Dalby (2018) proposed the concept of environmental security to encompass relative inequalities in environmental resources as a source of envy, disagreement, and conflict among human groups. Rising competition between groups of people has resulted in resource wars between poor and rich regions (Renner, 2002).

Over time, researchers have proposed a variety of interconnected variables that may impact environmental security. Early research suggested that acute human conflict can result from environmental change, specifically direct association of environmental degradation and scarcity with conflict among groups and "nation-states" (Homer-Dixon, 1991). Other research has examined a strong one-way, two-factor interaction between the human-based valuations of the environment and a generalized assessment of "human security" (Dalby 2018; Lee 2018). In this two-factor interaction between the human-based valuation of the environment and a generalized assessment of human security, the driver is the magnitude of disparity in an environmental resource of value, necessity, or strategic advantage (Conca and Beevers 2018; Gleditsch 1998). The more significant the difference between the assessed value of environmental resources and the availability of those resources, the more likely the prospect of conflict. Accelerators in this type of interaction may include the nature and degree of civil or social instability or the status of human security and change in the relative status of environmental resources, whether through time or by comparison between regions.

In contrast to socio-political perspectives, Klubnikin and Causey (2002) viewed potential interactions between the environment and human populations from an ecological perspective. Specifically, they argued that environmental change dynamics underlie a strong three-factor interaction among environmental security, human security, and defence security. Stated differently, changes in the natural ecology of the environment may drive significant interactions among and between these factors. Some are two-factor interactions like environmental status and human resource actions (Dalby 2018; Lee 2018). Other changes, not previously recognized in this context, include intra- and international environmental prerogatives in protection activities, the acquisition of resources, and the use of unprocessed and processed natural resources. Thus, to better understand drivers and interactions resulting in changes in environmental security homeostasis and how to address it, we pose the following questions: Does a pragmatic environmental security framework exist to make sense of the challenges, threats, and realities that affect ecological, human, and defence security in the polar regions? What is a better way to unify scientific research and multiple viewpoints, and how does that work?

In this chapter, we argue that challenges, threats, and realities in polar regions may be associated with changes in ecological, human, and defence security conditions. These conditions may contribute to the predictability of the overall status of environmental security in the polar regions and may structure future strategic discourse. We present a tripartite environmental security framework comprising ecological, human, and defence security, and discuss the use of multi-track diplomacy to navigate plausible polar scenarios that may affect the North American Arctic security landscape.

Challenges, Threats, and Realities

Challenges in Polar Regions

In broad aspect, the polar regions are like other areas of the world: they are international landscapes structured by multi-national geopolitical interactions, they have long histories as economic centres for renewable and non-renewable resource extraction, and they have substantial terrestrial and marine environments. In other ways, the polar regions differ by their relative isolation from population centres, lack of substantial built infrastructure, and extreme cold environmental conditions. Both broad features present challenges and opportunities. Distinct challenges include the tyranny of time and space and the uncertainty and lack of cohesive and responsive systems encompassing a multitude of shortfalls in areas critical for humans to thrive, not least of which is a robust logistics environment, the complexity of the polar ecosystem, and differing stakeholder values and motivations.

The Arctic and Antarctic share similarities but are nevertheless distinct from each other. Both are major components of the cryosphere, thus have glaciers and icebound environments, and are distinguished by low precipitation. Major differences include geography, political structure, and human occupation. The Arctic region is dominated by a central ice-covered ocean and surrounded by coastal terrestrial environments that are all sovereign territories; Indigenous peoples have occupied the Arctic region for thousands of years, and the coastal biotic environment is dominated by terrestrial-based plants and animals. By contrast, the Antarctic region is dominated by an ice-covered continent surrounded by the Southern Ocean. It is shaped by history and governed by international treaties (Sheikh, Vaughn, and Procita 2021). There are no sovereign territories or permanent inhabitants. The coastal environment is dominated by marine birds and mammals, with only a few isolated areas with any vegetation. As we discuss below, these ecological and geopolitical aspects play a significant role in structuring the security environment of the polar regions. We focus on the Arctic region, given its greater complexity of social, environmental, and geopolitical realities, and reflect on its differences and similarities with the Antarctic region.

Threats

Threats to environmental security may be interruptions in homeostasis in the ecological, human, and defence realms. In the polar regions, a critical threat is a lack of situational awareness. This may negatively affect the comprehension of baseline conditions, which in turn may lead to unforeseen changes without foresight into what and how to change.

Realities

The polar regions are experiencing profound physical changes: reduced sea ice, thawing permafrost, wildfires, diminished shore-fast ice, precipitation events, and increasing storm severity. Generally, researchers expect continued change, particularly in the form of reduced ice coverage at the peak of the summer season. Specifically, current climate research indicates that the Arctic maritime region is experiencing a decrease in sea ice extent and thickness (and thus "volume") due to changes in atmospheric and maritime conditions. Associated with changes in the Arctic Ocean and the adjoining Bering, Beaufort, and Chukchi Seas, which are associated with the US Arctic Extended Economic Zone, are a number of fine-scale changes in the marine environment's physical, chemical, and biological characteristics, most of which are projected to continue through the twenty-first century. Research suggests that in maritime and coastal regions, terrain frozen for more than a millennium may thaw, creating unique challenges for residents affecting infrastructure, eroding coastal and riverine environments, and jeopardizing current ways of life in villages and small communities (Huntington and Pungowiyi, 2009). Associated with these disruptions are ecological perturbations in Arctic flora and fauna, such as invasive species like beavers and killer whales, along with changes in resident species.

The "New Arctic"

As physical changes continue, the region is more readily accessible to a broader range of actors, vessels, and marine activities (Causey and Greaves, 2021). Some research indicates that by the mid-2030s, Canada's Northwest Passage and Russia's Northern Sea Route may be more reliably open from midsummer to autumn. Increasingly, forecasters predict that transpolar maritime routes may become navigable by ice-hardened vessels and vessels following in convoys behind icebreaking ships as early as the late 2020s or early 2030s. This access could facilitate further changes if commercial maritime traffic commences large-scale efforts and significantly reduces the distance to transit between Asia and Europe via a transpolar maritime route. While a transpolar route connecting Europe and East Asia reduces transit time and allows for substantially larger vessels when compared to the Panama Canal or the Suez Canal routes, neither distances nor vessel size necessarily dictates route-determination decisions by commercial shippers, particularly for container and cargo vessels that compete for tightly scheduled pier space at on-load or destination ports (Causey and Greaves 2021; Churchill 2015). Commercial marine transits in the polar regions, and the Arctic in particular, are governed by the International Maritime Organization's Polar Code. There is the relative lack of service ports and ports of refuge, inconsistencies as regards quality and frequency of marine weather forecasts, unpredictable insurance requirements and costs, and other factors (McDorman and Schofield, 2015).

Indigenous peoples increasingly seek to take advantage of shifts in the Arctic environment as diminishing ice creates changes in access. At the same time, Indigenous peoples have inhabited the North American Arctic for millennia and have created irreplaceable cultures and resilient communities adapted to the harsh difficulties of the region (Huntington and Pungowiyi, 2009). However, this resilience is challenged in new and unanticipated ways with increased cultural and material influences from lower latitudes and a physical environment that is less predictable, all of which affects traditional subsistence-based lifestyles.

Intra- and Interstate Interactions

In the past four to five decades, the Canadian and the US federal governments, the State of Alaska, and Canadian territories have enacted legislation and policies intended to address actions from the preceding century that affected Indigenous Arctic residents in North America. However, new questions have arisen about whether further legislation and policies are needed to preserve and protect communities from the array of influences from lower latitudes. Catalyzed by physical environmental changes and broader geopolitical considerations, interest in the Arctic continues to evolve. What has remained relatively constant among Arctic nations is an interest in continuing to seek ways to preserve the region as an area of collaboration and peace; however, with continued changes in the environment, competition over resources resulting from increasing access in the Arctic may arise (Palosaari and Tynkkynen, 2015). Although the Arctic is militarized, the region is not generally characterized as a zone of armed conflict. Arctic nations base military systems in the region for national defence readiness and active assistance in diverse homeland security operations. For example, Russia has deployed civilian and military infrastructure and systems to the Arctic, such as the S-400 Triumph anti-aircraft weapon and Bastion mobile coastal missile systems. The regional defence measures pursued by the United States include expanding fifth-generation fighter jets (F-22s and F-35As) and anti-ballistic missiles in Alaska to protect against intercontinental missile attacks. Considering rising security concerns, the leadership of the United States Coast Guard has testified before Congress about the potential need to arm icebreakers in the future. Additionally, China has introduced the concept of the Polar Silk Road (Willis and Dupledge, 2015). This action, combined with attempts to use Arctic resources to "pursue national interests" and investments in the region, sets the stage for a potential power competition not seen since the close of the Cold War. Other non-Arctic nations and actors, including the Japanese, the United Kingdom, the Netherlands, Germany, and the European Union, demonstrate interests spanning a wide variety of areas, ranging from alternate transit routes, foreign trade, and marine transport to the exploration of rare earth minerals, fishing, tourism, and scientific research. Additionally, with the North American Arctic, regional Canadian and Alaskan law-enforcement organizations note a rise in illicit activities.

Maritime security and safety issues in lower latitudes may eventually manifest in the Arctic maritime, and limited Canadian and US law-enforcement resources are needed to cover the vast yet sparsely populated region. Patrolling and policing for illicit human trafficking, illegal fishing, unregulated mineral extraction, and unsafe tourism practices present an array of complex issues that will likely worsen as opportunists and criminals conduct activities that often go undetected. An additional concern is the lack of understanding of risk and the insufficient capability to address increasing vessel traffic in vulnerable regions, such as the Bering Strait.

These concerns extend to non-maritime areas whose economic zones and border regions are for the most part unpatrolled and unsecured. As illicit activities are to likely increase, so will the risk to local, regional, national, and global security.

The polar regions are vast, and although these regions are largely associated with the maritime domain, the regions also include land, air, space, and cyber realms. The polar regions are sparsely populated. In the Arctic, there are only four million inhabitants (in Antarctica, no permanent residents exist). Thus, there are approximately four million unique local perspectives on life in the Arctic. This number does not account for outside perspectives. Views of reality are shaped by geographical location, cultural values, physical and mental attributes, and political and economic conditions, for both individuals and groups. Multiple perspectives from outside the Arctic and multiple external perspectives of uninhabited Antarctica further add to the complexity of security perspectives in the polar regions.

Tripartite Environmental Security Conceptual Framework

These factors discussed above can be aggregated within a tripartite environmental security (TES) framework as a practical way to unify trans-disciplinary research and activities (see figure 1.1 below). Use of a TES framework approach can lead to a deeper understanding of the variables and interactions affecting environmental security in the polar landscape. These components—categorized in one of three realms: ecological security, human security, and defence security—interact to contribute to the totality of environmental security in the polar regions. The outcomes of these interactions among and between components and sub-components can be predictable or unpredictable. Interruptions to desirable states and unknown factors and interactions, however, may result in instability and unpredictability. TES provides a visualization of threshold management in a constant temporal environment to secure solidarity measurements. In addition, the framework enables the exploration of polar scenarios that may extend beyond the region.

A review of environmental security literature found that perspectives on this topic are diverse and varied: as a component (Dalby, 1992), as a consequence (Gudev 2016; Loring and Gerlach 2015) and/or as a driver

Figure 1.1. Components of tripartite environmental security (TES).

Dynamics of Interaction

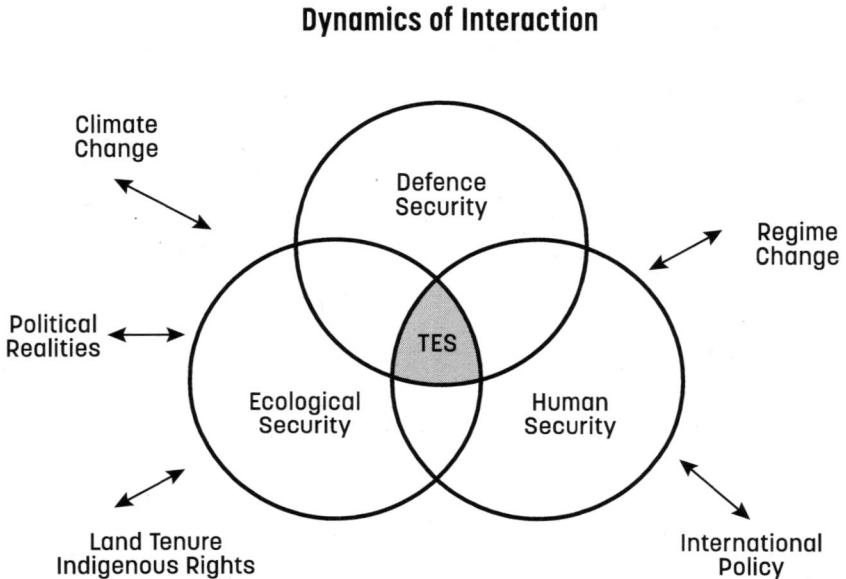

(Berner et al. 2016; Fillion et al. 2016) of human security. Environmental security is also viewed as an antagonist (Gudev, 2016), as a facilitator (Ford 2009; Greaves 2016), or as a mitigating factor (Watts et al. 2017; White et al. 2007). Environmental security can be considered a summary outcome of these factors (Eicken et al. 2011; Stokke 2011), or of none of these (Doel et al. 2014). Varying definitions stem primarily from the lack of a single operating assumption with which to unify multiple perspectives and understandings in the literature. Further, regardless of the perspective, many terms are used interchangeably and thus the discussions so far have been obscured by lack of a collective understanding of the components and their interactions (Bazely et al. 2014; Ebinger and Zambetakis 2009).

Environmental Security as a Function of Ecological Security, Human Security, and Defence Security

Ecological Security

For this discussion, we begin by redefining traditional definitions of environmental security as ecological security to delineate between often overlapping definitions of ecology and environment; we then map these onto the TES framework. Ecological security is a statement of the relative stability of ecological processes. Changes in the polar regions may be either predictable or unpredictable. In the Arctic, rapidly thawing permafrost with consequent coastal erosion (Stokke, 2011) and melting and retreating sea and land ice (Eicken et al. 2011; Greaves 2016) may strongly interact with human security (Churchill, 2015). Furthermore, changes in habitat and species distribution will have a direct effect on food and water security, primarily (though not exclusively) by changing distributions of traditional subsistence food items (Huntington, Loring, and Gannon 2018; Medeiros et al. 2017; Natcher et al. 2016). Such changes will present a challenge to local adaptation efforts. This weakening of the internal structure of environmental interconnections may be conceptualized as a weakening of "ecosystem health" or ecological complexity. Still, direct measurement of these changes has vexed environmental ecologists from the onset of focused study (Klubnikin and Causey, 2002; 2005).

Human Security

Introduced and championed by the United Nations and summarized in the *Our Common Future* report by the World Commission on Environment and Development (1987), the concept of human security is contextual and determined by local people and communities. In the Arctic, local knowledge and local contexts are informed by history, tradition, and experience—a concept both evident and essential (Huntington and Pungowiyi 2009). Bazely et al. describe human security as providing "a framework in which local peoples can identify issues and solutions that will increase their security, and many policies, pathways, and options become available" (2014, 139). By contrast, environmental security is a statement of the relative stability of ecological processes (Klubnikin and Causey 2002).

Ecological status is classified into three categories: predictable (stable), reaching stability, or becoming unstable. Elevated levels of ecological unpredictability or instability in the Arctic, such as rapidly thawing permafrost with consequent coastal erosion (Stokke, 2011) as well as melting and retreating sea and land ice (Eicken et al. 2011; Greaves 2016) will be strongly interacting factors for human security.

Various measures can be utilized, such as productivity, population growth, or decline; however, few describe the whole state. The literature suggests that no single variable or assessment sufficiently describes the complexity of interactions between human security and environmental stability interactions (Hoel, 2015). Further research is needed to explore interactions among and between factors and to test and expand on this integrative framework.

Defence Security

Lack of situational awareness may result in misinformation, misunderstanding, or misplaced action, thereby risking a potential "security dilemma" (Byers, 2020). Until recently, defence security in polar regions—that is, nation-state assessment of threat and consequence—was often described as a distant, low-level factor of little consequence (Byers 2019; Gabrielsson and Sliwa 2014). As a result, Arctic security has traditionally been left to defence actors, militaries, and coast guards, and in the case of non-defence-related security, the Arctic Council. However, defence security in the polar regions often involves using more than just militaries; it involves diplomacy, information, military, and economics (or DIME). Given the evolving challenges, threats, and realities in the defence-security landscape, the complexities at play in the polar regions require an expanded range of powers that complement the DIME approach: finance, intelligence, and law enforcement (or DIME-FIL). Unlike DIME, DIME-FIL is not as widely addressed in the literature. But these are important factors when it comes to establishing priorities of effort within a security framework in a region with an existing history of co-operation among actors. The United States is not alone in considering these additional factors; China and Russia have long employed additional elements of power (Rodriguez, Walton, and Chu 2020).

Environmental Conflict

There are many different issues and combinations that may be character-ized as environmental conflict, but there are at least four general inter-actions relevant to the polar regions (Lee, 2018). *Territorial and resource conflict* derives from limited access to resources and can lead to conflict that ranges from minor skirmishes to full-scale war fought for specific resources (i.e., "resource wars") (Renner 2002). *Extraterritorial resource conflict* is based in the control of resources through claims made outside of the boundaries of nation-state. *Conflict using the environment* results in environmental destruction in war and in the denial of strategic resources. *Environment in conflict* occurs when the environment is used to wage war. We use the term "conflict" intentionally to describe a general disagree-ment or struggle, rather than one specifically tied to aggressive disputes or armed intervention. The gradient of responses to conflict can span from parliamentary resolutions to armed conflict or outright war. Several types of environmental conflict relate directly or indirectly to the consequences associated with war and are beyond the scope of this discussion.

The study of environmental conflict reveals several commonalities (Lee, 2018). The relative abundance of a resource can be a strong driver of environmental conflict. The United States' purchase of Alaska from Russia was made with strong consideration of the availability of fur seals, a valu-able natural resource that was a suitable replacement for the increasingly limited supply of beaver elsewhere in the mid-nineteenth-century United States. Later, the discovery of gold, and more recently an interest in other valuable minerals, has led to increasing competition between developers and environmentalists, culminating in the highly charged debate within the State of Alaska over the Pebble Mine copper and gold development in Bristol Bay, involving Alaska Native groups, local people, environ-mental activists, and the mining industry (National Parks Conservation Association, 2019).

Links between the state of environmental resources and conflict are often indirect (Gleditch 1998; Swain and Ojendal 2019). Lack of potable water, whether caused by human activities, drought, or climate change, is a global concern, and one that increasingly manifests in the Arctic. Immediate responses are often possible when public health is affected;

however, long-term responses often require regional, state, or federal action, involving complex funding, timing, and alternative negotiation (Causey and Edwards 2008; Essak 2018; Mackenzie et al. 2013; Ruscio, Brubaker, and Glasser 2015).

In polar regions, all responses—immediate to long-term—can be summarized in two categories: environmental access and environmental control.

Environmental access occurs when participants have unequal access to resources; this is often termed territorial resource conflict (Lee, 2018). Typical cases of this type of environmental conflict include degradation or disruption of ecological resources or ecosystem functions, including "eco-system services" such as water quality, and soil stability. This may occur naturally, through fire, erosion, or weather, or it may be the result of human-created pollution or over- or under-use of existing resources. In this case, the conflict concerns specific resources and is often of an intra-state nature. Typical cases in Arctic regions involve access to potable water and restrictions on subsistence hunting and gathering (Huntington, Loring, and Gannon 2018).

Conflict over *environmental control* involves disputes for resources that lie outside of territorial limits. These occur when significant dispar-ities as regards environmental resources exist between regions (Homer-Dixon, 1991); perhaps new means of acquisition are being developed, or a new resource is discovered. Typical cases for polar regions involve control or management of coastal fisheries or subsurface seabed claims in the Arctic and Southern Oceans (Ørebech, 2016).

Changes in environmental factors and associated conflict rarely occur simultaneously. Sometimes the change in the abundance or availability of an environmental resource is small, with only incremental effects de-tectable. Over time, the effects amass, and human activities are affected at a scale that behaviour is affected. An example of this is shore erosion in coastal villages in Alaska. In the coastal villages of Kaktovik, located on the Beaufort Sea, and Shishmaref, located on the Chukchi Sea, chan-ges in environmental factors have been noticed by local people for years, but only in the past decade have the aggregated effects spurred external actors to address the impacts on these local communities. Changes in the environment in these coastal communities resulted in a need to relocate at great expense, which then gave rise to the questions of by whom and how the associated costs would be paid: by local villages, associated tribal authorities, state, or federal resource providers? In most active cases in the Arctic region and across the State of Alaska, these issues remain unresolved (Sutter, 2017).

The Advent of Defence Security as an Interactor

For many inhabitants of the United States, the Arctic region is a distant, remote, and relatively unimportant region located at the top of the map. Accordingly, the Arctic is deemed intractable, inaccessible, and the haven of polar bears and Indigenous hunters (Doel et al. 2014; Nopens 2010). Likewise, Antarctica is characterized as a region of penguins, seals, and visiting scientists, differing only in that the region is located at the bottom of a Mercator projection map.

Characteristics of polar regions include small populations above the Arctic Circle. Approximately four million people are year-round residents of the Arctic, roughly 50 per cent of whom live in Russia, all with limited infrastructure and a history of international co-operation or an absence of international conflict. Antarctica has no permanent inhabitants. Instead, it is principally a destination for visiting scientists and support personnel associated with research activities. Typical assessments of the polar regions as regions of co-operation have been attributed to a lack of underlying drivers of conflict consequently resulting in peace, co-operation, and stability.

The concept of limited conflict in the polar regions due to similarities and isolation is flawed. Differences in geography, land tenure and ownership, history, economics, and governance exist. When viewed through a geographical lens, the Arctic is an ice-covered polar ocean surrounded by the low-population coastal regions of nation-states. By contrast, the Antarctic is an uninhabited continent surrounded by an ice-covered stretch of the Southern Ocean. Antarctica fits the definition of *terra nullius*; however, the Arctic rarely has been so considered. A few small and isolated localities—Svalbard and the North Pole—fit that definition. However, the Arctic is home to various Indigenous peoples whose presence and land tenure predate European explorations and inhabitation, whereas Antarctica has none. In this sense, the closest equivalency for the polar regions is in marine transportation: the use of and access to polar regions from the beginning have been primarily by sea. Thus, traditional concepts of free passage apply to both the Arctic and the Antarctic (Burgess et al. 2017).

Multi-Track Diplomacy

Track One Diplomacy

Track one diplomacy is a *traditional* diplomatic interaction, otherwise known as *official diplomacy*: "an instrument of foreign policy for the establishment and development of contacts between governments of different states through the use of intermediaries mutually recognized by the respective parties" (Magalhães, 1988). This type of formal, state-to-state interaction follows traditional protocols and is exercised by diplomats, government officials, and heads of state (Mapendere, 2006). This approach has its strengths and weaknesses. A key strength is that negotiators speak with the full authority of the entities they represent. A disadvantage is that apolitical considerations often supersede political ones.

Track Two Diplomacy

Track two diplomacy is defined as "unofficial, informal interaction between members of adversary groups or nations that aim to develop strategies to influence public opinion . . . [or] organize human and material resources in ways that might help resolve their conflict" (Montville, 1991). A key strength of track two diplomacy is the unofficial nature of the interactions and the opportunity for incremental iterations that advance ways of achieving reconciliation through lower-risk engagement. Negotiating parties are not inhibited by political or constitutional power; however, they have limited ability to influence foreign policy and political power structures (Mapendere, 2006). Regardless, track two diplomacy is often employed by negotiating powers, and is a key tool employed by the US Department of State and the diplomatic agencies of other nation-states for issues that are not deemed crises and that require time or knowledge to reach a consensus or agreement. In the past several decades, an alternative approach to conflict or crisis diplomacy has expanded from the original two tracks to nine tracks or more (Diamond and McDonald, 1996). A comprehensive discussion of all tracks is beyond the scope of this chapter.

Instead, we focused on tracks one and two above and discuss an alternative below.

Track One and a Half Diplomacy

To fill the gap between tracks one and two, environmental security experts have recently developed the concept of track one and a half diplomacy (Staats, Walsh, and Tucci 2019). Originally described as "long-term unofficial facilitated joint analysis among negotiators," track one and a half is defined as follows:

> Public or private interaction between official representatives of conflicting governments or political entities such as popular armed movements, which is facilitated or mediated by a third party not representing a political organization or institution. Such interaction aims to influence attitudinal changes between the parties to change the political power structures that caused the conflict. (Mapendere 2006, 69)

Track one and a half diplomacy differs from tracks one and two in both the status and the diversity of participants. Here, a third party, not representing a nation-state or political entity, acts as a negotiator. Further, the negotiating participants are official representatives of the conflicting groups. In track two diplomacy, the negotiating parties are often influential citizens, including former government leaders and formal officials. Track on and a half diplomacy, also known as hybrid diplomacy, blends the features of tracks one and two to enable resolution and agreement (Mapendere, 2006).

Whether intended or not, the Arctic Council is considered by some a notable example of track one and a half diplomacy. It seeks to identify, and often works to resolve, environmental security concerns in the Arctic (Sarson et al. 2019), though matters of "hard" security are not addressed. Similarly, several participating entities have described the Arctic Council as a model of multi-track diplomacy (Conley and Zagorski, 2017). The Arctic Council includes eight Arctic nation-states: Canada, the Kingdom of Denmark (Greenland), Finland, Iceland, Norway, Russia, Sweden, and the United States, and six international organizations representing Arctic

Indigenous peoples, as well as other entities with observer status. Some researchers suggest that despite the fact that the Arctic Council lacks the formal ability to create, implement, or enforce treaties, working as it does entirely by consensus, it has been able to address many non-security-related Arctic issues (Heininen and Finger 2018; Rowe and Blakkisrud 2014; Sergunin and Konyshev 2014). However, there is considerable debate as to whether and how these processes should or could be advanced into a more formalized set of governance policies (Stokke, 2015).

A Pragmatic Approach to Environmental Security in the Polar Regions

Based on an informed understanding of existing models, and an examination of outcomes of policies and practices, our approach is both pragmatic and integrative, connecting multiple perspectives and formal inquiries to deliver on a continual basis actionable knowledge to address environmental security in the polar regions, with a principal focus on the Arctic. Advancing an improved posture of environmental security in the polar regions may enable the ability to identify the risks of a changing polar physical ecosystem categorized and then reconciled against factors that matter across the diplomacy, information, military, economics, finance, intelligence, and law-enforcement DIME/DIME-FIL construct.

An analytic investigation of the three-factor environmental security paradigm first introduced by Klubnikin and Causey (2002) will contribute to practical and applicable problem-solving capabilities with which to address current and future challenges, threats, and realities. We believe this approach addresses the dichotomy between various perspectives on environmental security and published research to produce previously unavailable knowledge. The dual nature of truth and knowledge from beliefs allows for a range of practical and useful environmental security solutions to address a wide range of challenges, threats, and realities. This approach provides a foundation and a conceptual framework to identify, categorize, and assess ecological security, human security, defence security attributes, and interactions. Unpredictability may be the norm in environmental security, but the desired outcome is predictability. These interactions may result in either homeostasis (stability), or positive or negative interruptions to homeostasis. The principles of pragmatism (Peirce, 1935) used to design TES promote the ongoing researcher-practitioner partnership and promote the development of practical solutions that enhance environmental security in the polar regions.

The response to complex and diverse problems is flexibility and a diversity of solution sets derived from multiple perspectives, a transdisciplinary approach, objective and subjective explorations, and qualitative and quantitative research strategies. The TES framework attempts to identify and assess consequences and interruptions to homeostasis and helps focus for challenge-prevention measures. TES acknowledges the spatial and temporal qualities of threats, challenges, and realities, and the interconnectedness of perspectives and published scientific research.

Discussion

Changes across the polar regions, and associated variations in the impact of these changes, mean that the nature of environmental security in the Arctic is rapidly transforming. Old scenarios and solutions may no longer be relevant. This applies not just to the nature of potential disasters, but also to the way security actors respond. Changing conditions in the Arctic Ocean and surrounding coastal regions demonstrate the need for security and defence professionals to seek and account for environmental security factors in order to reduce risk and better accomplish their missions to secure and defend their respective territories.

Arctic security has traditionally been left to defence actors such as navies, other armed forces, or associated national coast guards. However, law-enforcement organizations, other security personnel, and finance professionals have an increasingly vital role to play. Challenges, threats, and realities will continue to evolve and will need to be addressed, including through search and rescue, disaster mitigation, and humanitarian aid. This raises the question of the role of geopolitics in regional development and governance: Will geopolitics become increasingly competitive, or will it tilt toward a greater degree of peaceful co-operation as Arctic states either maintain the status quo or become even more mindful of the common threats they face and the attendant need for regional stability? To date, Arctic stakeholder relationships have remained relatively peaceful and co-operative; however, associated threats and capacity challenges may result from changes in the environment, increased tourism and maritime activity, and geopolitical tensions among and between Arctic stakeholders. Conversely, the Antarctic region remains governed by the Antarctic Treaty (United Nations, 1959). Nevertheless, both signatory and non-signatory nations will have to address and reconcile governance measures in the future, without an existing body, along the lines of the Arctic Council, that they can leverage as a venue of co-operative dialogue.

Growing security and operational risks continue to evolve; this includes defining the level of risk for a maritime incident in the Arctic and how to respond to challenges posed by increasing globalization and economic activity, criminal activity, smuggling, and policing. Impacts associated with diminishing ice affect subsistence harvesting, culture, safety, transportation, and building in the Arctic region. Traditional villages are at risk from these changes, thereby affecting the people of the region. The opening of greater commercial possibilities in the Arctic Ocean, especially as non-Arctic countries invest in the region, raises questions about the global impact of these changes. Actors in both Canada and the United States must contemplate risk-mitigation strategies. While general awareness, as well as some overarching plans, already exist, the multiple actors involved means that there is no single, shared perspective as regards issues like funding or political intentions.

It is imperative that we improve charting in the high latitudes and make additional investments in hydrographic mapping of the Arctic region to address challenges like supply-chain management and tourism safety. While the lack of such hydrographic mapping in the region has long been recognized, as marine traffic continues to rise across the circumpolar North, so does the risk to mass maritime response operations and their ability to potentially save hundreds to thousands of passengers on vessels in distress due to the impacts of uncharted obstacles.

In the United States, while the need to commit to a new generation of icebreakers has received some recognition, the pace of development thus far has not matched the rising, security-driven need to replace dated platforms and deliver new capacities. Canada offers icebreaking capabilities that contribute to North America's overall defence posture. Further, we must better synthesize and visualize Arctic sea ice and associated risks and hazards for maritime operation for nations, industry, and Arctic communities. This aligns with the Arctic Council's broader goals to enhance Arctic marine safety, protect Arctic people and environments, and build Arctic maritime infrastructure.

However, some security experts identify the challenge of rising great power competition, primarily among the People's Republic of China, the Russian Federation, and the United States, as one of the principal factors demonstrating the need for greater collaborative efforts in the polar regions, and especially the Arctic. There is a potential disconnect between the hope for continued Arctic exceptionalism and the reality of the strategic geopolitical tensions that were reignited in January 2007 with the return of Russian Long Range Aviation overflights across much of the Arctic. While collaboration often assumes a normative function among Arctic nations, Russia's manoeuvring and its opaque defence-planning process continue to create uncertainty and the potential for rising tension and risk of miscalculation. Additionally, non-Arctic national actors claiming sovereignty over some part of the region may pose threats to peaceful geopolitical relations in the Arctic Ocean by introducing military activities that, if not carefully messaged and understood, may also escalate tensions and risks. Whereas competition and the potential for confrontation in and through the Arctic are substantially less than they were during the Cold War, there is nonetheless a risk of miscalculation and the possibility of rising tension and conflict. Management of this tension and the associated potential for escalation has not been fully resolved among Arctic regional militaries, and it must therefore remain a focus.

Local Community Preparedness

In addition to threats arising from great power rivalries in the Arctic, there are also a host of challenges when it comes to building community preparedness for natural and human-created disasters. This demonstrates the need to make connections between state and non-state actors, such as the Alaska Federation of Natives and the United States military, including the United States Coast Guard. With their mutual interest in ensuring security in the Arctic, established security and defence forces and Indigenous communities in Alaska and Canadian coastal communities can increase their efforts to share knowledge and improve their preparedness and community resilience (Fabbi, 2015).

Due to permafrost thawing and changing hydro- and thermodynamics, the environmental transformation of the Canadian Arctic is outpacing the design of new infrastructure. The transformation of the environment affects all communities, challenging locally based security strategies and traditional subsistence lifestyles. Arctic communities can provide critically needed infrastructure bases during emergencies and security events. A dynamically changing environment requires more flexibility in planning as well as greater preparation for stochastic events.

The changing environment influences all communities in some ways. Access to old hunting routes is becoming more difficult, affecting cultural identity as well as food security. Overall, the sustainability of local communities is at risk. Yet sustainable communities are essential to Arctic security—a case in point being the Canadian Rangers community patrol groups. These play a critical role in patrolling northern territories. Such community-based observers and defenders are a citizen-security force, adapted to the harsh and difficult environment of the North American Arctic.

Nevertheless, environmental change challenges even these basic security practices. Concern about supply chains and the logistics involved in sustaining communities and local security teams in the Arctic remain acute. For example, the transportation of essential commodities, such as fuel, to remote Arctic villages across Canada is poised between stability and instability, and this is especially troubling when security agencies rely on these communities to provide temporary infrastructure bases during emergencies or security events. We must therefore address challenges related to infrastructure and remote resourcing in order to reduce risk and improve security in the North American Arctic.

The Role of Environmental Intelligence

As the Arctic's physical environment becomes increasingly dynamic, more information on weather and climatic conditions is needed to improve domain awareness and understanding and to form the core of a new environmental security relationship between defence forces and security communities. In particular, the US National Weather Service (NWS), as one operational arm of the Department of Commerce's National Oceanic and Atmospheric Administration, routinely receives questions and requests for information related to the ice forming or thawing in the Arctic. The NWS believes there is a need for inter-agency and international collaboration and coordination when it comes to answering these questions. At risk are potentially large energy projects and marine environments—for example, a potential fifteen billion barrels of oil in the Chukchi Sea and another estimated eight billion barrels in the Beaufort Sea.

While increased human activity in the polar regions, and especially in the Arctic, is likely to increase, such activity in the associated ecological environment remains difficult to model and forecast with precision due to lack of data, whether satellite, terrestrial, or marine based. This comes at a time when the associated aspects of a changing environment are increasingly dynamic, and less amenable to forecasting. As a result, there is a need for increased efforts in support of sustained, internationally coordinated environmental observations at various echelons, from the local to the regional and to pan-Arctic, so as to advance and provide needed data to support better forecasting. Current forecasting methods, while helpful, are limited in their ability to predict long-term changes. Most forecasts are predicated on hindcasts; they are therefore useful predictors of the future only if the future resembles many of the facets of the past.

Increased demand for fish protein, mineral wealth, and petrochemicals may drive industry and nations to further develop Arctic ecosystems, despite their having signed on to restraining moratoriums toward the Arctic. Marine traffic may continue to rise, and with such traffic, increased concerns about safety and our ability to respond to disasters as more ships ply the region's poorly sounded waters. A future Arctic will likely include increased cruise ship and liquefied natural gas transport, and increased transits in hard-to-navigate and unpredictable areas due to the presence of sea ice in waterways such as the Northern Sea Route, Transpolar Sea Route, and Northwest Passage, thereby introducing the potential for increased risk (Churchill, 2015). Difficult terrain, extreme cold weather conditions, and cycles of light and darkness, among other factors, must be factored into the region's already limited and expensive transportation and communication infrastructure and networks.

In the polar regions, and particularly in the Arctic, there is also a need for better technologies and the improved use of existing technologies, such as finding replacements for tracked land vehicles, advocating for an increased maritime surface presence for the United States military, and in particular the US Navy and US Coast Guard, and layering intelligence tools for added capacity. Similarly, we must develop better tools to assess long-term ice and climate predictions and aid safe operations. In addition, there is a need to integrate well-established traditional Arctic knowledge with current research-derived knowledge from the scientific community and to better share and understand available knowledge. Environmentally precise information for security, economic, and transit purposes is currently difficult to obtain.

The inability to secure maritime approaches to the North American Arctic regions underscores all areas of weakness in Canada and the United States. This stems from an overall level of sustained commitment. Various departments and agencies in Ottawa and Washington sponsor studies, strategies, initiatives, and papers that address the importance of the Arctic and the need to secure each country's respective national interests in the region. However, the sustained commitment of resources to the area, particularly in ensuring individual national interests, remains lacking. The economic strength of both Canada and the United States can advance each nation's Arctic security in the face of growing great power competition within the region. Still, concerted efforts to devote resources and implement strategies and policies are needed.

A Pragmatic Approach

The pragmatic approach we propose utilizes an ecological understanding of this complex system. Delineating the interaction framework for the Arctic and Antarctic in these contexts may provide a clearer understanding of changes in these regions. Current research indicates that the effects of climate change on the polar regions are becoming increasingly apparent (Palosaari and Tynkkynen, 2015). The consequent impact on human systems and regional, national, and international settings is recognized as having potentially profound implications on multi-state actions (Burnett and Adger 2007; CNA Military Advisory Board 2014; Doel et al. 2014; Heininen 2016; Stokke 2011). The concept of environmental security as a three-factor interaction complex involving environmental stability, human security, and defence security that structures activities within the

Arctic region is now receiving greater attention from interested parties (Doel et al. 2014), but much work remains.

We offer a pragmatic approach and the tripartite environmental security framework in order to improve our understanding of the complexities of the polar regions. The TES model includes factors and their constituent components and will help describe and quantify the effects that environmental status—whether stable or moving to a new regime state—may have on the other interacting components of TES. Applying this approach and framework to complex challenges, threats, and realities may improve our understanding of changes in the polar regions. Moreover, these conditions may contribute to the predictability of the overall status of environmental security in the polar regions and may structure future strategic discourse.

Conclusion

In this chapter we have shown that the challenges, threats, and realities of polar environmental security can be addressed within a conceptual framework comprising ecological security, human security, and defence security. Formal and informal diplomacy, including multi-track diplomacy, facilitates solutions for these difficult issues, specifically by use of track one and a half diplomacy (Staats, Walsh, and Tucci 2019) with Arctic stakeholders from Canada, Norway, the United Kingdom, and the United States (ADAC, 2019). While much work remains if we are to address environmental security in the polar regions, researchers have begun to look more closely at the perceived drivers, interactions, and outcomes of various scenarios, and have categorized these actions into the components of TES: ecological, human, and defence security. Our research here suggests that a relative abundance of natural resources may be a principal driver of environmental conflict (Lee, 2018). Links between environmental resources and conflict have often been found to be indirect (Causey and Edwards 2008; Essak 2018; Mackenzie et al. 2013; Ruscio, Brubaker, and Glasser 2015), and change in environmental factors and associated conflict rarely co-occur.

At the nexus of these and other changing conditions are concerns about risk and resiliency, examples of which manifest at all levels: local, regional, national, and global. Multi-track diplomacy (Conley and Zagorski 2017; Sarson et al. 2019), as employed in the Arctic Council and in an ADAC–Trent University workshop (ADAC, 2019), hold promise. Still, challenges like risk comprehension and such realities as the differing perspectives and values of stakeholders remain. Additionally, little is known about the risk comprehension and risk literacy of stakeholders working to advance environmental security issues in uncertain conditions.

Transforming traditional approaches to environmental security in the polar regions may involve testing our conceptual framework, addressing issues using multi-track diplomacy, and conducting relevant research into future studies and workshops. Additional areas for future research include more mixed-method environment security research bridging theories and known issues affecting the polar regions. Such efforts should go a long way toward the co-production of new and highly valuable knowledge, science, and solutions, thereby strengthening polar and Arctic security by contributing to the predictability of the overall status of environmental security in the polar regions, potentially structuring future strategic discourse.

REFERENCES

ADAC (Arctic Domain Awareness Center). 2019. *North American Arctic Marine and Environmental Security Workshop: Assessing Concern, Advancing Collaboration.* Anchorage, AK: Arctic Domain Awareness Center. https://arcticdomainawarenesscenter.org/Downloads/PDF/Arctic%20MaLTE/ADAC_Arctic%20MaLTE%202019_CANUS_Arctic%20Maritime%20and%20Environmental%20Security_Report_190109.pdf.

Bazely, D. R., J. Christensen, A. J. Tanentzap, and G. H. Gjorv. 2014. "Bridging the Gaps between Ecology and Human Security." In *Environmental and Human Security in the Arctic,* edited by G. H. Gjorv, D. R. Bazely, M. Goloviznina, A. J. Tanentzap, 129–50. New York: Routledge.

Berner, J., M. Brubaker, B. Revitch, E. Kreummel, M. Tcheripanoff, and J. Bell. 2016. "Adaptation in Arctic Circumpolar Communities: Food and Water Security in a Changing Climate." *International Journal of Circumpolar Health* 75:33820. DOI: 10.3402/ijch.v75.33820.

Burgess, J., L. Foulkes, P. Jones, M. Merighi, S. Murray, and J. Whitacre. 2017. *Law of the Sea: A Policy Primer.* Medford, MA: Fletcher School of Law and Diplomacy, Tufts University. https://sites.tufts.edu/lawofthesea/files/2017/07/LawoftheSeaPrimer.pdf.

Burnett, J., and W. N. Adger. 2007. "Climate Change, Human Security, and Violent Conflict." *Geography* 26:639–55.

Byers, M. 2019. "Cold, Dark, and Dangerous: International Cooperation in the Arctic and Space." *Polar Record* 55:32–47. DOI: 10.1017/S0032247419000160.

———. 2020. "Arctic Security and Outer Space." *Scandinavian Journal of Military Studies* 3:183–96. DOI: https://doi.org/10.31374/sjms.56.

Causey, D., and S. V. Edwards. 2008. "Ecology of Avian Influenza Virus in Birds." *Journal of Infectious Disease* 197 (Suppl. 1): S23–33. DOI: 10.1086/524991.

Causey, D., W. Greaves. 2021. "Climate Change: Reshaping the Face of the Canadian and Circumpolar Arctic." In *Beyond the Cooperation-Conflict Conundrum: Proceedings of an Arctic Security Webinar Series*, edited by P. W. Lackenbauer and P. Mason, 23–48. NAADSN Special Reports. Peterborough, ON: North American and Arctic Defence and Security Network.

Churchill, R. 2015. "The Exploitation and Management of Marine Resources in the Arctic: Law, Politics and the Environmental Challenge." In *Handbook of the Politics of the Arctic*, edited by L. C. Jensen and G. Honneland, 147–84. Northampton, MA: Edward Elgar Publishing.

CNA (Center for Naval Analysis) Military Advisory Board. 2014. *National Security and the Accelerating Risks of Climate Change*. Alexandria, VA: CNA Corporation.

Conca, K., and M. D. Beevers. 2018. "Environment and Conflict." In *Handbook of Environmental Conflict and Peacebuilding*, edited by A. Swain and J. Ojendal, 54–72. New York: Routledge.

Cokely, E. T., M. Galesic, E. Schulz, S. Ghazal, and R. Garcia-Retamero. 2012. "Measuring Risk Literacy: The Berlin Numeracy Test." *Judgment and Decision Making* 7:25–47.

Conley, H. A., and A. Zagorski. 2017. "The Arctic." In *A Roadmap for U.S.-Russia Relations*, edited by A. Kortunov and O. Oliker, 23–35. Boulder, CO: Rowman and Littlefield.

Dalby, S. 1992. "Ecopolitical Discourse: 'Environmental security' and Political Geography." *Progress in Human Geography* 16 (4): 503–22. DOI: 10.1177/030913259201600401.

———. 2018. "Climate Change and Environmental Conflicts." In *Handbook of Environmental Conflict and Peacebuilding*, edited by A. Swain and J. Ojendal, 42–53. New York: Routledge.

Diamond, L., and J. McDonald. 1996. *Multi Track Diplomacy: A Systems Approach to Peace*. West Hartford, CT: Kumarian Press.

Doel, R. E., R. M. Friedman, J. Lajus, S. Sorlin, and U. Wrakberg. 2014. "Strategic Arctic Science: National Interests in Building Natural Knowledge—Interwar Era through the Cold War." *Journal of Historical Geography* 44:60–80. DOI: 10.1016/j.jhg.2013.12.004.

Ebinger, C. K., and E. Zambetakis. 2009. "The Geopolitics of Arctic Melt." *International Affairs* 85 (6): 1215. DOI: 10.1111/j.1468-2346.2009.00858.x.

Eicken, H., J. Jones, F. Meyer, A. Mahoney, M. Druckenmiller, M. V. Rohith, and C. Kambhamettu. 2011. "Environmental Security in Arctic Ice-Covered Seas: From Strategy to Tactics of Hazard Identification and Emergency Response." *Marine Technology Society Journal* 45 (3): 37–48. DOI: 10.4031/MTSJ.45.3.1.

Essak, S. Y. 2018. "Environment: The Neglected Component of the One Health Triad." *Lancet Planetary Health* 2 (6): e238–39. DOI: 10.1016/S2542-5196(18)30124-4.

Fabbi, N. C. 2015. "Inuit Foreign Policy and International Relations in the Arctic." In *Handbook of the Politics of the Arctic*, edited by L. C. Jensen and G. Honneland, 482–500. Northampton, MA: Edward Elgar Publishing.

Fillion, M., T. A. Kenny, S. Weshe, A. Philibert, and L. H. M. Chan. 2016. "Impacts of Environmental Change on Food Security in the Canadian Arctic." *International Journal of Circumpolar Health* 75:1.

Ford, J. D. 2009. "Vulnerability of Inuit Food Systems to Food Insecurity as a Consequence of Climate Change: A Case Study from Igloolik, Nunavut." *Regional Environmental Change* 9:83–100. DOI: 10.1007/s10113-008-0060-x.

Gabrielsson, R., and Z. Sliwa. 2014. "Arctic—the New 'Great Game' or Peaceful Cooperation?" *Baltic Security Defence Review* 16:203–33.

Garcia-Retamero, R., A. Sobkow, D. Petrova, D. Garrido, and J. Traczyk. 2019. "Numeracy and Risk Literacy: What Have We Learned So Far?" *Spanish Journal of Psychology* 22:E10. DOI: 10.1017/sjp.2019.16.

Ghazal, S., E. T. Cokely, and R. Garcia-Retamero. 2014. "Predicting Biases in Very Highly Educated Samples: Numeracy and Metacognition." *Judgment and Decision Making* 9:15–34.

Gigerenzer, G., interview by David Brockman. 2011. "Annual Question 2011: What Scientific Concept Would Improve Everybody's Cognitive Toolkit?" Edge.org, accessed 21 July 2022. https://www.edge.org/response-detail/10624.

Gleditsch, N. P. 1998. "Armed Conflict and the Environment: A Critique of the Literature." *Journal of Peace Research* 35 (3): 381–400. DOI: 10.1177/0022343398035003007.

Greaves, W. 2016. "Arctic (in)Security an Indigenous Peoples: Comparing Inuit in Canada and Sami in Norway." *Security Dialogues* 47 (6): 461–80. DOI: 10.1177/0967010616665957.

Gudev, P. A. 2016. "[Non-Military Threats to the Arctic Security]." *Mirovaya Ekonmika I Mezhdunarodnye Otnosheniya* 60:72–82.

Heininen, L. 2016. "Security of the Global Arctic in Transformation—Potential for Changes in Problem Definition." In *Future Security of the Global Arctic: State Policy, Economic Security and Climate*, edited by L. Heininen, 12–34. London, Palgrave Pivot.

Heininen, L., and M. Finger. 2018. "The 'Global Arctic' as a New Geopolitical Context and Method." *Journal of Borderlands Studies* 33 (2): 199–202. DOI: 10.1080/08865655.2017.1315605.

Hoel, A. H. 2015. "Oceans Governance, the Arctic Council and Ecosystem-based Management." In *Handbook of the Politics of the Arctic*, edited by L. C. Jensen and G. Honneland, 265–80. Northampton, MA: Edward Elgar Publishing.

Homer-Dixon, T. F. 1991. "On the Threshold: Environmental Changes as Causes of Acute Conflict." *International Security* 19:5–40.

Huntington, H. P., and C. Pungowiyi. 2009. "Indigenous Perspectives." *Norwegian Polar Institute Report Series* 129:11–17.

Huntington, H. P., P. A. Loring, and G. Gannon. 2018. "Staying in Place during Times of Change in Arctic Alaska: The Implications of Attachment, Alternatives, and

Buffering." *Regional Environmental Change* 18:489–99. DOI: 10.1007/s10113-017-1221-6.

Klubnikin, K., and D. Causey. 2002. "Environmental Security and Conflict: Paradigm for the 21st Century." *Journal of Diplomacy and International Relations* 3:104–33.

———. 2005. "Beyond Trees: Forests, War, and Uneasy Peace." *European Tropical Forest Research* 43:27–28.

Kortunov, A., and O. Oliker, eds. 2017. *A Roadmap for U.S.-Russia Relations. A Report of the CSIS Russia and Eurasia Program and the Russian International Affairs Council.* Lanham, MD: Rowman and Littlefield.

Lee, J. R. 2018. "Environment and Conflict." In *Handbook of Environmental Conflict and Peacebuilding*, edited by A. Swain and J. Ojendal, 17–28. New York: Routledge.

Loring, P. A., and S. C. Gerlach. 2015. "Searching for Progress on Food Security in the North American North: A Research Synthesis and Meta-Analysis of the Peer-Reviewed Literature." *Arctic* 68 (3): 380–92. DOI: 10.14430/arctic4509.

Mackenzie, J. S., M. Jeggo, P. Daszak, and J. A. Richt. 2013. *One Health: The Human-Animal-Environment Interfaces in Emerging Infectious Diseases.* Berlin: Springer.

Magalhães, C. J. 1988. *The Pure Concept Our Diplomacy.* New York: Greenwood Press.

Mapendere, J. 2006. "Track One and a Half Diplomacy and the Complementarity of Tracks." *Culture of Peace Online Journal* 2:66–81. https://peacemaker.un.org/sites/peacemaker.un.org/files/TrackOneandaHalfDiplomacy_Mapendere.pdf.

McDorman, T. L., and C. Schofield. 2015. "Maritime Limits and Boundaries in the Arctic Ocean: Agreements and Disputes." In *Handbook of the Politics of the Arctic*, edited by L. C. Jensen and G. Honneland, 207–26. Northampton, MA: Edward Elgar Publishing.

Medeiros, A. S., P. Wood, S. D. Wesche, M. Bakaic, and J. F. Peters. 2017. "Water Security for Northern Peoples: Review of Threats to Arctic Freshwater Systems in Nunavut, Canada." *Regional Environmental Change* 17:635–47. DOI: 10.1007/s10113-016-1084-2.

Montville, J. 1991. *Track Two Diplomacy: The Arrow and the Olive Branch.* Vol. 2 in *The Psychodynamics of International Relations*, edited by V. D. Vokan, J. Montville, and D. A. Julius, 161–75. Lexington, MA: Lexington Books.

Natcher, D., S. Shirley, T. Rodon, and C. Southcott. 2016. "Constraints to Wildlife Harvesting among Aboriginal Communities in Alaska and Canada." *Food Security* 8:1152–67. DOI: 10.1007/s12571-016-0619-1.

National Parks Conservation Association. 2019. "Position on the Pebble Mine Project." National Parks Conservation Association, 23 October 2019. https://www.npca.org/articles/2328-position-on-the-pebble-mine-project.

Nopens, P. 2010. "The Impact of Global Warming on the Geopolitics of the Arctic: A Historical Opportunity for Russia?" *Egmont Security Policy Briefs* 8: 1–9. https://www.egmontinstitute.be/the-impact-of-global-warming-on-the-geopolitics-of-the-arctic-a-historical-opportunity-for-russia-2.

Ørebech, P. T. 2016. "Terrus Nullis, Inuit Habitation and Norse Occupation—with Special Emphasis on the 1933 East Greenland Case." *Arctic Review on Law and Policies* 7:20–41. DOI: https://doi.org/10.17585/arctic.v7.262.

Palosaari, T., and N. Tynkkynen. 2015. "Arctic Securitization and Climate Change." In *Handbook of the Politics of the Arctic*, edited by L. C. Jensen and G. Honneland, 87–104. Northampton, MA: Edward Elgar Publishing.

Peirce, C. S. 1935. *The Collected Papers of Charles Sanders Peirce*. Edited by C. Hartshorne and P. Weiss. Vols. 1–6. Cambridge, MA: Harvard University Press.

Renner, M. 2002. *The Anatomy of Resource Wars*. Worldwatch Paper No. 162. New York: Worldwatch Institute, NY.

Reyna, V. R., W. L. Nelson, P. Jean, and N. F. Dieckmann. 2009. "How Numeracy Influences Risk Comprehension and Medical Decision Making." *Psychological Bulletin* 135:943–73. DOI: 10.1037/a0017327.

Rodriguez, C. A., T. C. Walton, and H. Chu. 2020. "Putting the FIL into DIME." *Joint Forces Quarterly* 97. https://ndupress.ndu.edu/Media/News/News-Article-View/Article/2106566/putting-the-fil-into-dime-growing-joint-understanding-of-the-instruments-of-pow/.

Rowe, E. W., and H. Blakkisrud. 2014. "A New Kind of Arctic Power? Russia's Policy Discourses and Diplomatic Practices in the Circumpolar North." *Geopolitics* 19:66–85. DOI: 10.1080/14650045.2013.789863.

Ruscio, B. A., M. Brubaker, J. Glasser, W. Hueston, and T. W. Hennessy. 2015. "One Health—A Strategy for Resilience in a Changing Arctic." *International Journal of Circumpolar Health* 74:27913. DOI: 10.3402/ijch.v74.27913.

Sarson, L., V. Muzik, B. Ray, G. Gambrell, L. Yona, and R. Comeau. 2019. "The Model Arctic Council: Simulated Negotiations as Pedagogy and Embodied Diplomacy." *American Review of Canadian Studies* 49:105–22. DOI: 10.1080/02722011.2019.1570955.

Sergunin, A., and V. Konyshev. 2014. "Russia in Search of its Arctic Strategy: Between Hard and Soft Power?" *Polar Journal* 4:69–87. DOI: 10.1080/2154896X.2014.913930.

Staats, J., J. Walsh, and R. Tucci. 2019. "A Primer on Multi-Track Diplomacy: How Does It Work?" US Institute for Peace, 31 July 2019. https://www.usip.org/publications/2019/07/primer-multi-track-diplomacy-how-does-it-work.

Sheikh, P. A., B. Vaughn, and K. Procita. 2021. *Antarctic: Overview of Geopolitical and Environmental Issues*. CRS Report R46708. Washington, DC: Congressional Research Service Report. https://sgp.fas.org/crs/misc/R46708.pdf.

Stokke, O. S. 2011. "Environmental Security in the Arctic." *International Journal* 66 (4): 835–48. DOI: 10.1177/002070201106600412.

———. 2015. "Institutional Complexity in Arctic Governance: Curse or Blessing?" In *Handbook of the Politics of the Arctic*, edited by L. C. Jensen and G. Honneland, 328–51. Northampton, MA: Edward Elgar Publishing.

Sutter, J. D. 2017. "Tragedy of a Village Built on Ice." CNN, 29 March 2017. https://www.cnn.com/2017/03/29/us/sutter-shishmaref-esau-tragedy/index.html.

Swain, A., and J. Ojendal. 2018. "Environmental Conflict and Peacebuilding: An Introduction." In *Handbook of Environmental Conflict and Peacebuilding*, edited by A. Swain and J. Ojendal, 1–13. New York: Routledge.

United Nations. 1959. Antarctic Treaty. 1 December 1959, 402 UNTS 71. https://treaties.un.org/doc/Publication/UNTS/Volume%20402/volume-402-I-5778-English.pdf.

Watts, P., K. Koutouki, S. Booth, and S. Blum. 2017. "Inuit Food Security in Canada: Arctic Marine Ethnoecology." *Food Security* 9:421–40. DOI: 10.1007/s12571-017-0668-0.

WCED (World Commission on Environment and Development). 1987. *Our Common Future*. Oxford: Oxford University Press.

White, D. M., S. C. Gerlach, P. Loring, A. C. Tidwell, and M. C. Chambers. 2007. "Food and Water Security in a Changing Arctic Climate." *Environmental Research Letters* 2:045018. DOI: 10.1088/1748-9326/2/4/045018.

Willis, M., and D. Dupledge. 2015. "How We Learned to Stop Worrying about China's Arctic Ambitions." In *Handbook of the Politics of the Arctic*, edited by L. C. Jensen and G. Honneland, 388–407. Northampton, MA: Edward Elgar Publishing.

The Evolving Geopolitics of Polar Regions

Heather N. Nicol and Lassi K. Heininen

Polar Geopolitics: An Overview

A variety of different national, historical, cultural, political, and scientific perspectives and perceptions inform our understanding of polar geopolitics. In the Arctic, these intersect in different ways with nation building and national interest, as well as with region building. As to whether Arctic and Antarctic geopolitics are in any way comparable, it is useful to remember that the geopolitical landscapes of either region are deeply and historically contingent. The exploration of the Arctic and Arctic waters by European explorers and whalers began in the sixteenth century, but Indigenous peoples had already lived in the region for centuries, even millennia. While explorers were bringing back early accounts of a Eurasian and American Arctic, Antarctica was still a legendary continent of dubious status, believed to exist within a southern sea. Captain Cook may have discovered the island of South Georgia in 1775, but exploration of the Antarctic only began in earnest in the nineteenth century by Russian and then British explorers (Willson, Frog, and Bertell 2018; Dodds 2002, 2012). By the time the main era of Antarctic exploration began, the *terra firma* of the Arctic region had been largely mapped and entirely claimed by the eight Arctic states.

Both polar regions, once they had been discovered by Europeans, were witness to a flurry of further exploration and mapping, claiming of territory, and exploitation of natural resources. Explorers, whalers, sealers, hunters, scientific researchers, and state-sponsored expeditions were among the earliest historical actors who sought to discover new resources, routes, and territories. Despite their differences, all were motivated by very similar desires and the common ambitions of colonialism. This included accumulation of wealth, nation building, and dreams of establishing empires that extended European power overseas. Supported by national governments, these projects were highly colonial. The geopolitics of empire dominated these projects, and they were clearly competitive in nature.

The Arctic and Antarctic continue to excite the geopolitical imagination, but today, it is globalization, rapid climate change, and greater degrees of accessibility that are opening the Arctic region to new environmental, geographical, and geopolitical realities (ACIA 2014). What these new "realities" mean for Arctic states and Antarctic stakeholders is uncertain. The Arctic region is governed by eight different sovereign states in conformity with their own domestic interests and international legal conventions (for example, the UN Convention on the Law of the Sea concerning the Arctic Ocean) and by forums for intergovernmental co-operation (such as the Arctic Council). The result has been remarkable geopolitical stability and peaceful intergovernmental co-operation. While in recent months the collaborative work of the Arctic Council (AC) has been paused, consistent with the Western community's condemnation of the Russian invasion of Ukraine, it remains true that geopolitical order has been remarkably stable in the North. Rules and international agreements negotiated through the AC, and outside of it, still hold.

On the other side of the world, however, the Antarctic is today governed and controlled by an international Antarctic Treaty System (ATS). The ATS has had a damping effect on the geopolitics of competition by forbidding militarization of the continent and imposing strict regulations for resource utilization (Dodds 2012; Heininen and Zebich-Knos 2011; Hemmings, Rothwell, and Scott 2012). The Madrid Protocol has imposed a moratorium on resource exploitation as a part of the treaty system, ensuring that the Antarctic and sub-Antarctic regions will remain an environmentally protected area over the near future (Watts 1992; Hemming et al. 2012). Looking beyond the mid-twenty-first century, however, a degree of uncertainty attends the question of exactly what new developments will shape the geopolitics of this region. Some experts remain convinced of the continuing peaceful use of the Antarctic, as well as the continuing prohibition of resource extraction, while others suggest that, similar to the Arctic region, there could be a "resource race" (Dodds 2012; Heininen and Zebich-Knos 2011), even though the notion of an abundance of Antarctic resources is itself speculative (Watts 1992).

Given that governance structures in the Arctic and Antarctic are deeply divergent (one an international treaty system, the other co-operation involving both national governments and non-state actors), are there lessons that apply to both regions? It is now common for scholars, as well as the popular press, to narrate the geopolitics of the Arctic region using one of two opposing understandings of geopolitical events: "co-operative" or "competitive" (Nicol and Heininen, 2013; Østhagen 2017). The Antarctic is less often described as a potential zone of competitive tension, but this analytical frame has nonetheless begun to take hold given current global tensions and the anticipation of change—rightly or wrongly—to the Antarctic's treaty system in years to come. Yet few examine, critically or comparatively, what either co-operation (Heininen 2004; Fenge 2013) or competition (Borgerson 2008; Huebert 2013) means, or has meant, for the geopolitics of both regions relative to larger issues of colonialism or post-colonialism, realism and neo-realism, neo-liberalism, interdependence, or globalization (Heininen and Finger 2017; Heininen and Southcott 2010; Dittmer et al. 2011; Dodds 2010; Dodds and Nuttall 2015). Are the challenges facing northern and southern polar regions now similar, despite these regions' different histories and governance structures? Will their geopolitical futures be similar?

In this chapter, we conclude that if there is a growing threat that polar geopolitics could become competitive as a result of geostrategic considerations surrounding increased shipping, pressures for resource development, and disputed maritime claims, this is offset by a greater developing awareness of the threats related to climate change (see Causey, Kee, and Dunkle, this volume) and the development of a comprehensive understanding of human security over time (Heininen and Exner-Pirot 2019; Kee 2019; Nicol and Barnes 2019). Although imagining what the future holds for the geopolitics of the region is a speculative exercise, it is clear that subsequent developments will influence the way in which states' geopolitical interests and agendas interact with broader notions of comprehensive security—whether this be at the global, regional, or domestic levels. These are different for northern and southern polar regions.

The International Context

It is worth looking at the larger international systems that shape geopolitics within both circumpolar regions. Polar geopolitical processes are, and always have been, intimately tied to broader processes of international relations, global development, and geographical change (Heininen and Southcott 2010). Today, both polar regions currently find themselves situated within a global context characterized by shifting international relations, as "hot spots" of grand environmental challenges and therefore as critical spaces for collaborative scientific knowledge. Both regions remain exemplars of co-operative governance and peaceful relations. However, while there is a clear argument to be made for the uniqueness of the polar regions as zones of peace in a more tumultuous global geopolitical context, a peaceful, co-operative future is not assured. This is particularly true for the Arctic, where much focus has recently been directed at events in Russia and the Ukraine, and the potential for "spillover" into an Arctic conflict. Here, there is also speculation about new military-security agendas in the context of a global polar resource race, competition for maritime space, and shipping and transportation developments (Borgerson 2008; Dodds 2012; Dodds and Nuttall 2015; Heininen 2013; Heininen and Zebich-Knos 2011; Huebert 2010; Sheng 2022).

While there is much more recent speculation about the militarization of the Arctic, in the Antarctic, the longevity of peaceful geopolitics seems more assured. There have been suggestions that this is due to the treaty system now in place, and that, despite the well-established national context of its governance, the Arctic should emulate this arrangement. There have indeed been several treaties or binding agreements negotiated in the Arctic in recent decades, and indications are that more could be possible. However, a region-wide binding treaty there, as in the Antarctic, remains improbable. To date, however, there remain high levels of geopolitical stability in the region, maintained by the strength of constructive functional co-operation. Treaties aside, Arctic co-operation has been resilient despite clear challenges, and can be seen, thus far, as "exceptional" (Heininen 2022; see also Arctic Council 2021).

Overall, both regions are increasingly subject to very similar types of security and geopolitical narratives, shaped by similar concerns about climate change and melting ice, as well as by the increasingly ambitious agenda of many non-Arctic states in the areas of scientific research and regional geopolitics. But there are foundational differences too, making the notion that there can be a singular history of "polar geopolitics" problematic. The following discussion explores these similarities and differences, beginning with a brief overview of geopolitical thought pertaining to the region, and concluding with thoughts about the future of geopolitics in both the Arctic and Antarctic. Again, we caution against a singular, all-embracing notion of polar geopolitics in favour of a more nuanced, comparative one.

Geopolitical Definitions: Situating the Poles in a Global Geopolitical Framework

The history of polar geopolitics reflects national processes of nation building and state sovereignty. But it also reflects global processes, such as growing international scientific cooperation (see International Arctic Science Committee 2015). Both polar regions have been incorporated into the global system through a series of geopolitical agendas that range from satisfying the specific political-economic ambitions of colonizing states and their competitive empire-building narratives (see Chaturvedi 2000; Dodds 2002, 2012; Dodds and Nuttall 2015; Grant 2010; Roberts 2011), to classical and competitive (i.e., realist) perspectives (e.g., Cold War politics that had the effect of implicating the region in East-West conflict; see Farish 2010; Heininen 2004; Lackenbauer and Farish 2007; Östreng 2008), to the current post–Cold War era of international (environmental) co-operation (Byers 2008; English 2013; Heininen 2013; Nicol and Heininen 2013; Østhagen 2017; Young 2012).

The following discussion recounts both the development of these different interpretive strands of "polar geopolitics" and their points of convergence. It is particularly interesting to trace how specific geopolitical threads or narratives have grown out of a series of distinct international events and perspectives, rather than the strategic assessments of any one particular Arctic state. To this end, we show the way in which both polar regions have historically been constructed and positioned within the larger imperial, colonial, realist, and neo-realist discourses and geopolitical frameworks of their time. As Owens (2015) suggests, the stories we tell of European, Russian, and North American polar exploration and subsequent territorial claims—that is to say, the history of polar geopolitics itself—reflects a deeply colonial mindset. The narrative lenses through which such projects were understood promoted classical geopolitical understandings framed by realist international relations. Realist because classical geopolitics is one variety of realist international relations, offering "description of the spatial aspects of power politics . . . modified by technology and economics, and their strategic implication ensuring states" (Owens 2015, 467); "classic" because its geopolitical assumptions rest on the presumption that the power of the state has "some relation to the territory that it occupies, controls, or influences," while "resources and strategic potential, the sources of state power, are unequally distributed worldwide" (2015, 467).

Such geopolitical thinking also emphasizes the strategic importance of technologies in geopolitical assessments and prediction, promoting a military or traditional security focus on a limited number of factors, such as territorial integrity, natural resources, and national interest. Classical geopolitics is not, however, the only framework that informs the contemporary analysis of polar spaces (Tuathail and Dalby 1998). There are, in fact, a number of other important geopolitical frameworks (Agnew 2003), including that of critical geopolitics, a more recent framing of geopolitical thought that examines the factors influencing the constructed nature of geopolitical discourse. Critical geopolitics recognizes that in addition to territory and state power—themselves constructed entities according to critical geopolitical theory—are a plethora of other influences such as ideology, knowledge (as power), identity or cultural and social assessments, and the environment (e.g., Heininen, Ahola, and Frog 2014).

While critical geopolitics have created a contemporary framework through which to understand the constructivist nature of international relations, more recently, there has been an even greater recognition of how geopolitical frameworks intersect with and are influenced by environmental agency. Climate change and unpredictable weather events have forced national defence agencies in the polar regions to rethink the roster of "threats" to their territories. The effect has been twofold. On one level, the growing need for a large-scale environmental response in response to the increasing threat to life and limb from events triggered through natural processes has resulted in a reorientation of competitive geopolitics around realist or neo-realist concerns (Borgerson 2008). On another level, it has directed state agencies toward functional co-operation in the areas of environmental protection and science, and has fostered a broader understanding of human security, due to states' common interests in transnational co-operation, in particular in the Arctic (Heininen 2022; Nicol 2020). It has also been highly oriented toward decolonization.

We undertake this discussion about the different ways in which polar geopolitics have been conducted because it contextualizes our geopolitical analysis going forward. The informing narratives of classical geopolitics and its colonial mindset is considerably different from that of critical geopolitics as it is practised today. But today's geopolitical framing of polar regions, no matter how critical, must now recognize a new type of strategic challenge: climate change and environmental deterioration. In this novel scenario, new understandings of human security shape new strategic assessments of national interest that are existential in nature and related to environmental change. When exploring geopolitics in the context of both polar regions, then, changes to the geopolitical framing of events matter. They determine the extent to which it can be claimed that there is such thing as "polar geopolitics"—that is to say, a geopolitics that encompasses both polar regions. In a volume such as this, which seeks to undertake comparative analysis of both polar regions, it is important to understand where and when polar geopolitics converges, and where and when it does not.

Histories of Polar Exploration: the Arctic

The rise of international interest in the northern polar region began in earnest in the nineteenth century. Over much of the late nineteenth and early twentieth centuries, polar exploration, and its associated strategic interests, reflected a state-centred geopolitical narrative embedded in imperialist and global colonial systems. These narratives reflected the thinking of late nineteenth-century geopolitical theorists like Halford Mackinder, the founder of what has subsequently become known as the field of "classical" geopolitics. Mackinder promoted and codified realist geopolitics "based on the influence of the natural environments defined by geography and technology" (Wu 2018, 787). This view suggested that certain parts of the world were simply more strategically valuable than others. The Arctic was seen as being on the periphery of the world, and of little importance.

Although in the grand balance, the polar regions' importance lay less in the claiming of a specific piece of territory and more in the symbolic importance of circumnavigation of that territory,[1] the Arctic and Antarctic nevertheless had their purposes. While the circumpolar North itself was peripheral (though populated by Indigenous peoples in North America and Eurasia), during the late nineteenth and early twentieth centuries the Arctic Ocean increasingly became a venue for a popularized geopolitics, one heavily influenced by externally produced representations of "Arcticness." The values of scientific prowess and masculinity were embodied in the stories of polar explorers who conquered this harsh, unforgiving, and wild environment, in turn accruing prestige on behalf of their national governments. The race for the North Pole (and its southern counterpart) made tremendous newspaper copy worldwide, and eager audiences consumed this news with interest and excitement. Indeed, the geopolitics of the late nineteenth and early twentieth centuries posited the Arctic and Antarctic as frontiers that served several state-centric purposes (Heininen and Nicol 2008). These included the testing of Victorian values, encouraging the rising power of the United States, contextualizing the enduring power of the Russian Empire, and propagating a racialized discourse prizing masculinity and northern hardiness (Dodds 2002, 2012; Dodds and Nuttall 2015). The geopolitics of this era constructed a space for American "know-how," while giving breadth to European and Russian interests. It was, simultaneously, a "civilizational geopolitics" (see Agnew 2003) rich in an imagery of naturalizations as much as "a framework of analysis for policy and strategy in world politics" (Wu 2018, 787). Thus, while the polar regions served as frontiers for civilization, or as paths to riches, they also invited a race for the survival of the fittest and strongest, and provided narratives for heroic and even self-indulgent exploration. This was a highly competitive view of global relations. Wu has called this geopolitical meme a "modern geopolitics," one whose origins lie "in fin de siècle Europe in response to a series of technological changes." The result was the creation of a "closed political system" as European geographic discoveries and imperialist competition extinguished the world's "frontiers'" (2018, 786). And, because the Arctic and Antarctic were some of the few remaining frontiers, their discovery, exploration, and mapping were justified with reference to realist thinking on political and environmental relationships. Here, again, polar geopolitics marched in step with contemporary geostrategic thinking. So pronounced was this view of the deterministic relationship between natural order and political balance that Halford MacKinder (1904) wrote that the world had entered a post-Columbian age characterized by a "closed" political system. But, in the European and North American imagination in particular, unclosed territory existed still in the form of the polar regions. Here, the so-called Heroic Age of exploration led by Shackleton, Scott, Amundsen, and others was just getting under way (see Dodds 2002, 2012; Roberts 2011).

True to the requirements of classical geopolitics, then, the main discourses associated with the northern and southern polar regions came from outside. Abstract and simplified, yet embedded in colonial and hegemonic ambitions, they were inspired by the realist geopolitical assessments of the period. Both polar regions, by this time, had been deliberately constructed in British, European, and North American newspapers and journals as a "frontier" or "no man's land," and in doing so fulfilled the romantic, and decidedly Victorian, visions of any number of European states with an interest in polar exploration (see Dodds 2002, 2012; Dittmer et al. 2011; Gale Ambassadors 2019).

While popular imagination in much of the world was focused on the North American Arctic and Britain's Heroic Age in the Antarctic, the Russian Arctic was also under construction, as settlements and towns (for example, Arkhangelsk and Kola) were built for the benefit of the Russian Empire. While Russia had "sold" Alaska to the United States in 1867, this did not signal its retreat from the Arctic region more generally. A railway was constructed from Murmansk to Saint Petersburg in the early twentieth century, for example, to strengthen northern infrastructure and to promote regional development in the vast tracts of the Russian North (Gale Ambassadors 2019; Yarovoy 2014).

Despite the strategic positioning of the northern polar region in the global narratives referencing empire and power, these narratives did not represent a direct threat to global stability. For example, after Britain transferred the Arctic Archipelago to Canada, Canadian claims to sovereignty over its Arctic islands and waters (advanced according to the sector principal in 1909; see Cavell 2014) largely fell on deaf ears. True, expeditions and efforts to claim various islands within the archipelago were occasionally launched by other nations (Grant 2010), but for most, including the United States, these remained peripheral and sporadic. Some nations challenged Canada's sovereignty over certain Arctic islands before agreement as to the extent of ownership was complete, but these territories and disagreements were of little real importance to the larger global community.

In the European Arctic, there was, however, a growing interest in control and ownership of Arctic waters and archipelagos by the early twentieth century (for example, those between Norway and Russia on Svalbard and Novaya Zemlya). Nonetheless, open disputes were avoided.[2]

Overall, geopolitics in the North, in the late nineteenth and early twentieth centuries, could be considered "classic" in orientation. The race for the North Pole saw nations compete, sometimes to the death of their expeditionary teams, to reach this iconographic place. Yet the competition remained geopolitically benign; Cook, Peary, Byrd, Amundsen, and others mounted expeditions, but their goals were less about conquest than national prestige. By the mid-twentieth century, the race had been subsumed by the Cold War, with control of the Arctic for strategic purposes resulting in a need for military bases, exploitation of strategic national resources, and a great reliance on science. These were symbolic as well as strategic concerns.

History of Polar Exploration: the Antarctic

Meanwhile, the Antarctic saw its own Heroic Age develop and the attendant development of an Antarctic version of classical geopolitical thought. While the region was considered less strategically significant in the late eighteenth and earlier nineteenth centuries, it nonetheless remained on the agendas of European powers. That said, it was more important to sealers and whalers than navy expeditions. That changed in the late nineteenth century. The Antarctic remained on the periphery of a resource frontier for global markets long after the Arctic had been converted to a region of states and national interests (see Grant 2010; Heininen and Zebich-Knos 2011). It also remained a virtual *terra nullius*, or no man's land, well into the first decade of the twentieth century, in ways that the Arctic was not.

But increasingly, in the early twentieth century, the world powers became more interested in claiming this far-flung polar continent. As if to make up for lost time, the United States sent scientific expeditions to Antarctica in the early twentieth century, while Britain attempted to "paint the Antarctic pink" through its expeditions in the region. British explorers suffered a series of temporary setbacks, as Amundsen and his fellow Norwegians entered the race for the South Pole, effectively challenging the British Empire's attempted expansion on the southern continent (Dodds 2002, 2012). Nonetheless, by the early twentieth century, Europe, the United Kingdom, the United States, and Russia met in the Antarctic. Their efforts prioritized the exploitation of marine resources and the collection of scientific data. Yet even this early geopolitics of the Antarctic was less about establishing settlements and more about acquiring geographical knowledge and scientific prowess. Above all else, it was about the building of a narrative and imagery with which to project power through new military and scientific technologies.

Unlike the Arctic region, however, the Antarctic—although it had been important to late nineteenth-century empire-building projects in much the same way the Arctic had been—remained in a state of "legal limbo" during the first half of the twentieth century. By 1907, the governments of Argentina, Australia, Great Britain, Chile, France, New Zealand, and Norway had all made claims on the region. However, these were not recognized by the global system (Joyner 1998). The apportioning of the Antarctic continent was disputed and contested, so much so that no clear state colonies or boundaries emerged. Instead, the Antarctic was the object of an international effort to create a "management plan" in an attempt to diffuse these territorial claims (Dodds 2002, 2012; Heininen and Zebeich-Knos 2011; Joyner 1998; Roberts 2011). Nonetheless, the launch of the now famous Antarctic expeditions of Scott, Shackleton, and others in the century's early decades were narrated according to classical geopolitical discourses: the search for the last place on earth and the closing of the globe to new territorial claims.

The early history of Antarctic exploration and exploitation serves to underscore the fact that, much like the Arctic, the "big picture" has always been a necessary aspect of the geopolitical constructions of global power in the polar regions. And, in the late nineteenth and early twentieth centuries, it was clear that the big picture was increasingly oriented toward Arctic and Antarctic exploration, territorial claims, and sovereignty facilitated by a colonial governance system implemented through technologies of state power (Heininen and Nicol 2008). Nonetheless, outcomes differed widely. By mid-century, one polar region was fragmented among eight Arctic states, the other consolidated under an international treaty system that awarded no one single country sovereign rights.

The Mid-Twentieth Century: Geopolitics, Military Security, and the Cold War

As we have seen, during the first half of the twentieth century, the development of the polar regions, whether for scientific, empire-building, or realist strategic purposes, clearly facilitated the advancement of state interests and domestic agendas. This was a geopolitical era that emphasized occupation and/or control of physical space and natural resources (Dougherty and Pfaltzgraff 1990, 58–67). By mid-century, war and the Cold War had changed the landscape. The Arctic, once considered an area with vast potential for the exploitation of natural resources (and the development of scientific knowledge), was increasingly seen as a military space for the performance of sovereignty, national security, and other state interests.[3] In the European North, the Barents Sea become increasingly strategic, first due to German capabilities in submarine warfare in the North Atlantic, and the interest during the Second World War in utilizing a newly found nickel deposit in Pechenga/Petsamo (then a Finnish territory); and second, due to the presence of Soviet naval bases for strategic submarines on the Kola Peninsula during the Cold War. The latter were intended to ensure nuclear deterrence against the United States (Heininen 1991). Correspondingly, in the North American North, military securitization of the Arctic advanced because of a fear of Soviet missiles, leading to the construction of the Distant Early Warning Line (Coates et al. 2008).

These developments placed vast—although fragmented (by national territory)—areas of the circumpolar region within a realist international relations framework that perpetuated a geopolitical narrative focused on military threat. In this realist-inspired "military-security" model of geopolitics, the Arctic was often abstracted and simplified, portrayed as a space needing robust expressions of sovereignty (Heininen 1991; Nicol 2015; Till 1987). It also validated an "ideological geopolitics" (see Agnew 2003) whereby the so-called Free World and the Communist Bloc were pitted against each other, with the Arctic serving as a buffer zone.

Thus, if the Second World War and the subsequent Cold War saw Arctic geopolitics take on a newfound importance in the European, Asian, and North American North, it also saw the North incorporated into new models of international relations (Østhagen 2020). Any number of researchers (e.g., Bone 2012; Coates et al. 2008) have suggested that the Second World War transformed the Arctic from a backwater into an area of international importance. No longer the frontier for Victorian and early twentieth-century exploration, the Arctic, from a North American perspective, took on a new significance as a place where the world was divided between two ideological camps and two superpowers (Coates et al. 2008). The Canadian North, in particular, "became a military bridge, and its geopolitical role in world affairs involved providing a safe, inland supply route to the European and Pacific theaters of war" (Bone 2012, 87).

This situation ensured that North American Arctic security was shared between Canada and the United States, and that military infrastructure was developed to mobilize troops, weapons, and radar surveillance throughout this contiguous region (Farrish 2010; Lackenbauer 2010; Lackenbauer and Farrish 2007). In the European Arctic, however, no such bridge developed, as the region became a border, though a peaceful one, between the North Atlantic Treaty Organization (NATO) and the Soviet Union.

In the Antarctic, tensions also mounted during this period. Although this was arguably for different reasons, classical geopolitics still framed international thinking in the region. A number of interested states had laid a claim to the Antarctic continent, and this, "coupled with increased human presence on the continent, became so contentious that many in policy-making circles worldwide agreed that an international effort was needed jointly to work out a management plan for Antarctic to protect it from human expansionist incursions and possible destruction from war" (Heininen and Zebich-Knos 2011, 208). By the late 1940s and early 1950s, the continued exploration of the Antarctic region for minerals and subsequent state claims had brought the region to a tipping point. The claims of states like Great Britain for sectors of the Antarctic—especially the Falkland Islands (Malvinas)—and its encouragement of other nation-states to do likewise, put them at odds with South American nations like Argentina and Chile, which traced their right to the same Antarctic territories through the fifteenth century's Treaty of Tordesillas, and as such regarded the Antarctic as an "imperial inheritance". (Dodds 2002).

This phase of geopolitics, with its jockeying for Antarctic territory, created the context for a mounting of tensions in the region (Dodds 2012; Heininen and Zebich-Knos 2011). But it also brought about greater pressure for a solution to these tensions. This came in the form of the Third International Polar Year (IPY) (part of the 1957–58 International Geophysical Year (IGY)[4] and the subsequent Antarctic Treaty of 1959. Dedicated to "the peaceful advancement of the world," the Antarctic was henceforth characterized as an area of co-operation thanks to a treaty system that formed the basis for a lasting sharing of space, and a series of conventions to ensure the preservation of Antarctic fauna, flora, and environments (Heininen and Zebich-Knos 2011; Joyner 1998). As Watson (2009) reminds us, "The existing dispute over the Arctic is similar to the one that transpired approximately fifty years ago over Antarctica. At that time, seven nations were vying for Antarctic territory. These nations resolved their conflicting claims through the Antarctic Treaty, thereby establishing a legal framework of joint governance over the continent" (326).

Although advocates of a single-treaty polar governance scheme often see the Antarctic Treaty as a single binding treaty, it is not. Instead, the Antarctic Treaty is one of several significant agreements that the Australian government uses to guide its Antarctic program. Another is the Protocol on Environmental Protection to the Antarctic Treaty (the so-called Madrid Protocol). It provides for comprehensive protection of Antarctica and expands the range of earlier provisions regarding protection of the Antarctic environment. In doing so, its article 7 protects the land and marine environments and ecosystems lying below 60 degrees south latitude by prohibiting "activity relating to mineral resources except scientific research activity." It will expire fifty years after its entry into force in 1998 (United Nations 1998; see also Heininen and Zebich-Knos 2011). Other agreements include:

- Agreed Measures for the Conservation of Antarctic Fauna and Flora (1964) (entered into force in 1982)

- The Convention for the Conservation of Antarctic Seals (1972)

- The Convention for the Conservation of Antarctic Marine Living Resources (1980)

- The Convention on the Regulation of Antarctic Mineral Resource Activities (1988; although it was signed in 1988, it was subsequently rejected and never entered into force)

With the creation of this system of agreements and treaties, the era of classical geopolitics came to an end in the Antarctic region. It was henceforth replaced by "a different vision—one that was potentially far removed from the contest between nations for defined sovereign rights" (Dodds 2012, 60; see also Roberts 2011). The Antarctic Treaty itself provides for use of Antarctica for peaceful purposes only, including the facilitation of scientific research in Antarctica, international scientific co-operation, the exercise of the rights of inspection provided for in article 8 of the treaty, questions relating to the exercise of jurisdiction in Antarctica, and preservation and conservation of the region's living resources.

New Realities: The Twenty-First-Century Arctic and Environmental Co-operation

The end of a competitive, classical, and indeed military-oriented geopolitics arrived in the North somewhat later than in the southern polar region. Although there are structural and legal differences between the two areas, the point is that, to date, environmental and scientific co-operation—whether through one or many binding agreements—has proven to be the most effective means for regional governance designed to exclude any form of military activity, as well as for dialogue. Tensions have been met through cultivating greater degrees of structural efficiency, co-operation, and efficacy. By the 1990s, Cold War military confrontation in the North had diminished (Lackenbauer 2010), as had the Arctic's perceived role as a space for geopolitical confrontation (Coates et al. 2008). As Heininen (2013), Wilson Rowe and Blakkisrud (2013), and others have reminded us, in contrast to the high levels of militarization that characterized the Cold War Arctic, there was a proliferation of environmental, scientific, social, and even military co-operation just after the collapse of the Soviet Union. After Gorbachev's 1987 "Murmansk Speech" and the subsequent the fall of the Berlin Wall, a more general concern with environmental co-operation and stability grew. This was a turning point in the Cold War, and it meant a significant paradigm shift from confrontation toward co-operation. This was in many ways the beginning of the modern Arctic era (Heininen, Jalonen, and Käkönen 1995).

Indeed, NATO and the Warsaw Pact began to play increasingly smaller roles in the Arctic, while regional agreements favouring environmental co-operation were to replace them as instruments for international comity, facilitating what Chaturvedi (2000) called a shift from "confrontation" to "cooperation," diminishing the conceptual importance of the Arctic as a theatre for military confrontation. Even where tensions lingered in some post–Cold War arenas, a strategic focus on military activities and confrontation was overshadowed by growing concern for environmental issues, such as long-range air and water pollution and nuclear safety (Heininen 2013).

Similar to what occurred in the late 1950s with the ATS, the Arctic region retained its saliency on the international stage, but in new ways. As its military role diminished, the importance of international co-operation in many fields such as environmental protection, research, and higher education grew, as did the range of actors and agencies who could play a legitimate role in regional governance. The late twentieth century saw a broad and expansive "North" that included not only all of the Arctic states (see Young 2000), but also non-state actors, such as Indigenous peoples' organizations, sub-national governments, and non-governmental organizations, which were all very much concerned with the environment (Heininen 2004).

The story of the development of the Arctic Council and the circumpolar North is worth repeating here to explain how new geopolitical narratives have come to define the region. It begins with the now Murmansk Speech by Russian president Mikhail Gorbachev in 1987 (Pravda 1987). This set the stage for the development of a series of regimes, treaties, agreements, and regional organizations through which an "international North" and a new international space for Arctic geopolitics was subsequently constructed (Fenge 2013; Keskitalo 2004; Heininen, Jalonen, and Käkönen 1995; Young 2000). For example, the Arctic Environmental Protection Strategy, launched in 1991, was supplanted five years later by the establishment of the Arctic Council. With its focus on environmental protection and co-operative institutional arrangements, the Arctic Council initiative suggested that Arctic geopolitics would now subsume earlier institutional and international arrangements. For some, the point of the new Arctic geopolitics and its regional institutions was to create an encompassing treaty system, much like the Antarctic Treaty (see Young 2000); it has not, however, been supported by the Arctic states.

In addition to ushering in a period of relative geopolitical quiet, the agenda pursued by the Arctic Council began to reshape the region. The 2004 *Arctic Human Development Report*, for example, identified the following as the main themes of Arctic international relations and geopolitics during the early twenty-first century: increased circumpolar co-operation by Indigenous peoples' organizations and sub-national governments; region building, with nations serving as major actors; and the promotion of a new kind of relationship between the Arctic and the outside world with regard to functional co-operation in non-military policy fields such as environmental protection and science (Heininen 2004). All this suggested that, if in the outside world new geopolitical perspectives were gaining ground, the Arctic might play the role of a "zone of peace," thereby living up to Gorbachev's dream. The major characteristic of geopolitical discourse in the early twenty-first century was its stability (Heininen 2004), institutional co-operation (Fenge 2013; Keskitalo 2004; Young 2000), and self-determination (Zellen 2009a, 2009b).

All of this is to say that, although the 1950s saw the development of an international treaty for the Antarctic, it was not until the late twentieth century that Arctic geopolitics was reimagined through the lens of institutional co-operation, and in particular through the Arctic Council (AHDR 2004; Heininen and Nicol 2007; Keskitalo 2004; Østhagen 2017). Moreover, definitions of security were changing apace. The paramount importance of military security was slowly replaced by the notion that security was a broadly defined concept implying environmental security and human well-being, not just national security (Heininen and Exner-Pirot 2019; Nicol and Barnes 2019).[5]

However, while co-operation was the norm in the Arctic during the opening years of the twenty-first century, this did not preclude a focus on territorial sovereignty or a new emphasis on competition for Arctic Ocean spaces. Border disputes assumed an increasing importance as the first decade of the twenty-first century closed. The United States renewed its Arctic security position, for example, through a series of presidential directives in 2008 and 2010 that reflected a renewed interest among American policy-makers (Nicol 2020). This was the first time since the Cold War that the United States had overtly indicated its concern with Arctic Ocean regional stability and security. A similar concern was echoed by Canadian governmental representatives at the time, who increasingly articulated a military presence in the North to protect Canada's national sovereignty and military-security interests (Huebert 2010). Potential disputes over Canadian claims to the Northwest Passage, US and Canadian disputes concerning international boundaries in the Beaufort Sea, and other unresolved boundary issues were believed to be potential powder kegs that were exacerbated by the increase of economic activities in the region. Unlike Norway and the Russian Federation, which managed to agree on the shelves of the Barents Sea, there was division over which states were entitled to influence determinations concerning allocation of the Arctic Ocean coastal states. The latter is determined through the provisions of the United Nations Convention on the Law of the Sea (UNCLOS).

Similarly, China's heightened interest in the Arctic, as well as that of certain European non-Arctic states, has triggered a larger discussion about what exactly constitutes an Arctic state or an Arctic stakeholder (Lasserre 2010), and about the role of these actors in regional co-operation. China's potential "threat" as an external national presence in the Arctic was somewhat moderated by the acceptance of new observer states, including China, into the Arctic Council in 2013. Still, China's interest in the Arctic was thought to foreshadow a future in which the race for resources in the North would trigger conflict. Building on the commonly held assumption that melting sea ice will allow for better access to the strategic resources needed for North American and Eurasian states to achieve energy security, the emerging discourse argued that conflict rather than co-operation would characterize the future of Arctic governance. The planting of a Russian flag under the Arctic Ocean in the area of the North Pole was interpreted as a provocation in this regard. Likewise, the impact of climate change on polar sea ice has created a flurry of interest in the region, both in terms of the implications for natural resource exploitation (mostly hydrocarbons) as well as the potential impacts of intensified shipping. There was renewed concern about the potential status of the Northwest Passage. In Canada in particular, this heightened dialogue about state sovereignty and national security has provoked what Dodds (2010) called a return to the colonial-like territorial mappings of great powers. Instead of furthering co-operation and a focus on matters of human security (broadly defined), this new geopolitical discourse suggested the potential emergence of "Arctic boom or doom" or "Arctic paradox" scenarios, as unlikely as they might seem (Palosaari 2012; Zellen 2009a, 2009b).

However, as Wilson Rowe and Blakkisrud (2013) have reminded us, "many official statements are somewhere in between these two extremes of cooperation or competition." And furthermore, though the Arctic states dominating the region "are searching for a balance between environmental protection and economic activities, and proclaim that there must be such a balance, there is ambivalence when it comes to environmental protection versus economic development" (Heininen et al. 2019, 249–53). The result has been the institutionalization of a geo-economic perspective in the Arctic that promises sustainable development and resiliency as a complement to peaceful international co-operation through a series of regional and global economic institutions. This neo-liberal re-mapping of geopolitical space acknowledges the unlikelihood of resource wars and conflict within the Arctic region. Much of the contemporary analysis of post–Cold War geopolitical co-operation in the Arctic is thus concerned with the role of Arctic states in brokering co-operation and facilitating inclusion (English 2013; Lackenbauer, Nicol, and Greaves 2017; Śmieszek and Koivurova 2017).

Environmental Cooperation: The Twenty-First-Century Antarctic

Is there a comparable movement toward twenty-first-century co-operative geopolitics in the southern polar region? Here, the legacy is somewhat different as regards state sovereignty, Indigenous peoples, and the structure of intergovernmental co-operation. There is, for example, no state sovereignty in the Antarctic, only deferred claims. Moreover, there are no Indigenous peoples in a sense that would align with the normative definitions of various UN declarations and conventions, only people working at state-sponsored research stations. The Antarctic Treaty System is an umbrella term for multiple treaties and agreements capable of maintaining the degree of co-operation necessary for a peaceful Antarctic. It is ably supported by the annual Antarctic Treaty Consultative Meeting (ATCM). Our research suggests that over the years since the establishment of the ATCM, such meetings have covered at least thirty-nine broad themes ranging from "co-operation with other organizations" to "exchange of information" to "multi-year strategic work plans." Environmental protection, the operation of the ATCM, and protected areas are also on the list, as are numerous mechanisms concerning the reporting and monitoring of research stations, projects, and operational activities. The point is that much like the Arctic Council, such monitoring, meeting, and reporting systems are key not just for effective science, but for bringing about co-operation and compliance as well. Environmental co-operation is deeply embedded, broadly consultative. Where that occurs, other forms of co-operation follow.

Indeed, if in the future, the consensus clause of the Madrid Protocol lapses, there are fears that strategic competition for potential resources in Antarctica and the Southern Ocean could lead to greater geopolitical tensions. However, this only serves to underline the need for greater consultative analysis of the ATS and its emphasis on environmental co-operation. As the Arctic Council has shown, the strength of environmental co-operation lies in its focus, the commitment of its members and observers, and, present circumstances aside, the fact that military-security is excluded from discussion. In contrast, the ATS has managed unprecedented geopolitical tensions simply by establishing an effective platform for managing regional, and in particular scientific co-operation, by establishing the continent's status as a non-militarized area within a binding agreement: "Antarctica shall be used for peaceful purposes only" (see National Science Foundation n.d.). Can these two different models achieve the same ends?

Speculating on the Future

The most enduring and mainstream discourse concerning Arctic geopolitics remains the one that sees geopolitical stability as the result of institutional co-operation, particularly in the context of the Arctic Council and other international bodies that focus on functional co-operation, mainly for environmental protection and, increasingly, for human security (Byers 2017; Heininen 2022). This narrative of geopolitical stability and co-operation is supported by the Arctic states through their commitment to co-operating on sustainable development and the protection of the polar environment. Such commitment reflects these states' common interest in decreasing military tension and increasing political stability and promoting trans-boundary co-operation on environmental protection and a host of other issues. It also includes regional organizations and sub-national actors whose growing agency is derived from ongoing processes of decolonization and neo-liberalism, among them Indigenous peoples' organizations, regional organizations, and territorial governments (see Heininen 2004, 2013; Shadian 2014; Wilson Rowe 2019).[6]

While in the past, the challenges faced by both polar regions included national conflict and competition for territory, which to a large extent defined the regions' respective geopolitical importance, today new strategic challenges affect this assessment. We see changing definitions of security as the climate changes and local environments become unstable. We also see a greater concern with community and the safety of regional inhabitants and infrastructures (Hemmings, Rothwell, and Scott 2012; Menezes and Nicol 2019; Nicol 2010). Indeed, environmental security has emerged as a one of the greatest geostrategic challenges in both regions (Heininen and Nicol 2007; Hemmings, Rothwell, and Scott 2012; Kee et al. 2019). Moreover, there are similar concerns about the activities of some states that cannot, by any stretch of the imagination, be considered "polar," not least because of their lack of geographical proximity to the polar regions. Although the instruments for controlling such activities are in place in both regions, it would be fair to say that this does not prevent speculation and some degree of concern about how "peaceful" agreements can be used to contain more concerted or militant agendas.

Conclusions

Many geopolitical rationales and criteria have been used to assess the polar regions. However, while the Arctic and the Antarctic are very different places (geographically, environmentally, demographically, and from the point of view of international law), and while each has its own unique geopolitical history, there are nonetheless some real similarities in the geopolitics of these regions, which have been shaped by the broader political interests of nation-states. This is particularly true of the way in which both polar regions have been positioned within a geopolitical tradition of colonialism, empire building, and the strengthening of state power, as well as the way in which each region was explored and claimed with reference to a scientific curiosity that was used to appropriate the polar regions to serve state interests. The Antarctic Treaty established the Antarctic as "a natural reserve devoted to peace and science" (see APECS n.d.). Although the potential for geopolitical competition is not seen as a near-term threat in the Antarctic region, some experts fear that such competition may cause problems in the long term. Although there is no treaty system in the Arctic comparable to the ATS, the Arctic Council has built a successful environmental agenda and established a series of working groups and programs aimed at fostering environmental co-operation and peaceful circumpolar coexistence. For more than two decades, it has maintained the Arctic as a zone of peace by playing an active policy-shaping role, all in the face of the rising pressure of increasing economic activity and the more forceful annunciation of national security interests. To these we can add a host of new challenges, such as the outbreak of war in Ukraine and the potentially more aggressive role of China in polar lands and waters.

On the other hand, it is also true that both regions have been positioned within a larger international framework of customary law and legal regimes, and in a multi-national context of functional co-operation. The trend is most probably toward the continued institutionalization of relations and co-operation in both polar regions through treaties and agreements, governance organizations, and forums and networks.

The biggest geopolitical similarity between both poles, however, has been the environmental co-operation that forms the basis of successful polar co-operation. Indeed, the concern is that, if the Madrid Protocol's consensus requirement lapses, the resource potential of Antarctica and the Southern Ocean will drive strategic competition in the future. This could lead to greater geopolitical tensions, which only goes to indicate the need for greater consultative analysis of the ATS and its emphasis on environmental co-operation. As the Arctic Council has shown, the strength of co-operation is in its focus on the environment, and the commitment of its consultative members. The ATS must therefore ensure that in the future it is reinforced by strong national support, that its flexibility and complexity is enhanced to allow for sectoral as well as territorial management, and that it remains inclusive of member states' interests.

In short, the ATS is an effective way to manage new geopolitical tensions as they develop, simply because it has established an effective platform for managing regional co-operation without reference to military or security imperatives. For this reason, the experience of the Arctic Council is perhaps as important to the Antarctic as the ATS's experience managing Arctic environments may be in the future.

That said, we have seen that the geopolitical interest in polar regions has shifted focus and frameworks several times over the past two centuries or more. Beginning with the curiosity of polar explorers, these regions have been drawn into the international system, first through realist/classical geopolitical narratives, and then through more critical geopolitical narratives based on co-operative relations and agreements that stressed functional co-operation—often scientific and environmental—rather than confrontation. There is no reason to assume that this will change in the near future so long as the institutions of Arctic governance can withstand the political crises that are now challenging our ability to engage in co-operation. Although there are structural and legal differences between the two polar regions, the point is that to date, environmental co-operation—whether through one or many binding agreements—has proven to be the most effective means to achieve the sort of regional governance designed to foster dialogue and exclude any form of military activity.

Tensions have been met through the cultivation of greater degrees of structural efficiency, co-operation, and efficacy. Currently, the Antarctic is still considered as a "global commons" (Sheng 2022) that has served and continues to serve the benefit of humankind; the Arctic, for its part, has the potential to serve as a model of mutually beneficial co-operation for peaceful coexistence.

The question we have pursued in this chapter, however, is not whether classical geopolitics is still a useful framework through which to explain the geostrategic similarities between the two polar regions, but rather, how the geopolitics of polar regions has survived, transformed, and retained their saliency within larger strategic and increasingly global frameworks even as the explanatory power of classical geopolitics wanes. We affirm the continuing role of geopolitical perspectives in a world where environmental and economic co-operation has eclipsed realist geopolitical assessments. Different rationales and normative strategic doctrines have continuously informed states' engagement with Arctic and Antarctic locales. These changing rationales have, however, played out in similar ways at both ends of the earth, so that in the early twenty-first century, the geopolitical concerns that inform both polar regions are themselves informed by similar co-operative international relations. Here, growing concern about the changing environment and climate, peaceful political relations, and the need for stability and the rule of international law and treaties prevail.

NOTES

1   Consider, for example, the famous British explorer Sir John Franklin, whose failed expedition to the Northwest Passage triggered a massive and protracted search-and-rescue effort that spanned centuries (Grant 2010). Similarly, the Finnish-Swedish explorer Nordenskiöld sailed through the Northeast Passage in the 1870s to connect the Atlantic Pacific Oceans, as England and Holland had attempted to do a few centuries earlier (Gale Review 2019).

2   This was true even when tensions became even more pronounced after the Bolshevik Revolution of 1917 and the Russian Civil War (1918–20).

3   In North America, for example, major wartime projects included the building of the Alaska Highway and Northwest Staging Route by the US government (a highway and series of airstrips for ferrying aircraft); the Norman Wells and Canol Pipeline projects

(developed to enhance energy security and supplies for US bases in Alaska); Project Crimson, a series of airfields in the eastern Canadian Arctic; and the military complex built at Goose Bay in Labrador, which served as a US air base during the Second World War (Dougherty and Pfaltzgraff 1990; see also Bone 2012).

4   The IPY is an interdisciplinary international scientific program focusing on the unique environment of the Arctic and the Antarctic: "The First IPY, from 1881 to 1884, involved 11 nations and was the first coordinated international polar research activity ever undertaken, inspiring subsequent international research programs. There was a Second IPY in 1932–1933 involving 40 nations, and a Third IPY in 1957–1958 (67 nations) that was also called the International Geophysical Year or IGY because it included research outside the Polar areas. Planning for the Fourth IPY, 2007–2008, started in 2004" (NOAA n.d.)

5   Nonetheless, it was not all clear sailing, as the Arctic states excluded military security from the Arctic Council agenda. There was also the question of who was to speak for international Arctic co-operation and at what scale, best represented by the meetings of the Arctic Ocean littoral states in Greenland in 2008 (the Ilulissat Declaration 2008) and in Canada in 2010 (at Chelsea, Quebec). The meetings at Ilulissat and Chelsea effectively narrowed down the rightful discussants of Arctic sovereignty and security to those Arctic littoral states recognized under the law of the sea, particularly those who had ratified the UN Convention on the Law of the Sea. The notion that there was a core "Arctic 5," as well as a larger "Arctic 8," emerged. Alongside this, however, were increasing attempts to better position the voices of permanent participants within the Arctic Council, and to strengthen the role of the Arctic Council itself. While not diminishing the importance of co-operation, this was a reminder that beneath the veneer of friendship and collaboration, Arctic states retained their own, often disparate, national interests and agendas (see Bailes and Heininen 2012; Heininen et al. 2020; Östreng 2017).

6   The Inuit Circumpolar Council, for example, issued its own declaration on Arctic resource sovereignty in response to its exclusion from the deliberations of the coastal Arctic states in the Ilulissat Agreement (ICC 2009). The role for Indigenous peoples in Arctic international relations and geopolitical narratives is, therefore, changing (Nicol 2010, 2017). In particular, the involvement of Indigenous peoples' organizations as permanent participants is an increasingly important ethical consideration in Arctic Council negotiations, despite inadequacies in funding (Shadian and Gamble 2017).

REFERENCES

ACIA (Arctic Climate Impact Assessment). 2014. *Impacts of a Warming Arctic: Arctic Climate Impact Assessment.* Cambridge: Cambridge University Press.

Agnew, J. 2003. *Geopolitics: Re-visioning World Politics.* New York: Routledge.

AHDR. 2004. *Arctic Human Development Report.* Akureyri, IS: Stefansson Arctic Institute.

APECS (Association of Polar Early Career Scientists). n.d. "The Madrid Protocol 25 Years On." Association of Polar Early Career Scientists, accessed 25 July 2022. https://apecs.is/news/polar-news/1569-madrid-protocol-25-years-on.html.

Arctic Council. 2021. "Reykjavik Declaration." Arctic Council, May 2021. https://oaarchive.arctic-council.org/handle/11374/2600.

Bailes, A. J. K., and L. Heininen. 2012. *Strategy Papers on the Arctic or High North: A Comparative Study and Analysis*. Reykjavík: Centre for Small State Studies Institute of International Affairs.

Bone, R. M. 2012. *The Geography of the Canadian North: Challenges and Issues*. Toronto: Oxford University Press.

Borgerson, S. G. 2008. "Arctic Meltdown: The Economic and Security Implications of Global Warming." *Foreign Affairs*, March/April. http://www.foreignaffairs.com/articles/63222/scott-g-borgerson/arctic-meltdown.

Byers, M. 2008. *Who Owns the Arctic?* Vancouver: Douglas and McIntyre.

———. 2017. "Crises and International Cooperation: An Arctic Case Study." *International Relations* 31 (4): 375–402.

Cavell, J. 2014. "Sector Claims and Counter-Claims: Joseph Elzéar Bernier, the Canadian Government, and Arctic Sovereignty, 1898–1934." *Polar Record* 50 (254): 293–310.

Chaturvedi S. 2000. "Arctic Geopolitics: Then and Now." In *The Arctic: Environment, People, Policy*, edited by M. Nuttall and T. V. Callaghan, 441–58. Amsterdam: Harwood Academic Publishers.

Coates, K., P. W. Lackenbauer, B. Morrison, and G. Poelzer. 2008. *Arctic Front: Defending Canadian Interests in the Far North*. Toronto: Thomas Allen and Son.

Dittmer, J., S. Moisio, A. Ingram, and K. Dodds. 2011. "Have You Heard the One about the Disappearing Sea Ice: Re-casting Arctic Geopolitics." *Political Geography* 30:202–14.

Dodds, K. 2002. *Pink Ice: Britain and the South Atlantic Empire*. London: I. B. Tarius.

———. 2010. "Flag Planting and Finger Pointing: The Law of the Sea, the Arctic and the Political Geographies of the Outer Continental Shelf." *Political Geography* 29 (2): 63–73.

———. 2012. *The Antarctic: A Very Short Introduction*. Oxford: Oxford University Press.

Dodds, K., and M. Nuttall. 2015. *The Scramble for the Poles: The Geopolitics of the Arctic and Antarctic*. Cambridge: Polity Press.

Dougherty, J. E., and R. L Pfaltzgraff. 1990. *Contending Theories of International Relations: A Comprehensive Survey*. New York: Harper and Row.

English, J. 2013. *Ice and Water: Politics, Peoples, and the Arctic Council*. Toronto: Allen Lane.

Farish, M. 2010. *The Contours of America's Cold War*. Minneapolis: University of Minnesota Press.

Fenge, T. 2013. "The Arctic Council: Past, Present and Future Prospects with Canada in the Chair from 2013 to 2015." *Northern Review* 37 (Fall): 7–35.

Gale Ambassadors. 2019. "Adolf Erik Nordenskiöld—A Great Arctic Explorer of the Nineteenth Century." *Gale Review*, 18 March 2019. https://review.gale. com/2019/03/18/adolf-erik-nordenskiold-a-great-arctic-explorer-of-the-nineteenth-century/.

Grant, S. 2010. *Polar Imperative: A History of Arctic Sovereignty in North America*. Vancouver: Douglas and McIntyre.

Heininen, L. 1991. *Sotilaallisen läsnäolon ympäristöriskit Arktiksessa—Kohti Arktiksen säätelyjärjestelmää*. Tampere Peace Research Institute, Research Report No. 43. Tampere, FN: Tampere Peace Research Institute.

———. 2004. "Circumpolar International Relations and Geopolitics." In *Arctic Human Development Report*, 207–25. Akureyri, IS: Stefansson Arctic Institute.

———. 2013. " 'Politicization' of the Environment: Environmental Politics and Security in the Circumpolar North." In *The Fast-Changing Arctic: Rethinking Arctic Security for a Warmer World*, edited by B. S. Zellen, 35–55. Calgary: University of Calgary Press.

———. 2022. "The Post–Cold War Arctic." In *Global Arctic: An Introduction to the Multifaceted Dynamics of the Arctic*, edited by M. Finger and G. Rekvig, 109–27. Cham, CH: Springer.

Heininen, L., J. Ahola, and E. Frog. 2014. " 'Geopolitics' of the Viking Age? Actors, Factors and Space." In *Fibula, Fabula, Fact: The Viking Age in Finland*, edited by J. Ahola and E. Frog with C. Tolley, 296–320. Vantaa, FI: Finnish Literature Society.

Heininen, L., K. Everett, B. Padrtova, and A. Reissell. 2020. *Arctic Policies and Strategies—Analysis, Synthesis, and Trends*. Helsinki: International Institute for Applied Systems Analysis and Ministry for Foreign Affairs of Finland.

Heininen, L., and H. Exner-Pirot. 2019. *Climate Change and Arctic Security: Searching for a Paradigm Shift*. London: Palgrave Pivot.

Heininen, L., and M. Finger. 2017. "The 'Global Arctic' as a New Geopolitical Context and Method." *Journal of Borderlands Studies* 33 (2): 199–202.

Heininen, L., O.-P. Jalonen, and J. Käkönen. 1995. *Expanding the Northern Dimension*. Tampere Peace Research Institute, Research Report No. 61. Tampere, FN: Tampere Peace Research Institute.

Heininen, L., and Heather N. Nicol. 2007. "The Importance of Northern Dimension of Foreign Policies in the Geopolitics of the Circumpolar North." *Geopolitics* 12:133–35.

———. 2008. "Canada and the New Geopolitics of the North Pacific Rim." In *Seeking Balance in a Changing North: The Proceedings Papers from the 5th Northern Research Forum Open Assembly in Anchorage, Alaska* (Plenary Session 1: The Future of Northern Cooperation). http://www.nrf.is.

Heininen, L., and C. Southcott, eds. 2010. *Globalization and the Circumpolar North*. Fairbanks: University of Alaska Press.

Heininen, L., and M. Zebich-Knos. 2011. "Polar Regions—Comparing Arctic and Antarctic Border Debates." In *Ashgate Research Companion to Border Studies*.

Part II: Geopolitics: State, Nation and Power Relations, edited by D. Wastl-Walter, 195–217. London: Ashgate.

Hemmings, A. D., D. R. Rothwell, and K. N. Scott. 2012. *Antarctic Security in the Twenty-First Century.* New York: Routledge.

Huebert, R. 2010. *The Newly Emerging Arctic Security Environment.* Calgary: Canadian Defence and Foreign Affairs Institute.

———. 2013. "Submarines, Oil Tankers and Icebreakers." *International Journal* 66 (4): 809–24.

ICC (Inuit Circumpolar Council). 2009. *A Circumpolar Inuit Declaration on Sovereignty in the Arctic.* Inuit Circumpolar Council, April 2009. https://www.itk.ca/wp-content/uploads/2016/07/Declaration_12x18_Vice-Chairs_Signed.pdf.

Ilulissat Declaration. 2008. "Arctic Ocean Conference in Ilulissat, Greenland, 27–29 May 2008." (August): 12–13.

Joyner, C. C. 1998. *Governing the Frozen Commons: The Antarctic Regime and Environmental Protection.* Columbia: University of South Carolina Press.

Kee, R. 2019. "Key Issues to Arctic Security." In *North American Arctic: Themes in Regional Security,* edited by D. W. Menezes and H. N. Nicol, 93–115. London: University College London Press.

Keskitalo, E. C. E. 2004. *Negotiating the Arctic: The Construction of an International Region.* London: Routledge.

Lackenbauer, P. W. 2010. "Mirror Images? Canada, Russia, and the Circumpolar World." *International Journal* 65 (4): 879–97.

Lackenbauer, P. W., and M. Farish. 2007. "The Cold War on Canadian Soil: Militarizing a Northern Environment." *Environmental History* 12 (4): 921–50.

Lackenbauer, P. W., H. Nicol, and W. Greaves. 2017. *One Arctic: The Arctic Council and Circumpolar Governance.* Ottawa: Canadian Arctic Resources Committee.

Lasserre, F. 2010. *China and the Arctic: Threat or Cooperation Potential for Canada.* China Papers No. 11. Toronto: Canadian International Council.

MacKinder, H. J. 1904. "The Geographical Pivot of History." *Geographical Journal* 23:421–37.

Menezes, D. R., and H. N. Nicol, eds. 2019. *North American Arctic: Themes in Regional Security.* London: University College London Press.

National Science Foundation. n.d. "The Antarctic Treaty." National Science Foundation, accessed 25 July 2022. https://www.nsf.gov/geo/opp/antarct/anttrty.jsp.

Nicol, H. N. 2010. "Reframing Sovereignty: Indigenous Peoples and Arctic States." *Political Geography* 29 (2): 78–80.

———. 2015. *The Fence and the Bridge: Geopolitics and Identity along the Canada–US Border.* Waterloo, ON: Wilfrid Laurier University Press.

———. 2017. "From Territory to Rights: New Foundations for Conceptualising Indigenous Sovereignty." *Geopolitics* 22:794–814.

———. 2020. "The Evolving North American Arctic Security Context: Can Security Be Traditional?" In *The Palgrave Handbook of Arctic Policy and Politics*, edited by K. Coates and K. Holroyd, 455–72. London: Palgrave Macmillan.

Nicol, H., and J. Barnes. 2019. "Resilience, Environment and Economic Development in the Canadian Arctic." In *Canada's Arctic Agenda: Into the Vortex*, edited by J. Higginbotham and J. Spence, 111–17. Waterloo, ON: Centre for International Governance Innovation.

Nicol, H. N., and L. Heininen. 2013. "Human Security, the Arctic Council and Climate Change." *Polar Record* 50 (1): 80–85. doi:10.1017/S0032247412000666.

NOAA (National Oceanic and Atmospheric Administration). n.d. "The International Polar Years." PMEL Arctic Zone, accessed 25 July 2022. https://www.pmel.noaa.gov/arctic-zone/ipy.html.

Østhagen, A. 2017. "Geopolitics and Security in the Arctic: What Role for the EU?" *European View* 16 (2): 239–49. https://doi.org/10.1007/s12290-017-0459-1.

———. 2020. *The Nuances of Geopolitics in the Arctic*. The Arctic Institute, 7 January 2020. https://www.thearcticinstitute.org/nuances-geopolitics-arctic/.

Östreng, W. 2008. "Extended Security and Climate Change in the Regional and Global Context: A Historical Account." In *Politics of the Eurasian Arctic: National Interests and International Challenges*, edited by G. R. Thorsteinsdottir and E. E. Oddsdottir, 16–30. Akureyri, IS: Northern Research Forum and Ocean Future.

———. 2017. "The Arctic Council and the 'One Arctic': A Historic Stocktaking of Some Circumpolar Challenges, Dilemmas and Inconsistencies." In *One Arctic: The Arctic Council and Circumpolar Governance*, edited by P. W. Lackenbauer, H. Nicol, and W. Greaves. Ottawa: Canadian Arctic Resources Committee.

Owens, M. T. 2015. "In Defense of Classical Geopolitics." *Orbis* 59 (4): 463–78. https://doi.org/10.1016/j.orbis.2015.08.006.

Palosaari, T. 2011. "The Amazing Race." *Nordia Geographical Publications* 40 (4): 13–30.

Pravda. 1987. "Speech by Mikhail Gorbachev at a Formal Meeting in Murmansk on 1 October 1987." *Pravda*, 5 October 1987.

Roberts, P. 2011. *The European Antarctic: Science and Strategy in Scandinavia and the British Empire*. London: Palgrave.

Shadian, J. M. 2014. *The Politics of Arctic Sovereignty: Oil, Ice, and Inuit Governance*. London: Routledge.

Shadian, J. M., and J. Gamble. 2017. "One Arctic . . . but Uneven Capacity: The Arctic Council Permanent Participants." In *One Arctic: The Arctic Council and Circumpolar Governance*, edited by W. Lackenbauer, H. Nicol, and W. Greaves, 142–57. Ottawa: Canadian Arctic Resources Committee.

Sheng, E. L. 2022. *Arctic Opportunities and Challenges: China, Russia and the US Cooperation and Competition*. Palgrave Macmillan.

Śmieszek, Małgorzata (Gosia), and Timo Koivurova. 2017. "The Arctic Council: Between Continuity and Change." In *One Arctic: The Arctic Council and Circumpolar Governance*, edited by W. Lackenbauer, H. Nicol, and W. Greaves, 1–26. Ottawa: Canadian Arctic Resources Committee.

Till, G. 1987. *Modern Sea Power*. London: Brassey's.

IASC (International Arctic Science Committee). 2015. "Integrating Arctic Research: A Roadmap for the Future" [Toyoma Conference Statement]. Arctic Science Summit Week, Toyama, Japan, 23–30 April 2015. https://icarp.iasc.info/images/articles/Themes/ASSW_Conference_Statement.pdf

Tuathail, G. O. U., and S. Dalby. 1998. *Rethinking Geopolitics*. London: Routledge.

United Nations. 1998. Protocol on Environmental Protection to the Antarctic Treaty. https://www.ats.aq/e/protocol.html.

Watson, M. 2009. "An Arctic Treaty: A Solution to The International Dispute over the Polar Region." *Ocean & Coastal Law Journal* 14 (2): 307–34.

Watts, A. 1992. *International Law and the Antarctic Treaty System*. Cambridge: Grotius Publications.

Willson, K., E. Frog, and M. Bertell. 2018. *Contacts and Networks in the Baltic Sea Region: Austmarr as a Northern Mare Nostrum, ca. 500–1500 CE*. Amsterdam: Amsterdam University Press.

Wilson Rowe, E. 2019. *Arctic Governance: Power in Cross-Border Cooperation*. Manchester: Manchester University Press.

Wilson Rowe, E., and H. Blakkisrud. 2013. "A Normal Great Power? Russia and the Arctic." *Policy Options*, 1 May 2013. https://policyoptions.irpp.org/magazines/arctic-visions/a-normal-great-power-russia-and-the-arctic/.

Wu, Z. 2018. "Classical Geopolitics, Realism and the Balance of Power Theory." *Journal of Strategic Studies* 41 (6): 786–823. DOI: 10.1080/01402390.2017.1379398.

Yarovoy, G. 2014. "Russia's Arctic Policy. Continuity and Changes." In *International Relations and the Arctic. Understanding Policy and Governance*, edited by R. W. Murray and A. Dey Nuttall, 191–233. Amherst, NY: Cambria Press.

Young, O. 2000. *The Internationalization of the Circumpolar North: Charting a Course for the 21st Century*. Akureyri, IS: Stefansson Arctic Institute.

———. 2012. "Arctic Politics in an Era of Global Change." *Brown Journal World Affairs* 14 (1): 165–78.

Zellen, B. S. 2009a. *Arctic Doom, Arctic Boom: The Geopolitics of Climate Change in the Arctic*. Santa Barbara, CA: ABC Clio.

———. 2009b. *On Thin Ice: The Inuit, The State and the Challenge of Arctic Sovereignty*. Lanham. MD: Lexington Books.

3

Polar Disaster Diplomacy: Geostrategies for Norway

Ilan Kelman

Disaster Diplomacy

A disaster, by definition, is when people, human constructions, or human interests are harmed beyond their ability to cope themselves (UNDRR 2019). Given this focus on human impacts, from the beginnings of disaster studies through to current understandings (Gaillard 2019; Hewitt 1983, 1997; Lewis 1999, 2019; O'Keefe, Westgate, and Wisner 1976; Rodríguez, Donner, and Trainor 2018; Wisner 2004), disaster research has accepted that processes and phenomena from nature, such as high or low temperatures, storms and floods, earthquakes, and volcanic eruptions, are not disasters per se, but can sometimes be hazards. When a hazard interacts with elements of society unprepared for it or unable to deal with it, then a disaster can occur. One consequence is the preference in disaster studies for avoiding the phrase "natural disaster" on the premise that disasters are caused by society, rather than nature (Chmutina and von Meding 2019; Gaillard 2019; Kasdan 2019; O'Keefe, Westgate, and Wisner 1976; Staupe-Delgado 2019). Not differentiating between natural and non-natural disasters also permits studying all forms of disasters together, whether hazards emerge from nature (e.g., meteorite strikes), technology (e.g., chemical spills), or society (e.g., riots).

Given this starting point and the basic definitions, environmental conditions in the Arctic and Antarctic can be hazards but are not disasters. Much is said of these locations often being harsh, dangerous, and challenging, especially in relation to temperature, wind, storms, snow, ice, and waves, along with wildlife like polar bears and orcas. Large swathes of the Antarctic are also hazardous with respect to high elevation. When intersecting with people's and societies' vulnerabilities, a long history of a variety of disasters results in both the Arctic and the Antarctic (Finnish Red Cross 2018; Jabour 2007; Munk School of Global Affairs 2014), though plenty of examples exist of managing in both places without succumbing to vulnerabilities (e.g., Mileski et al. 2018; Sellheim, Zaika, and Kelman 2019; Taylor and Gormley 1997). These experiences demonstrate that action can be taken individually and collectively in developing and pursuing geostrategic futures so that hazards do not become disasters. This does not always occur, meaning a continual need for response, recovery, and reconstruction.

Some of these actions for dealing with disasters—before, during, and after—can mean co-operation and conflict among numerous parties, including independent state governments, many of which have or claim interests in the Arctic or the Antarctic. Seven states make territorial claims in the Antarctic: Argentina, Australia, Chile, France, New Zealand, Norway, and the United Kingdom. All of these countries, except Norway, claim a sector from the continent's shoreline to the South Pole. Norway's claim does not accept a sector-based approach and thus does not place explicit northern or southern limits on its claim (Government of Norway 2014–15). Russia and the United States maintain the basis for potentially claiming territory in the future.

At the other end of the globe, five states border the Arctic Ocean—Canada, Denmark (through Greenland), Norway, Russia, and the United States—with Finland, Iceland, and Sweden also having territory above the Arctic Circle. Iceland's territorial waters extend above the Arctic Circle, whereas Sweden's and Finland's do not. From these two sets of countries, the only one with claims at both poles is Norway. Other countries express interest. For instance, as part of its geostrategic futures, the United

Kingdom has been positioning itself as an Arctic country or, at minimum, a country with significant Arctic interests (e.g., Depledge 2018), with the Scottish government and its Arctic strategy (Scottish Government 2019) being one driver. Meanwhile, countries at lower latitudes get involved in affairs of one or both poles, with examples being China, the Czech Republic, India, Poland, Singapore, and South Korea. For formal territorial involvement in both regions, Norway remains unique and thus serves as a useful case study for exploring similarities and differences in interstate ventures for strategically addressing polar disasters, especially with respect to improvements in the future.

One research area for examining the implications of disaster-related work for co-operation and conflict as part of geostrategic futures is "disaster diplomacy." Disaster diplomacy examines how and why reducing disaster risk, preventing disasters, responding to situations, and recovering from them do and do not influence different forms of peace and conflict (Kelman 2012, 2016). Much disaster diplomacy research has focused on violent conflict and countries deemed to be "enemies," such as Greece and Turkey from the 1950s to the 1990s (Ker-Lindsay 2007), Cuba and the United States when Fidel Castro led Cuba (Glantz 2000), and climate change possibly influencing sub-Saharan conflict (Buhaug 2010; Burke et al. 2009). This field expands to how non-violent political disputes or disagreements could be influenced by disaster diplomacy alongside non-state-based parties.

A large amount of disaster diplomacy work has also focused on environmental hazards. Greece-Turkey disaster diplomacy has been influenced primarily by earthquakes (Ker-Lindsay 2007). Cuba-US disaster diplomacy has been mainly climate- and weather-related (Glantz 2000), although Glantz (2000) also discussed how wind patterns could have distributed fallout over the southern United States from an incident at Cuba's Juragua Nuclear Power Plant, if the plant had ever been completed. The few detailed disaster diplomacy case studies not involving environmental hazards include poisoning in Morocco in 1959 (Segalla 2012) and Southeast Asia's regional haze over previous decades (Brauer and Hisham-Hashim 1998; Islam, Pei, and Mangharam 2016). Other work (e.g., Whittaker et al. 2018) has developed health diplomacy and medical diplomacy within a disaster diplomacy framework. Aspects of disaster diplomacy are being explored for polar regions (e.g., Kontar 2018; Kontar et al. 2018; Nikitina 2017; Pincus and Ali 2016).

All this theoretical and empirical work on disaster diplomacy has so far not been able to provide evidence for new, lasting diplomacy based on only disaster-related activities. Instead, disaster-related activities are frequently used as one excuse among many to pursue pre-desired diplomatic pathways, whether for co-operation or for conflict. This approach sometimes leads to short-term influences that are invariably superseded by interests in and priorities regarding non-disaster-related factors, with examples being changes in leadership, the inertia of historical dislike, or preference for geopolitical gain over dealing with disasters.

Given this background on disasters and disaster diplomacy, as well as the unique geostrategic position of Norway in relation to the Arctic and the Antarctic, this chapter provides the first exploration of polar disaster diplomacy using Norway as a case study to consider some wider implications. The focus is on state-based diplomacy to provide a baseline for discussion. The next section examines possibilities for Norway's polar disaster diplomacy. Norway's geostrategic interests are then considered within understandings of "enemies." Conclusions provide possible analogues for polar disaster diplomacy.

Norway

Norway has typically prided itself on being a neutral state seeking peace (Leira 2013), and therefore has worked actively to end conflicts, such as in Sri Lanka (Moolakkattu 2005) and the Middle East (Jones 1999). Since the forced union with Sweden in 1814, followed by full independence in 1905, Norway has not been involved in extensive interstate violent conflicts, apart from Nazi Germany's invasion and occupation of 1940 to 1945 during the Second World War. Norwegian troops have seen combat in several post–Second World War overseas wars under international auspices—namely, the North Atlantic Treaty Organization (NATO) and the United Nations (UN).

Norway has nonetheless been involved in other forms of political conflict. As a founding member of NATO in 1949, and with a land border with the Union of Soviet Socialist Republics (USSR) until 1991 and then Russia, the country has always been assumed to be at the front line of violent and non-violent Cold War conflict. In the high Arctic, this relationship becomes complicated regarding the archipelago of Svalbard. Svalbard is a sovereign territory of Norway, but it is governed by the Svalbard Treaty (1920) providing rights for livelihood and commercial activities to the citizens of countries that have signed the treaty. The USSR ratified the treaty in 1935 and Russia is currently one of forty-six treaty signatories. Irrespective of the Cold War and contemporary tensions between the USSR/Russia and other countries, Norway was and is bound to co-operate with the USSR/Russia regarding Svalbard.

Co-operation in relation to the Svalbard Treaty does not necessarily entail disaster-related activities. Norway's stance is clear that Svalbard is sovereign Norwegian territory and so Norway has the responsibility for response, rescue, and recovery. The Joint Rescue Coordination Centre of Northern Norway is based in Bodø and is responsible for the region from 65 degrees North latitude to the North Pole, which covers all of Svalbard and its surrounding waters (Hovedredningssentralen n.d.). When disasters have occurred around Svalbard, Norwegian authorities have responded and led efforts even if in collaboration with other countries such as Russia when a Russian airplane crashed in 1996 killing 141 people (Olaisen, Stenersen, and Mevåg 1997), and when a Russian helicopter crashed in 2017 killing 8 people (AIBN 2018). The main Russian settlement on Svalbard is Barentsburg, and Russia has been pushing to lead search-and-rescue from there using its own personnel and equipment. Political tussles continue over this leadership issue, while co-operation also continues through joint training exercises, exchanges of information and equipment, and collaborative planning and meetings for scenarios such as oil spills, health concerns, and cruise ships sinking.

Norway-Russia interactions, co-operative and conflictual, in Arctic disaster-related activities have not been confined to the Svalbard Treaty area. Both countries are involved in numerous regional multilateral and bilateral efforts. The Barents Euro-Arctic Council has focused on disaster-linked topics such as transportation safety (BEAC 2019) and climate change (BEAC 2017). The Arctic Council covers disaster risk reduction through the Sustainable Development Working Group and covers disaster response through the Working Group on Emergency Prevention, Preparedness and Response. Russia-Norway direct co-operation occurs, for instance, through the Joint Norwegian-Russian Environment Commission for pollution disasters and the Norwegian-Russian Nuclear Commission for nuclear disasters. Norway and Russia coordinate the monitoring of Barents Sea maritime vessels through the International Maritime Organization (2012) agreement; although Norway controls its waters from Lofoten to the Russian border, and Russia is responsible for its waters from the Norwegian border to Murmansk. Mutual aid nonetheless shows operationally, such as when a Russian ship was foundering on the Rybachiy Peninsula on 18 December 2007, and a Norwegian rescue helicopter crossed the border to lift the crew to safety (Marchenko et al. 2015).

Throughout all the policies, talks, actions, and disagreements, this Norway-Russia Arctic disaster diplomacy has not shown evidence of wider impacts or spillover into other areas of interaction. As with all other disaster diplomacy case studies investigated so far (Kelman 2012, 2016), disaster-related activities for Norway in the Arctic have not been shown to create new, lasting diplomacy. Instead, co-operation tends to be confined to the disaster-related activities with other aspects of Arctic relations dominated by non-disaster factors. Examples are trade, culture—including cross-border Sámi links—and geopolitics (Wilson Rowe, 2018). Similar conclusions result for Norway when examining the Antarctic.

The Antarctic is governed by the Antarctic Treaty System (ATS), which applies to all areas south of 60 degrees south latitude. Many examples exist of countries with conflicts being jointly involved in aspects of the ATS, such as Argentina and the United Kingdom (both claimant countries for Antarctic territory) attending negotiation meetings in 1982 during the Falklands War (CCAMLR 1982); the USSR and the United States both joining at the initiation of the Antarctic Treaty in 1959 despite the Cold War; and North Korea joining as a non-consultative member in 1987, despite its relative international isolation and continuing threats to the region, with South Korea as a full ATS treaty party. The pattern within the ATS appears to be countries dealing with Antarctic matters without connecting to possibilities outside of the ATS area or permitting the links to influence other matters. If this pattern continues, then disaster-related activities, from an eruption of Mount Erebus to a cruise ship sinking, would not spill over into other diplomatic realms, instead continuing the pattern of disaster diplomacy's ineffectiveness.

Norway was an original signatory to the Antarctic Treaty, and as a country making territorial claims on the continent, it retains strong interest in the southern regions. Bouvet Island in the South Atlantic Ocean is outside the ATS area and is recognized as a dependency of Norway, while the Antarctic territories of Queen Maud Land and Peter I Island fall under the ATS claims provisions. Disaster-related activities for these three dependencies are limited due to the absence of permanent settlements and the low rate of people in their vicinity. Hazards are frequent and numerous such as the weather, icebergs, tsunamis, and volcanic eruptions as well as possibilities for pollution. Disasters are rare, and most disaster-related activities relate to either (1) pre-disaster actions through appropriate siting, construction, and maintenance of infrastructure along with personnel training, and (2) post-disaster actions of search and rescue.

Otherwise, the most prominent considerations would be shipping and aircraft incidents, mainly related to science, tourism, fishing, and exploration. For Bouvet Island outside of the ATS area, prospects remain for vessels used for mineral exploration or military purposes. Search and rescue in and around Bouvet Island and the ATS area is not straightforward since equipment and people are not available rapidly and environmental conditions often preclude deployment. The South Pole station is effectively inaccessible during the winter, and other stations might or might not have winter access. For instance, significant efforts for winter aircraft landings at McMurdo Station (outside the Norwegian claim area) started in 2015.

Perhaps one of the most political Antarctic disasters for Norway was the deaths in 1912 of the British explorer Robert Scott and four of his companions while returning from the South Pole after the Norwegian explorer Roald Amundsen and his team reached there first. Despite significant resentment in the United Kingdom at the time, and continuing debate today about the two expeditions and their competition, little major, long-term political fallout was evident. Amundsen and his mentor, the Norwegian explorer Fridtjof Nansen, continued representing Norway on the world stage for exploration, science, and international relations.

Major political differences emerge between the Arctic and Antarctic regions that influence Norway's disaster-related interests, roles, and activities. Much of the Arctic is owned by sovereign states, some of which use it for military purposes. In comparison, the Antarctic is governed by ATS, neither recognizing nor denying sovereign territory claims but prohibiting military uses. Many Indigenous peoples have long lived around the Arctic, and territorial discussions continue with the current governing states. As far as the evidence suggests, no peoples have established themselves in the Antarctic. Many parts of the Arctic are fairly easy to reach, with many settlements established and thriving alongside livelihood activities including all-season resource extraction and regular tourism. The Antarctic is expensive and difficult to get to, meaning that even if resource extraction were legal, it might not yet be financially or technically viable. Meanwhile, Antarctic tourism remains limited because it is expensive and onerous. Both regions fall under some similar international governance regimes for disaster-related activities such as the International Convention for the Safety of Life at Sea, or SOLAS Convention (IMO 1974), the International Convention on Maritime Search and Rescue, or SAR Convention (IMO 1979), and the International Code for Ships Operating in Polar Waters (IMO 2017). Pollution prevention and response are covered by another series of international protocols, as well as some that are region-specific such as through the Arctic Council and as part of ATS.

Could Norway link the two polar regions for disaster diplomacy? It would be possible if an active approach were taken, so that Norway explicitly aims for disaster diplomacy with a polar perspective. It is not clear that this approach would necessarily be in Norway's interest, unless there were a specific peace process in which Norway were trying to intervene. For instance, Sri Lanka and Middle Eastern countries as examples of Norway's previous attempts at brokering peace have thus far expressed limited interest in the polar regions. Could the two Koreas' ATS involvement provide a way for Norway to start with common ground leading to further talks? Similarly, during the 1982 Falklands War, could Norway have used the combatants' Antarctic interests to try to foster a non-violent resolution? Given that this conflict was over sub-Antarctic territories, it is highly unlikely.

Similarly, other factors indicate that, despite Norway's unique position with respect to neutrality and both poles, such efforts might not be successful. First, the overarching disaster diplomacy analysis is that disaster diplomacy processes are rarely successful because parties involved in disaster-related activities tend to prioritize non-disaster-related reasons for peace and conflict (Kelman 2012, 2016). Past failures do not preclude future successes, but caution would be needed in assuming that polar disaster diplomacy would work if Norway attempted it. Second, despite Norway's positioning of itself within diplomacy, its successes are debated, especially as shown by Sri Lanka and the Middle East, but also due to its early membership in NATO and its military roles overseas.

More specifically regarding possible contemporary case studies, it is not clear that Norway would necessarily be viewed as an appropriate player. For the Korean Peninsula, China is a significant party, especially as a somewhat-ally of North Korea. After Chinese activist Liu Xiaobo received the 2010 Nobel Peace Prize and was refused permission to leave China to receive the prize in Oslo, China instituted several retaliatory measures against Norway that took several years to achieve restitution. Would China trust Norway as a peace broker for the Koreas or would it pretend not to trust Norway to gain leverage? The same challenge could occur with another of the world's hot spots, Kashmir, since China and India are involved, and both these countries profess Arctic and Antarctic interests. Meanwhile, conflicts within or around Russia would not place Norway well as a neutral party due to Norway-Russia relations. Other major conflicts currently tend to have few parties with strong Arctic or Antarctic interests, with examples being the Democratic Republic of Congo, Yemen, Iraq, Iran, Afghanistan, Burma's treatment of the Rohingya people, and internal strife in and migration from Latin American countries (e.g., Colombia and Mexico).

Consequently, even if Norway wished to pursue polar disaster diplomacy, scope for doing so is constrained. One limitation to this conclusion is the assumption that polar disaster diplomacy would be led by Norway's government. This chapter is bound to state-based formal diplomacy, but the diplomacy and disaster diplomacy literatures explore possibilities beyond state-based interactions. This multi-track diplomacy could involve sub-national governments, supra-national organizations, media, business, non-governmental organizations, and private citizens such as philanthropists and celebrities (e.g., McDonald 2012). While the multi-track disaster diplomacy examples explored so far are characterized as being as unsuccessful as state-based disaster diplomacy, options remain for

Norway or Norwegians to pursue polar disaster diplomacy beyond state-based diplomacy.

Norway in Wider Perspectives: Beyond "Enemies"?

Norway's potential for, and lack of fulfillment of, state-based polar disaster diplomacy occurs within the context of trying to understand who a state-based "enemy" might be. The differences between the Arctic and the Antarctic become even more apparent, demonstrating that establishing parallels between the two regions might be tenuous.

In the Arctic, the paradigm has typically been of one enemy: The USSR and then Russia, especially since the other four countries bordering the Arctic Ocean, as well as Iceland, are NATO members, although Sweden and Finland are not. This discourse is about hostility from Russia in the Arctic, emphasizing storylines of re-militarizing the North and increasing military-related actions including flying bombers near NATO's Arctic territories (Laruelle 2014; Overland and Krivorotov 2015). In April 2018, Russia transported a floating nuclear power plant, the *Akademik Lomonosov*, along the coastline of nuclear-free Norway to reach Russia's Arctic (Lenton 2018), which was also seen as being provocative and asserting Russia's northern rights. Other analyses do not necessarily deny that Russia pursues its self-interests but explain that Russia tends to see Arctic co-operation as the best way to achieve its Arctic self-interests, evidenced by numerous agreements such as for fisheries and oil spills (Nikitina 2018; Wilson Rowe and Blakkisrud 2014). Some authors describe few prospects for a recurrence of Cold War attitudes and antipathy for the Arctic (Åtland and Pedersen 2008; Young 2019).

Even among NATO allies, territorial disputes around the Arctic remain (Pincus and Ali 2016). In May 2018, Canada and Denmark/Greenland set up a Joint Task Force on Boundary Issues to seek recommendations regarding their maritime boundary line in the Lincoln Sea, the Labrador Sea continental shelf overlap beyond two hundred nautical miles, and any land boundary across Hans Island. The United States continues to dispute Canada's sovereignty over the Northwest Passage (Pompeo 2019). Meanwhile, the current Russia-Norway land border was effectively established in 1326 and formalized in 1826, while their maritime boundary was delimited by the Barents Sea Treaty (2010). Consequently, it is not clear that the main antipathy around the Arctic comes from or is directed toward Russia. Russia and Finland, though, have exchanged plenty of violence across their shifting border, and Karelia remains an issue for the countries' relations (Raudaskoski and Laine 2018).

In contrast to the Arctic, few direct players in the Antarctic are enemies, and the international governance regime is about collaboration. Among countries claiming territory, the only recent violent conflict was between Argentina and the United Kingdom in 1982, and although this territorial dispute remains unresolved, the specific war was led by an Argentine president who held the role for less than six months. The United States and the USSR/Russia have retained their right to claim territory in Antarctica, leading to similar discussions as for the Arctic regarding the USSR/Russia and NATO. Chile and Argentina nearly came to war in 1978 over three islands and the surrounding sea at the southern tip of South America, with Argentina intending to occupy them in 1982 after a presumed victory in the Falklands. Since then, a series of agreements between the two countries has resolved most disagreements with commitments toward peaceful relations and amicably finalizing remaining disputes. The overlapping Antarctic claims of Argentina, Chile, and the United Kingdom could lead to problems if Antarctic territorial claims are ever accepted.

None of the issues seem to have affected disaster-related activities around the continent, mainly because many of these activities are governed by international law. For instance, when the Norwegian yacht *Berserk* set off its emergency beacon in McMurdo Sound in 2011, a New Zealand naval vessel responded, although it could not find the yacht and its three crew members. Violations of Antarctic law by the yacht's captain, who had been dropped off on the continent and so was not aboard the boat when it disappeared, were dealt with by Norway since the captain is Norwegian. Given that Norway and New Zealand have limited enmity anyway, how germane is the disaster diplomacy question in this instance?

The key is considering wider scopes for and implications of disaster diplomacy. Given disaster diplomacy's definition, it is important to consider connections, friendships, enmity, and disputes emerging from disaster-related activities that go beyond disaster-related activities. That is, the parties involved would not necessarily need to be enemies or even have pre-existing conflict. The difficulty, then, is that the starting point might be the truism that any interaction among people creates positive, negative, and neutral connections and often outcomes. Meanwhile, a long-standing literature exists examining a variety of dimensions of these questions (e.g., Olson and Drury 1997; Quarantelli and Dynes 1976).

Consequently, to understand polar disaster diplomacy and its relevance or otherwise, a balance is needed. In the Arctic, the USSR/Russia have played key roles as enemies, but there might be little else that is highly relevant from state-based disaster diplomacy among Arctic countries, apart from considering historical wars—and possible future ones. In the Antarctic, the disaster diplomacy question at the state-based level for claimant countries might remain with Argentina-Chile, Argentina–United Kingdom, and Russia, yet the absence of actual conflict at the moment decreases the relevance of any of these. Similar patterns are seen for some non-state-based case studies providing disaster diplomacy insights, such as disaster casualty identification (Scanlon 2006). For instance, passengers on board Air New Zealand Flight TE901, which crashed into Mount Erebus in 1979 killing all 257 people on board, had eight different nationalities. Because the aircraft was registered in New Zealand and the flight originated in and would have landed in New Zealand, the body recovery was led by New Zealand through the NZ Police Disaster Victim Identification Team.

In both the Arctic and Antarctic, however, questions arise regarding states from outside of the respective regions having polar interests. For example, some commentators describe an Arctic role for Australia (e.g., Halt 2014), but little in-depth scientific discussion has been published formally. At the moment, thirteen states—eight in Europe and (analyzed by Tonami 2016) five in Asia—and more than two dozen non-state groups have observer status at the Arctic Council. From a disaster diplomacy perspective, China and India are perhaps of most interest given previous analyses (see Kelman 2012, 2016; Venugopal and Yasir 2017; Weizhun and Tianshu 2005). China's first Arctic Policy (Government of China 2018) in effect mapped out a Polar Silk Road for connecting China to the Arctic and supporting Arctic initiatives (Glantz 2019). Both China and India maintain research stations in Svalbard, as do other non-Arctic countries including the Czech Republic and Poland. China and India also have research stations in the Antarctic, as do more than a dozen non-claimant countries, again including the Czech Republic and Poland.

From all this work, it currently appears that science-related collaboration is the most prominent interstate outcome of polar disaster diplomacy, as discussed for the Arctic by Kontar (2018) and Kontar et al. (2018) with applicability to the Antarctic. Thus far, no operational examples of disaster diplomacy potential could be found for countries outside the respective Arctic and Antarctic regions. As one instance, on 19 May 2019, a Svalbard avalanche killed two Polish scientists from the Polish research station, but the search and recovery operation was not linked to politics or to Norway-Polish relations, nor should it have been. The protocol was to inform Svalbard's Norwegian authorities that the two had failed to return to base so that these authorities could lead proper, safe, and effective actions for rescue or recovery.

This limited relevance of polar disaster diplomacy raises the question, as with Norway earlier, of whether or not countries should actively try to make it more relevant. If Australia wishes to be involved more in the Arctic or if India wishes to be involved more in both polar regions, should the government push disaster diplomacy as a possible entry point or leadership possibility? This would require the government making active choices to direct policy in favour of pursuing disaster diplomacy and to try to demonstrate successful polar disaster diplomacy.

Conclusions

This chapter has provided the first exploration of polar disaster diplomacy, considering pre-disaster and post-disaster actions, using Norway as a case study. Norway's unique position as the only country with territorial claims around both poles makes it geostrategically distinct with respect to its polar activities, and also provides it with many futures pathways, only some of which are represented in this chapter. In particular, since Norway does not operate in isolation, wider perspectives are covered, including but not limited to Norwegian interests, even if often from the perspective of relevance to Norway.

One area for further exploration is how unique polar situations really are from both geostrategic and futures perspectives. Could lessons from other situations be drawn up for, or apply from, the Arctic and Antarctic?

Two locations that could be parallels, especially for the Antarctic due to the lack of territorial sovereignty and the difficult accessibility, are the deep sea and outer space, including other celestial bodies. Could a governance system modelled on ATS be implemented for the moon, Mars, and beyond, especially given that disaster-related issues have some parallel challenges for risk reduction, search and rescue, and recovery? Similarly for the deep sea, would it be helpful to formulate and apply conventions similar to SOLAS, the SAR Convention, and the Polar Code?

From the analysis here corroborating the wider disaster diplomacy literature within geostrategic futures, if the goal is to bring together parties for long-term peace and co-operation within or based on the polar regions, then a focus on disaster-related activities is unlikely to be successful. This conclusion should not preclude interest in disaster-related activities to ensure that continuing work in the Arctic and Antarctic is as safe as feasible. Polar diplomacy, if it is desired for geostrategic futures, can still be pursued and achieved through other means.

REFERENCES

AIBN (Accident Investigation Board Norway). 2018. *Investigation of Air Accident in the Sea Near the Helicopter Base Outside Barentsburg, Svalbard, Norway.* Lillestrøm, NO: Accident Investigation Board Norway.

Åtland, K., and T. Pedersen. 2008. "The Svalbard Archipelago in Russian Security Policy: Overcoming the Legacy of Fear—or Reproducing It?" *European Security* 17 (2–3): 227–51. https://doi.org/10.1080/09662830802642470.

Barents Sea Treaty. 2010. Treaty between the Kingdom of Norway and the Russian Federation Concerning Maritime Delimitation and Cooperation in the Barents Sea and the Arctic Ocean. Oslo: Government of Norway; Moscow: Government of Russia.

BEAC (Barents Euro-Arctic Council). 2017. *Action Plan on Climate Change for the Barents Cooperation.* 2nd ed. Kirkenes, NO: Barents Euro-Arctic Council.

———. 2019. *Declaration of the Transport Ministerial Meeting of the Barents Euro-Arctic Council (BEAC), 12 September 2019.* Umeå, SE: Barents Euro-Arctic Council.

Brauer, M., and J. Hisham-Hashim. 1998. "Fires in Indonesia: Crisis and Reaction." *Environmental Science and Technology* 32 (17): 404A–407A. https://www.doi.org/10.1021/es983677j.

Buhaug, H. 2010. "Climate Not to Blame for African Civil Wars." *Proceedings of the National Academy of Sciences* 107 (38): 16477–82. https://doi.org/10.1073/pnas.100573910.

Burke, M. B., E. Miguel, S. Satyanath, J. A. Dykemae, and D. B. Lobell. 2009. "Warming Increases the Risk of Civil War in Africa." *Proceedings of the National Academy of Sciences* 106 (49): 20670–74. https://doi.org/10.1073/pnas.090799810.

CCAMLR (Commission for the Conservation of Antarctic Marine Living Resources). 1982. *Report of the First Meeting of the Commission for the Conservation of Antarctic Marine Living Resources (Hobart, Australia 25 May–11 June 1982).* Hobart, AU: Executive Secretary Commission for the Conservation of Antarctic Marine Living Resources.

Chmutina, K., and J. von Meding. 2019. "A Dilemma of Language: 'Natural Disasters' in Academic Literature." *International Journal of Disaster Risk Science* 10:283–92. https://doi.org/10.1007/s13753-019-00232-2.

Depledge, D. 2018. *Britain and the Arctic.* Cham, CH: Palgrave Macmillan.

Finnish Red Cross. 2018. *Red Cross Arctic Disaster Management Study.* Helsinki: Finnish Red Cross.

Gaillard, J. C. 2019. "Disaster Studies Inside Out." *Disasters* 43 (S1): S7–S17. https://doi.org/10.1111/disa.12323.

Glantz, M. H. 2019. 2000. "Climate-Related Disaster Diplomacy: A US–Cuban Case Study." *Cambridge Review of International Affairs* 14 (1): 233–53. https://doi.org/10.1080/09557570008400340.

———. *One Belt One Road: China's Long March Toward 2049.* Nepean, ON: Sumeru Press.

Government of China. 2018. *China's Arctic Policy.* Beijing: State Council Information Office of the People's Republic of China.

Government of Norway. 2014–15. *Norwegian Interests and Policy in the Antarctic.* Meld. St. 32 (2014–2015) Report to the Storting (White Paper). Oslo: Norwegian Ministry of Foreign Affairs.

Halt, B. 2014. "Poles Apart: The Case for an Australian Role at the Arctic Council." Australian Institute of International Affairs, 26 May 2014. http://www.internationalaffairs.org.au/news-item/poles-apart-the-case-for-an-australian-role-at-the-arctic-counci.

Hewitt, K., ed. 1983. *Interpretations of Calamity.* London: Allen and Unwin.

———. 1997. *Regions of Risk: A Geographical Introduction to Disasters.* London: Routledge.

Hovedredningssentralen. n.d. "Om Hovedredningssentralen." Hovedredningssentralen, accessed 23 August 2022. https://www.hovedredningssentralen.no/om-hovedredningssentralen/om-hovedredningssentralen.

IMO (International Maritime Organization). SOLAS. 1974. *International Convention for the Safety of Life at Sea* [SOLAS Convention]. London: International Maritime Organization.

———. 1979. *International Convention on Maritime Search and Rescue* [SAR Convention]. London: International Maritime Organization.

———. 2012. Resolution MSC.348(91). Adopted on 28 November 2012. Adoption of a New Mandatory Ship Reporting System "In the Barents Area (Barents SRS)." London: International Maritime Organization.

———. 2017. *International Code for Ships Operating in Polar Waters* [Polar Code]. London: International Maritime Organization.

Islam, M. S., Y. H. Pei, and S. Mangharam. 2016. "Trans-boundary Haze Pollution in Southeast Asia: Sustainability through Plural Environmental Governance." *Sustainability* 8 (499): 1–13. https://doi.org/10.3390/su8050499.

Jabour, J. 2007. "Underneath the Radar: Emergency Search and Rescue Insurance for East Antarctic Tourism." *Tourism in Marine Environments* 4 (2–3): 203–20. https://doi.org/10.3727/154427307784772066.

Jones, D. 1999. *Cosmopolitan Mediation? Conflict Resolution and the Oslo Accords.* Manchester: Manchester University Press.

Kasdan, D. 2019. "The Cure for Catastrophe: How We Can Stop Manufacturing Natural Disasters." *Disaster Prevention and Management* 28 (2): 299–300. https://doi.org/10.1108/DPM-04-2019-352.

Kelman, I. 2012. *Disaster Diplomacy: How Disasters Affect Peace and Conflict.* Abingdon, UK: Routledge.

———. 2016. "Catastrophe and Conflict: Disaster Diplomacy and Its Foreign Policy Implications." *Brill Research Perspectives in Diplomacy and Foreign Policy* 1 (1): 1–76.

Ker-Lindsay, J. 2007. *Crisis and Conciliation: A Year of Rapprochement between Greece and Turkey.* London: I. B. Tauris.

Kontar Y. Y. 2018. "Perspectives from an Early Career Scientist." In *The Future of Arctic Ocean Cooperation*, edited by R. W. Corell, J. D. Kim, Y. H. Kim, A. Moe, D. L. VanderZwaag, and O. R. Young, 162–72. Seoul: Korean Maritime Institute; Honolulu: East-West Center.

Kontar, Y. Y., T. Beer, P. A. Berkman, J. C. Eichelberger, A. Ismail-Zadeh, I. Kelman, J. L. LaBrecque, A. E. Sztein, and Y. Zaika, 2018. "Disaster-Related Science Diplomacy: Advancing Global Resilience through International Scientific Collaborations." *Science & Diplomacy* 7 (2). http://www.sciencediplomacy.org/article/2018/disaster-related-science-diplomacy-advancing-global-resilience-through-international.

Laruelle, M. 2014. *Russia's Arctic Strategies and the Future of the Far North.* New York: Sharpe.

Leira, H. 2013. " 'Our Entire People Are Natural Born Friends of Peace': The Norwegian Foreign Policy of Peace." *Swiss Political Science Review* 19 (3): 338–56. https://doi.org/10.1111/spsr.12044.

Lenton, D. 2018. "The Measure of Akademik Lomonosov." *Engineering & Technology* 13 (6): 10–11. https://www.doi.org/10.1049/et.2018.0612.

Lewis, J. 1999. *Development in Disaster-Prone Places: Studies of Vulnerability.* London: Intermediate Technology Publications.

———. 2019. "The Fluidity of Risk: Variable Vulnerabilities and Uncertainties of Behavioural Response to Natural and Technological Hazards." *Disaster Prevention and Management* 28 (5): 636–48. https://doi.org/10.1108/DPM-01-2019-0014.

Marchenko, N. A., O. J. Borch, S. V. Markov, and N. Andreassen. 2015. "Maritime Activity in the High North—The Range of Unwanted Incidents and Risk Patterns." Proceedings of the 23rd International Conference on Port and Ocean Engineering under Arctic Conditions, 14–18 June 2015, Trondheim, NO. https://www.poac. com/Papers/2015/pdf/poac15Final00109.pdf.

McDonald, J. W. 2012. "The Institute for Multi-Track Diplomacy." *Journal of Conflictology* 3 (2): 66–70. http://dx.doi.org/10.7238/joc.v3i2.1629.

Mileski, J., A. Gharehgozli, L. Ghoram, and R. Swaney. 2018. "Cooperation in Developing a Disaster Prevention and Response Plan for Arctic Shipping." *Marine Policy* 92:131–7. https://doi.org/10.1016/j.marpol.2018.03.003.

Moolakkattu, J. S. 2005. "Peace Facilitation by Small States: Norway in Sri Lanka." *Cooperation and Conflict* 40 (4): 385–402. https://doi. org/10.1177/0010836705058225.

Munk School of Global Affairs. 2014. *National Roundtable on Arctic Emergency Preparedness: Report of Proceedings.* Toronto: Munk School of Global Affairs.

Nikitina, E. H. 2017. Международное сотрудничество в снижении рисков природных бедствий в Арктике: Проблемы адаптации к последствиям климатических изменений. В кн.: Глобальные и национальные стратегии управления рисами катастроф и стихийных бедствий. Верескун А.В., Жданенко И.В. (ред.). Москва, МЧС России, 85–92.

———. 2018. "The SDGs and Agenda 2030 in the Arctic: An Arctic State Perspective." In *The Arctic in World Affairs: A North Pacific Dialogue on Arctic 2030 and Beyond: Pathways to the Future,* edited by R. W. Corell, J. D. Kim, Y. H. Kim, A. Moe, D. L. VanderZwaag, and O. R. Young, 337–49. Seoul: Korean Maritime Institute; Honolulu: East-West Center.

O'Keefe, P., K. Westgate, and B. Wisner. 1976. "Taking the Naturalness Out of Natural Disasters." *Nature* 260:566–7. https://doi.org/10.1038/260566a0.

Olaisen, B., M. Stenersen, and B. Mevåg. 1997. "Identification by DNA Analysis of the Victims of the August 1996 Spitsbergen Civil Aircraft Disaster." *Nature Genetics* 15:402–5. https://doi.org/10.1038/ng0497-402.

Olson, R. S., and A. C. Drury. 1997. "Un-therapeutic Communities: A Cross-National Analysis of Post-disaster Political Unrest." *International Journal of Mass Emergencies and Disasters* 15 (2): 221–38.

Overland, I., and A. Krivorotov. 2015. "Norwegian-Russian Political Relations and Barents Oil and Gas Developments." In *International Arctic Petroleum Cooperation: Barents Sea Scenarios,* edited by A. Bourmistrov, F. Mellemvik, A. Bambulyak, O. Gudmestad, I. Overland, and A. Zolotukhin, 97–110. Abingdon, UK: Routledge.

Pompeo, M. 2019. "Looking North: Sharpening America's Arctic Focus." Speech in Rovaniemi, FI, 6 May 2019. Washington: US Department of State. https://www. state.gov/looking-north-sharpening-americas-arctic-focus.

Pincus, R., and S. H. Ali, eds. 2016. *Diplomacy on Ice: Energy and the Environment in the Arctic and Antarctic.* New Haven, CT: Yale University Press.

Quarantelli, E. L., and R. R. Dynes. 1976. "Community Conflict: Its Absence and Presence in Natural Disasters." *Mass Emergencies* 1:139–52.

Raudaskoski, M., and J. Laine. 2018. "Changing Perceptions of the Finnish-Russian Border in the Post-Cold War Context." In *Post-Cold War Borders: Reframing Political Space in the EU's Eastern Europe*, edited by J. Laine, I. Liikanen, and J. W. Scott, 129–46. London: Routledge.

Rodríguez, H., W. Donner, and J. E. Trainor, eds. 2018. *Handbook of Disaster Research.* 2nd ed. Cham, CH: Springer.

Scanlon, J. 2006. "Dealing with the Tsunami Dead: Unprecedented International Co-operation." *Australian Journal of Emergency Management* 21 (2): 57–61.

Scottish Government. 2019. *Arctic Connections: Scotland's Arctic Policy Framework.* Edinburgh: Scottish Government.

Segalla, S. D. 2012. "The 1959 Moroccan Oil Poisoning and US Cold War Disaster Diplomacy." *Journal of North African Studies* 17 (2): 315–36. https://doi.org/10.1080/13629387.2011.610118.

Sellheim, N., Y. V. Zaika, and I. Kelman, eds. 2019. *Arctic Triumph: Northern Innovation and Persistence.* Basel, CH: Springer.

Staupe-Delgado, R. 2019. "Analysing Changes in Disaster Terminology over the Last Decade." *International Journal of Disaster Risk Reduction* 40 (101161). https://doi.org/10.1016/j.ijdrr.2019.101161.

Svalbard Treaty. 1920. Treaty between Norway, the United States of America, Denmark, France, Italy, Japan, the Netherlands, Great Britain and Ireland and the British Overseas Dominions, and Sweden Concerning Spitsbergen. Signed in Paris, 9 February 1920.

Taylor, D. M., and P. J. Gormly. 1997. "Emergency Medicine in Antarctica." *Emergency Medicine* 9 (3): 237–45. https://doi.org/10.1111/j.1442-2026.1997.tb00394.x.

Tonami, A. 2016. *Asian Foreign Policy in a Changing Arctic.* London: Palgrave Macmillan.

UNDRR (United Nations Office for Disaster Risk Reduction). 2019. "Terminology on Disaster Risk Reduction." UNDRR, accessed 14 December 2019. https://www.unisdr.org/we/inform/terminology.

Venugopal, R., and S. Yasir. 2017. "The Politics of Natural Disasters in Protracted Conflict: The 2014 flood in Kashmir." *Oxford Development Studies* 45 (4): 424–42. https://doi.org/10.1080/13600818.2016.1276160.

Weizhun, M., and Q. Tianshu. 2005. "Disaster Diplomacy: A New Diplomatic Approach?" *Shanghai Institute for International Studies International* Review (Spring): 111–24 [in Chinese].

Whittaker, C., A. Frühauf, S. J. Burthem, R. S. Parry, M. Kotikalapudi, Y. Liang, M. M. Barker, P. R. Patel, and I. Kelman. 2018. "A Disaster Diplomacy Perspective of Acute Public Health Events." *Disasters* 42 (S2): S173–S195. https://doi.org/10.1111/disa.12306.

Wilson Rowe, E. 2018. *Arctic Governance: Power in Cross-Border Cooperation.* Manchester: Manchester University Press.

Wilson Rowe, E., and H. Blakkisrud. 2014. "A New Kind of Arctic Power? Russia's Policy Discourses and Diplomatic Practices in the Circumpolar North." *Geopolitics* 19 (1): 66–85. https://doi.org/10.1080/14650045.2013.789863.

Wisner, B., P. Blaikie, T. Cannon, and I. Davis. 2004. *At Risk: Natural Hazards, People's Vulnerability and Disasters.* 2nd ed. London: Routledge.

Young, O. R. 2019. "Constructing the 'New' Arctic: The Future of the Circumpolar North in a Changing Global Order." *Outlines of Global Transformations* 12 (5): 6–24.

The Case for a Five Eyes Critical Minerals Alliance Focusing on Greenland

Dwayne Ryan Menezes

In August 2019, when it surfaced that the incumbent president of the United States had sought to purchase Greenland from Denmark, the world, not surprisingly, greeted the story with derision and incredulity. The idea that one country—no matter how large or powerful—could simply make an offer to purchase another country—no matter how unfamiliar or re-mote—seemed anachronistic at best, prompting the Danish prime min-ister, Mette Frederiksen, to dismiss the proposal as "absurd" and assert, "Greenland is not Danish. Greenland is Greenlandic." The very notion that Greenland was a mere appendage of Denmark that the latter could sell was highly problematic, leading Greenland's premier, Kim Kielsen, to state, "Greenland is not for sale."

Yet, by causing the world to sit up and take notice of this large Arctic island, Donald Trump may have unwittingly lifted the veil on Greenland's—and indeed the Arctic's—geostrategic importance to the United States and its allies more widely than ever before. The renewed em-phasis on Greenland in US foreign, defence, and security policy is much more explicable when viewed against the backdrop of Greenland's vast resource potential and increasing US-China great power competition. The relative abundance of several critical minerals, including rare earth ele-ments, in Greenland offers the United States and its allies the opportunity to reduce their dependence on China for resources essential to their defence and security, renewable energy, and high-tech sector needs and thus enhance their resource security and strategic competitiveness.

What makes the case of Greenland particularly interesting is that, despite the media hullaballoo about China's growing footprint in the Arctic, the three countries most prolific in Greenland's mining sector are the United Kingdom, Australia, and Canada, three of the United States' closest allies and, along with New Zealand, its partners within the Five Eyes (FVEY) alliance. By casting a spotlight on this oft-overlooked reality, this chapter prompts the question: Would greater and more concerted FVEY co-operation in, and with, Greenland be a more appropriate and effective strategy to address some of the more legitimate concerns and achieve some of the more reasonable objectives that may have fuelled the proposed US acquisition of Greenland, especially in relation to enhancing regional security, and building more diverse and resilient supply chains of critical minerals?

By focusing on the British, Australian, and Canadian commercial presence in Greenland instead of the more familiar US military presence there, this chapter will explore why Greenland should matter just as much to the FVEY alliance as a whole as it does to the United States. It will make the case for why concerted FVEY co-operation in and with Greenland would be invaluable to the resource security, defence, industrial, and climate ambitions of the five countries, as well as those of their European allies.

Look North: Greenland's Vast Resource Potential

Changing Arctic sea ice conditions have opened up the possibility of increased navigation along the Northern Sea Route, dramatically reducing the time it takes to ship goods between Asia, Europe, and North America, while presenting new opportunities for Greenland's waterways and port infrastructure. Likewise, the growing practicality and popularity of using polar air routes that result in substantial time and fuel savings on flights between North America, Europe, and Asia have opened up new opportunities for Greenland's airways and airport infrastructure. What makes Greenland so strategic, though, is not just where it sits geographically, but also what it holds resource-wise. In 2008, the US Geological Survey estimated that the three major basins off the coast of Greenland could yield up to the equivalent of fifty-two billion barrels of oil. Furthermore, a 2015 study found that Greenland could produce enough hydro power to meet its own needs and export the surplus to Nunavut, or Newfoundland and Labrador, and perhaps even further through an undersea cable (Pehora 2016). Greenland's fish-rich waters also make it one of the world's largest exporters of cold-water prawns, cod, haddock, halibut, and snow crab. Mineral-rich Greenland, moreover, holds large reserves of copper, zinc, lead, iron ore, nickel, titanium, cobalt, gold, precious gemstones, platinum-group metals, rare earth elements, and other minerals.

Growing Chinese Interest in Greenland

Greenland's—as also the wider Arctic's—vast resource potential has not escaped China's attention. In 2018, China outlined its ambitions to build a Polar Silk Road (as an extension of its Belt and Road Initiative) by developing Arctic shipping routes; vessels belonging to China's COSCO Shipping have plied the Northern Sea Route since 2013. China, furthermore, has actively pursued investment opportunities in Greenland's airport, port, and research infrastructure, as well as mining and energy sectors. In 2016, it was reported that Chinese mining company General Nice sought to take over the abandoned naval base at Grønnedal, but Danish prime minister Lars Løkke Rasmussen personally intervened to prevent it from doing so (Breum 2016). More recently, a Chinese construction firm, China Communications Construction Company, bid for Greenland's airport projects but withdrew after Denmark stepped in to finance the projects, reportedly in the face of mounting US concern over China's role with respect to Greenland's future air facilities (Shi and Lantaigne 2019).

When it comes to mining, Chinese firms, such as Shenghe Resources Holding Company Ltd., General Nice Development, China Non-Ferrous Metal Industry's Foreign Engineering and Construction Company Ltd., and China National Nuclear Corporation, have long had interests in Greenland, much to the consternation of the United States. Greenland sits on some of the world's largest deposits of rare earth elements, which are critically important to the United States, but for which the US is still heavily dependent on China, a dependence that China could weaponize in the US-China trade war. Although Greenland's new government, elected in April 2021, decided to halt one project and withdraw the licence from another, both of which had Chinese interests, the new government went ahead with existing plans to open a new representation in Beijing in November 2021, so the implications of recent developments on China's economic footprint in Greenland has yet to be seen. In the energy sector, two Chinese oil majors—China National Petroleum Corporation and China National Offshore Oil Corporation—had expressed interest in bidding for Greenland's onshore oil and gas blocks in 2021. However, in July 2021, Greenland's new government announced it would suspend all new oil and gas exploration to focus instead on combatting climate change, so again it will be of interest to see what opportunities—if any—China might wish to court next. China also serves as one of the largest markets for Greenland's fish exports. A 2017 study noted that Greenland attracted the highest levels of Chinese foreign direct investment as a percentage of GDP of all Arctic countries (Rosen and Thuringer 2017).

The Forgotten Giants: The British, Australian, and Canadian Economic Footprint in Greenland

While China undoubtedly has demonstrated significant interest in Greenland, the preoccupation with China has resulted in the United States overlooking the importance of other players, including its closest allies, in the region. Despite the media hullabaloo about China, it is the United Kingdom that, with the exception of Denmark, still commands the greatest economic footprint in Greenland, followed by Canada and Australia. The United Kingdom, Canada, and Australia, furthermore, have a long and rich history of resource exploration and development in Greenland. Geologists, prospectors, and explorationists from the United Kingdom and the wider English-speaking world have been instrumental in surveying and mapping the geology, as well as energy and mineral resources, of Greenland for the better part of two centuries. The United Kingdom, Canada, and Australia have remained relevant to Greenland over recent decades as home to some of the world's leading clusters of energy and mining expertise, the foremost centres of global energy and mining finance, and the biggest and most visible energy and mining companies.

In the case of the United Kingdom, energy firms such as BP, Royal Dutch Shell, and Cairn Energy, have been a key feature of Greenland's oil and gas exploration landscape. While BP and Shell were part of a consortium of companies that was granted a prospecting licence under the Kalaallit Nunaat Marine Seismic project as early as 1989, Cairn Energy had emerged as the biggest explorer in Greenland by 2011, though its US$1.2 billion campaign to drill eight wells proved unsuccessful. The United Kingdom's largest mining firms as well, Glencore, BHP, Rio Tinto, and Anglo American, have been involved in Greenland at various points. For instance, Rio Tinto was already prospecting in Kangerluarsuk, Isua, and Washington Land in the 1990s, and another UK-based firm, London Mining, acquired its Isua iron ore project from Rio Tinto in 2005. In 2013, London Mining was awarded a thirty-year licence to develop the Isua project, described then as "the largest commercial project to date in Greenland," though financial problems led to the transfer of its Greenlandic subsidiary to the Chinese company General Nice Development (BBC News 2013). Likewise, when BHP Billiton took over Canadian diamond producer Dia Met Minerals Ltd. in 2001, it acquired a majority interest in a joint venture engaged in diamond exploration in western Greenland (*Northern Miner* 2001). Incidentally, BHP and Rio Tinto are both Anglo-Australian joint ventures, while Glencore is an Anglo-Swiss company, and Anglo American has strong ties to both the United Kingdom and South Africa.

Although no mineral resources were mined in Greenland for a few years since the closure of its southern gold mine in 2013, the mining sector has grown steadily since then, and as of April 2021, Greenland had two active mines:

- In 2017, LNS Greenland, the sister company of Greenland Ruby and both part of the Norwegian family-owned LNS Group, commenced the production of rubies—positioned as the world's only conflict-free rubies—at its Aappaluttoq mine.

- In 2019, the TSXV-listed Canadian firm Hudson Resources started production at its White Mountain anorthosite mine, which it reports is the largest anorthosite occurrence, surpassed only by the moon.

As of February 2021, there were forty-one companies listed as holding mineral exploitation, exploration, and prospecting licences in Greenland. As we see in table 4.1 below, at least twenty-seven of these firms were largely or entirely British, Canadian, and Australian:

- United Kingdom: 16 firms were headquartered in, listed in, or substantially connected to the United Kingdom, even if they operated in Greenland through local subsidiaries.

- Canada: 7 firms were headquartered in, listed in, or substantially connected to Canada, even if they operated in Greenland through local subsidiaries.

- Australia: 6 firms were headquartered in, listed in, or substantially connected to Australia, even if they operated in Greenland through local subsidiaries.

- Of the firms mentioned above, 2 were connected either to both the United Kingdom and Canada or both the United Kingdom and Australia, so they have been counted only once in the total number of British, Canadian, and Australian mining firms operating in Greenland, bringing the total number to 27 rather than 29.

- This number does not include the 6 Danish firms, most of whose majority stake was held by a firm in the British Virgin Islands.

There have been several significant developments since spring 2021. In 2021, the ASX-listed, Perth-headquartered firm Eclipse Metals acquired full ownership of the Ivittuut project in southwestern Greenland, which is said to be "the world's largest historical cryolite mine with rare earth potential" (Eclipse Metals 2021) and potentially "the world's largest and only known source of naturally occurring cryolite" (Birney 2021). In August 2021, the Berkeley, California–based American firm KoBold Metals, backed by Bill Gates and Jeff Bezos, signed a joint venture (JV) agreement with the British mining firm Bluejay Mining, which would give it a 51 per cent stake in the Disko-Nuussuaq project in Greenland. In October 2021,

Table 4.1. British, Canadian, and Australian Licensees in the Mining Sector in Greenland (February 2021)

	Company	Listed address*	Notes
UK	Anglo American Exploration Overseas Holdings Ltd.	UK	LSE- and JSE-listed, London-headquartered
UK/SA	De Beers Marine (Pty) Ltd.	South Africa	Cape Town–based, part of London-headquartered De Beers Group, itself 85 per cent owned by Anglo American
UK	Bluejay Mining Plc.	UK	AIM- and FSE-listed, OTCQB-traded, London-headquartered
UK	Bluejay Mining Ltd.	UK	
UK	Disko Exploration Ltd.	UK	100 per cent owned by Bluejay Mining Plc.
UK	Dundas Titanium A/S	UK	
UK	Bright Star Resources Ltd.	UK	London-headquartered private limited companies that are subsidiaries of, or connected to executive chair of, AIM-listed Alba Mineral Resources
UK	Obsidian Mining Ltd.	UK	
UK	White Eagle Resources Ltd.	UK	
UK	White Fox Resources Ltd.	UK	
UK	Stallion Resources Ltd.	UK	
UK	Challenge Holdings Ltd.	UK	London-headquartered private limited company
UK	FBC Mining (BA) Ltd.	UK	London-headquartered private limited company
UK/AU	Longland Resources Ltd.	UK	Bristol-headquartered private limited company acquired by ASX-listed Conico in 2020
IE/UK	Resource 500 FeVTi Ltd.	Ireland	51 per cent owned by London-headquartered Gofer Mining Plc.
CA/UK	Nalunaq A/S	Greenland	Owned by Toronto-headquartered TSXV- and AIM-listed AEX Gold Inc.
CA	Greenland Resources Inc.	Canada	Toronto-headquartered private limited company
CA	Copenhagen Minerals Inc.	Canada	100 per cent owned by Greenland Resources Inc., but may be acquired by CSE-listed Cryptologic Corp. in 2021

Table 4.1. (*continued*)

	Company	Listed address*	Notes
CA	Hudson Resources Inc.	Canada	TSXV-listed, OTCQX-traded, Vancouver-headquartered
CA	Hudson Greenland A/S	Greenland	31 per cent owned by Hudson Resource Inc.
CA	North American Nickel Inc.	Canada	TSXV-listed, Toronto-headquartered
CA	Skaergaard Mining A/S	Greenland	Owned by CSE-listed, Vancouver-headquartered Major Precious Metals Corp.
AU	Greenfields Exploration Ltd.	Australia	Perth-headquartered private limited company
AU	Greenland Minerals A/S	Greenland	Subsidiary of ASX-listed, Perth-headquartered Greenland Minerals Ltd.
AU	Ironbark Zinc A/S	Australia	Subsidiary of ASX-listed, Perth-headquartered Ironbark Zinc Ltd.
AU	Rimbal Pty Ltd.	Australia	Perth-based private limited company
AU	Tanbreez Mining Greenland A/S	Australia	Subsidiary of Perth-based Rimbal Pty Ltd.

* Address of the company, as per Naalakkersuisut/Government of Greenland (2021).

shares in ASX/LSE/WSE-listed, London-, Perth-, Warsaw- and Karbonia-based Prairie Mining Ltd. (renamed since as GreenX Metals) rose after the firm entered into an earn-in agreement with Greenfields Exploration Ltd. that would see it acquire up to an 80 per cent stake in the Arctic Rift copper project in northeastern Greenland (Llinares Taboada 2021).

Over the same period, a new coalition government was elected in Greenland in April 2021, which, while supportive of mining in Greenland in general, has been strongly opposed to radioactive material extraction, raising questions about the future of ASX-listed Greenland Minerals's Kvanefjeld rare earths and uranium project, as well as uranium extraction in general. In May 2021, the French uranium miner Orano announced its decision to suspend exploration at its two sites in southern Greenland. In November 2021, the Government of Greenland passed legislation banning not only uranium mining but also the mining of resources with a uranium content above 100 parts per million (ppm) (Schøler 2021). Although the legislation will apply to licences issued only after 2 December 2021, and Greenland Minerals received its exploration licence before this date, the government has stated that the company cannot be granted the exploitation licence for which it has applied as this would constitute a new and separate licence (Newell 2021). In November 2021, Greenland also withdrew the Isua iron ore project licence of the Hong Kong–based Chinese mining firm General Nice Development on grounds of inactivity and failure to make guarantee payments (*Mining Technology* 2021).

Consequently, since February 2021, there have been new players from the FVEY countries entering the space, even if the future of one of the older Australian players remains uncertain. However, given the partial Chinese ownership of this firm and the withdrawal of the licence from another Chinese firm, recent developments have taken a much greater toll on China's economic influence in Greenland. As seen in the figures from February 2021 and the companies entering Greenland since, the United Kingdom, Canada, and Australia, moreover, are not just where many of the mining companies scoping out opportunities in Greenland originate, but are often where they choose to fundraise or seek expertise. Listing on exchanges in the three countries, as well as in the United States, has proven especially popular. Furthermore, the Government of Greenland regularly hosts Greenland Day events in both Canada and Australia—at, or following, mining conferences, such as the PDAC (Prospective and Developments Association of Canada) Convention in Toronto and the Australian Nickel Conference in Perth—to promote Greenland's resource potential and attract investment.

Given the extent to which the ownership, funding, and project activities of mining firms—especially British, Canadian, and Australian, but also American, Irish, and South African—may be intertwined through ownership structures, exchange listings, and pathways of co-operation, one might ask whether these national distinctions are or remain clearcut in practice. What complicates matters is that it is often the case that a firm registered or headquartered in one country may choose to list in another country or may be acquired by a firm listed in another country. As is apparent, many of the firms, or their parent companies, may also hold multiple listings—on exchanges such as the London Stock Exchange (LSE) and its Alternative Investment Market (AIM), the Toronto Stock Exchange Venture Exchange (TSXV), the Australian Securities Exchange (ASX), the Frankfurt Stock Exchange (FSE), and the Johannesburg Stock Exchange (JSE)—and trade in over-the-counter markets, such as OTCQB and OTCQX (part of OTC Markets Group), allowing them to access wider and more diverse pools of international capital.

Furthermore, as the firms currently producing in Greenland expand, and those prospecting or exploring eventually commence production, Greenland—owing to its resource potential and relative geographical proximity—is well placed to become one of North America's and Europe's leading import sources for a number of metals and minerals. Many of these firms may rely on British, Canadian, Australian, and American expertise and mining finance, as is already the case, and may also look to use or to develop processing operations in the United Kingdom, Canada, Australia, and the United States. Such pathways of future co-operation may also make national distinctions less relevant, meaningful, or valuable in comparison with international alliances when it comes to conceiving strategies to build secure, stable, sustainable, reliable, and resilient supply chains of critical minerals.

The following examples reveal some of the ways in which UK companies and exchanges are involved in Greenland's mining sector, and how connected they are with companies and exchanges beyond, especially in the United States, Canada, Australia, and South Africa:

- The AIM- and FSE-listed British firm Bluejay Mining is developing three projects in Greenland: the Dundas Ilmenite Project, which is the world's highest-grade mineral sand ilmenite (the key ore in titanium) project; the Disko-Nuussuaq Project, a magmatic and massive sulphide nickel-copper-platinum-cobalt project believed to host mineralization similar to the world's largest nickel/copper sulphide mine in Siberia; and the Kangerluarsuk Zinc-Lead-Silver Project. In 2019, it signed an agreement with Rio Tinto Iron and Titanium Canada, a member of the LSE- and ASX-listed Anglo-Australian mining giant Rio

Tinto Group, for further analysis of the ilmenite from the Dundas project. In August 2021, it also entered into a JV with Berkeley-based KoBold Metals, which would see the American firm pay US$15 million in exploration funding for a 51 per cent stake in the Disko-Nuussuaq project.

- The LSE- and JSE-listed British mining giant Anglo American—the world's largest platinum producer—is one of the largest mining firms and holds licences in Greenland, where it is undertaking polymetallic (copper-nickel-platinum group elements) exploration, as it is in Finland and Canada. Anglo American had also taken over the London-headquartered global diamond giant De Beers Group in 2011, with an associated Cape Town–based South African company—De Beers Marine (Pty) Ltd.—since obtaining an exploration licence for diamond exploration in Greenland.

- Another LSE- and JSE-listed British-Swiss mining giant, Glencore, is a significant shareholder at the ASX-listed Australian firm Ironbark Zinc and an offtaker for its Citronen project. Ironbark Zinc is developing the Citronen Zinc-Lead Project, which represents one of the world's largest undeveloped zinc-lead deposits with a resource of more than thirteen billion pounds in contained zinc and lead metal.

- In July 2020, the TSXV-listed Canadian firm AEX Gold, which has revived the Nalunaq Gold Project, and which currently holds the largest gold licence portfolio in Greenland, achieved a dual listing on the AIM, the sub-market of the LSE for small and medium-size companies, after raising GB£42.5 million through a placing and direct subscriptions.

This also brings us to what resources the British, Canadian, and Australian firms currently holding licences in Greenland are targeting. As evident in table 4.2 below, there is a substantial focus on base metals

Table 4.2. What Resources Are British, Canadian, and Australian Licensees in Greenland Exploring?

Licence holder	Minerals
Anglo American Exploration Overseas Holdings Ltd.	Disko-Nuussuaq: nickel, copper, platinum-group metals
	Svartenuk Halvø: nickel, copper, platinum-group metals
De Beers Group	Diamonds
Bluejay Mining Plc. and through its subsidiaries Dundas Titanium A/S Disko Exploration Ltd.	Disko-Nuussuaq Project: nickel, copper, platinum-group metals, cobalt
	Kangerluarsuk Project: zinc, lead, silver
	Thunderstone: potential for gold, nickel, copper, PGE, lead, zinc, uranium
	Dundas Ilmenite Project: ilmenite, titanium
Greenland Resources Inc. through Copenhagen Minerals	Malmbjerg Project: molybdenum
	Storø Project: gold
Greenfields Exploration Ltd.	Frontier Project: copper, nickel, tungsten
Greenland Minerals A/S	Kvanefjeld Project: rare earth elements, uranium, zinc, fluorspar
Hudson Resources Inc. and Hudson Greenland A/S	White Mountain (Qaqortorsuaq) Project: anorthosite
	Sarfartoq Project: rare earth elements, niobium, tantalum
Ironbark Zinc A/S	Citronen Fjord Project: zinc, lead
Longland Resources Ltd.	Ryberg Project: copper, palladium, gold, nickel, cobalt, platinum
Nalunaq A/S	Nalunaq and Tartoq: gold
North American Nickel Inc.	Maniitsoq Project: nickel, copper, cobalt
Resource 500 FeVTi Ltd.	Isortoq: vanadium, titanium
Rimbal Pty Ltd. and Tanbreez Mining Greenland A/S	Kringlerne Project: rare earth elements, niobium, tantalum, zirconium, hafnium, tungsten, arfvedsonite, feldspar
Skaergaard Mining A/S	Skaergaard Project: gold, palladium, platinum, titanium, vanadium, copper
Stallion Resources Ltd.	Motzfeldt: rare earth elements, niobium, tantalum
Alba Mineral Resources through its subsidiaries Obsidian Mining Ltd. White Eagle Resources Ltd. White Fox Resources Ltd.	Amitsoq Graphite Project: graphite
	Thule Black Sands Project: high-grade ilmenite
	Melville Bay Iron Project: iron ore, haematite, magnetite
	Inglefield Land: cobalt, copper, gold, vanadium, nickel, zinc, molybdenum

Source: Company websites and communication. See also Naalakkersuisut/Government of Greenland (2021).

(copper, lead, zinc), light metals (such as ilmenite, titanium, and magnesium), precious metals (such as gold, silver, and the platinum-group metals), iron and ferro-alloy metals (such as iron, nickel, cobalt, molybdenum, chromium, and niobium), industrial minerals (such as graphite, feldspar, and anorthosite), specialty metals (such as rare earth elements, zirconium, niobium, tantalum, and uranium) and gemstones (rubies, pink sapphires, and diamonds). These are all metals and minerals that the United Kingdom and its partners use and import quite considerably and that are vital to their defence and security, climate and energy policies, business growth, and industrial strategies. When it comes to rare earths in particular, the firms that appear to be of greatest interest—Greenland Minerals, Tanbreez, Hudson Resources, Stallion Resources, Eclipse Metals—are Australian, Canadian, or British, though the first has run into trouble due to the new government's opposition to, and introduction of, new legislation restricting radioactive material extraction.

It should be noted that the United Kingdom's economic footprint in Greenland extends beyond mining. As of October 2020, while there were at least twelve British companies holding twenty-eight mining licences in Greenland, there were also four UK entities holding licences for oil and gas exploration in Greenland, at least one UK firm exploring water and ice export opportunities from Greenland and, albeit not trade, a substantial UK research community engaged with research projects in Greenland. In addition, the United Kingdom is one of the leading sources of incoming tourists in Greenland, and several UK travel companies—including cruise companies—include Greenland in their itineraries. Furthermore, the United Kingdom is one of the largest markets for Greenland's fish and fish products and accounts for more than 10 per cent of Greenland's total exports. There is a substantial value chain that has developed around Greenlandic seafood in the United Kingdom, one that includes UK importers, processors, manufacturers, traders, distributors, wholesalers, retailers, and food-service channels (such as fish and chips shops, pubs, and restaurants). Given the United Kingdom's vast footprint in Greenland, it is as much in the interest of its Five Eyes and European partners, as it is in its own interest, to encourage a pivoting of UK foreign, defence, security, and trade policy toward Greenland and the cultivation of a new UK–Greenland Special Relationship. The same holds true for Canada,

Australia, New Zealand, and the United States, with their economic footprint also extending beyond mining to trade, investment, or co-operation in energy, water, tourism, fisheries, research, and defence and security (Menezes and Nicol 2019).

Rare Earth Elements: Critically Important to the Five Eyes Allies and Europe

The need for rare earths among the Five Eyes and European countries is critical, and Greenland's strengths are obvious. Rare earths, a group of seventeen elements (yttrium, scandium, and the fifteen lanthanides) are not necessarily rare in their occurrence, but so widely dispersed that they are rarely found in large concentrations. Rare earths are vital to the green energy transition, as well as for defence and security and hi-tech sectors.

Green Energy Transition

Rare earths are the building blocks of the green energy revolution, making their way into electric vehicles, battery storage, solar panels, and wind turbines. An average electric vehicle uses 66.3 kilograms of graphite, 53.2 kilograms of copper, 39.9 kilograms of nickel, 24.5 kilograms of manganese, 13.3 kilograms of cobalt, 8.9 kilograms of lithium, and 0.5 kilograms of rare earths (International Energy Agency 2021). The International Energy Agency estimates that, over the next two decades, the demand for lithium will grow forty times, graphite twenty-five times, and cobalt and nickel twenty times. Rare earth magnet demand is expected to increase fivefold by 2030. The electric vehicle sector alone is set to increase the demand for rare earths from 5,000 tonnes in 2019 to 70,000 tonnes in 2030. If President Biden is to achieve his goal of ensuring that 50 per cent of the cars sold in the United States in 2030 are zero-emission electric vehicles, then the United States will require ten times the amount of rare earths that it currently has (Koetsier 2021).

Likewise, the wider adoption of solar photovoltaic systems would lead to a surge in demand for the copper, cadmium, tellurium, gallium, indium, selenium, silicon, silver, and aluminum that go into solar panels. The adoption of wind turbines would lead to a spike in demand for the neodymium and dysprosium that make their way into permanent magnets used in the generators in the nacelles, and also for the copper, aluminum, steel, concrete, and fibreglass used in the towers and blades. The wind turbine market is projected to result in roughly 30 per cent of the global growth in the use of rare earth magnets (Ritter 2017).

A 2020 study commissioned by the European Commission noted that the demand for rare earths used in permanent magnets could increase 10 times by 2050, while the European Union would require up to 18 times more lithium and 5 times more cobalt in 2030, and around 60 times more lithium and 15 times more cobalt in 2050, for electric vehicle batteries and energy storage (European Commission 2020).

Defence and Security

Rare earths are also the lifeblood of the defence and security sector, being used in guidance and control systems (such as smart bombs, Tomahawk cruise missiles, Joint Direct Attack Munitions, Joint Air-to-Ground fin actuators, and Predator unmanned aircraft); defence electronic warfare (such as jamming devices, electromagnetic railguns, Ni Metal Hydride batteries, area denial systems, and long-range acoustic devices); targeting and weapon systems (laser targeting, air-based lasers, Laser Avengers, SaberShot Photonic Dispensers, and Future Combat Systems vehicles with laser weapons); and electric motors (such as Combat Hybrid Power Systems, integrated starter generators, hub-mounted electric traction drive technology, Zumwalt DDG 1000s, and Joint Strike Fighter electric aircraft). They are also used in communication (satellite communications, sonar transducers, radar technology, enhanced X-ray radiation detection, and Multipurpose Integrated Chemical Agent Alarms) and optical equipment and speakers (such as night-vision goggles) (Grasso 2013, 10–13).

When it comes to the amount of rare earths needed, according to a 2013 US Congressional Research Service report, a single F-35 Lightning II Joint Strike Fighter jet needs about 920 pounds (418 kilograms); a DDG-51 Aegis destroyer needs around 5,200 pounds (2,359 kilograms); while a single SSN-774 Virginia-class submarine requires 9,200 pounds (4,180 kilograms). Significant restrictions to the supply of rare earths can thus severely affect British and American defence and aerospace firms, such as BAE Systems, Rolls-Royce Holdings, Lockheed Martin, Northrup Grumman, Raytheon, and Boeing.

Tech Industry

Rare earths are also industrial gold where the high-tech sector is concerned, used in iPhones and iPods, LED screens, loudspeakers, computer hard drives, camera and telescope lenses, studio lighting and cinema projection, catalytic converters in cars, aircraft engines, aerospace components, vibration motors, lasers, microwave filters, glass polishing, nuclear batteries, superconductors, visors, electrical components, fibre optics, and X-ray and MRI scanning systems (BBC News 2012).

China's Dominance in Global Rare Earths Supply: Security Implications

Despite the critical importance of rare earths to their defence and security, energy, and technology sectors, the United Kingdom and its Five Eyes and European partners are greatly dependent on China for the supply and processing of rare earths and other critical minerals. China holds around 37 per cent (44 million metric tonnes) of the world's rare earth reserves, accounts for 58 per cent of the world's rare earth production, hosts around 95 per cent of the world's processing of raw ore, and is responsible for 90.5 per cent of the global total output of rare earth permanent magnets (ResearchInChina 2019). Likewise, 80 per cent of the world's electric vehicle batteries are produced in Japan, South Korea, and China. The control that China exercises across the supply chain is reflected in its status as the world's largest reserve, producer, consumer, processor, importer, and exporter of rare earths. This gives China the opportunity to wield tremendous power at every stage of the supply chain, making importing countries—whether in North America, Europe, or the Asia-Pacific—beholden to it.

The United States depends on China for 80 per cent of its rare earth supply. The European Union (EU) depends on China for 98 per cent of its rare earth element supply. The EU's 2020 List of Critical Raw Materials also indicated that China provides 38 per cent of the EU's supply of baryte; 49 per cent of its supply of bismuth; 93 per cent of its supply of magnesium; 47 per cent of its supply of natural graphite; 66 per cent of its supply of scandium; 45 per cent of its supply of titanium; 69 per cent of its supply of tungsten; and 39 per cent of its supply of vanadium (European

Commission 2020, 2–3). One must not forget that Asian rare-earth-producing or -processing countries, such as Myanmar, Thailand, Malaysia, and Vietnam, are also tied at the hip to China, either as exporters or through Chinese equity. Thus, even if the United States and its allies were to boost domestic production of rare earths, all it takes is for one weak link—whether represented by inadequate technical capabilities or project financing—for the entire supply chain to become dependent on China.

China has repeatedly demonstrated its willingness to deploy economic levers for geopolitical gain, with rare earths arguably the sharpest weapon in its arsenal. In September 2010, China halted the export of critical rare earth minerals to Japan in retaliation for its detention of the captain of a Chinese fishing trawler near some disputed East China Sea islands, causing the prices of rare earth minerals to soar (Bradsher 2010). In July 2020, China threatened to impose new sanctions on US defence contractor Lockheed Martin, which would cut off its supply of rare earth elements in retaliation for the US approval of an arms deal for Taiwan relating to air defence missiles made by the company (Tang and Philp 2020). Then, there are also the risks of China restricting the use of domestic rare earth production for domestic manufacturing industries, which would disrupt global production in all of the sectors that depend on rare earths (Smyth 2020a), and, conversely, of China defending its monopoly by flooding the global market with rare earths to lower their prices considerably, when necessary, thus drowning out new entrants (Smyth 2020b).

Rare earth elements have also emerged as China's weapons on standby in the US-China trade war: "Will rare earths become a counter weapon for China to hit back against the pressure the United States has put on for no reason at all?" asked China's *People's Daily* in May 2019. "The answer is no mystery," it replied unabashedly, adding later, "We advise the US side not to underestimate the Chinese side's ability to safeguard its development rights and interests. Don't say we didn't warn you!" (Wu 2019). By reducing its exports of rare earths, China could seriously disadvantage American, British, Canadian, Australian, and European firms. In November 2020, an analyst at a consultancy backed by the Chinese government disclosed that US weapons makers could be among the first companies targeted by export restrictions imposed by China (Yu and Sevastopulo 2021).

In February 2021, the *Financial Times* reported that China's Ministry of Industry and Information Technology proposed draft controls on the production and export of seventeen rare earth minerals in China, with government officials asking industry executives how severely companies in the United States and Europe would be affected if China restricted rare earth exports during a bilateral dispute. Reportedly, Beijing also sought to understand if the United States would have trouble making F-35 jets and how quickly it could secure alternative sources of rare earths and increase its own production capacity. While China's proposed guidelines would require rare earth producers to follow export-control laws that regulate shipments of materials that "help safeguard state security," with China's State Council and Central Military Commission having the final say on whether the list should include rare earths, not everyone is on board. Concern has been raised in some quarters that such export controls are a "double-edged sword" that might motivate China's rivals to accelerate their own production capacities and undermine China's dominance of the industry, and Chinese rare earth miners themselves are troubled about the enhanced power that such regulations would give China's Ministry of Industry and Information Technology to control their output (Yu and Sevastopulo 2021).

Reducing Dependence on China: The Search for Alternative Sources

While rare earths are also mined domestically in the United States, the Mountain Pass mine in California—for decades, the world's leading source of rare earths, and today the only active rare earth mining and processing facility in the United States—has had a checkered recent history, being moved into care and maintenance in 2015 before being revived in 2018. The 2015 bankruptcy of Molycorp, which owned Mountain Pass prior to MP Materials taking over, had triggered serious questions about the security and stability of the US supply of critical minerals. Although MP Materials, which purchased the mine in 2017, affirms a mission to "restore the full rare earth supply chain to the United States of America" and has received backing from the Pentagon, it has not succeeded in challenging China's dominance yet (MP Materials 2021a). This US-led consortium, paradoxically, includes China's Shenghe Resources Holding Company Ltd., which holds a non-voting 9.9 per cent minority interest, while the firm sends more than 50,000 tonnes of its rare earth concentrates to China for final processing and also depends entirely on Chinese customers for its annual revenue (Scheyder 2020). Its offtake agreement with Shenghe Resources commits all its rare earths concentrate to Shenghe until the re-payment of the Shenghe Offtake Advance (US$78 million), estimated to be in 2024 (Kozak 2021). Nevertheless, as the only active rare earths mine in the United States and "the largest rare earths producer in the Western Hemisphere," reportedly producing "approximately 15 percent of global rare earth content," MP Materials remains strategically important to the United States (MP Materials 2021b). As a case study, it highlights, how-ever, the control that China exercises over the global supply chains of rare earth elements.

The provision of funding by the Pentagon to MP Materials is of interest and signals the importance the US federal government places on securing the country's critical minerals supply chains by reducing import reliance on China and expanding domestic production and processing capacity in the United States. The United States also has other rare earth elements (REE) projects being developed at Hondo, Texas, by the Australian firm Lynas Corporation in partnership with Texas-based processing company Blue Line Corporation; at Round Top, Hudspeth County, West Texas, by New York–based USA Rare Earth LLC in partnership with Texas Mineral Resources Corporation; at Bear Lodge, Wyoming, by OTCQB-traded Rare Element Resources Ltd.; at Bokan Mountain in southeast Alaska by TSXV-listed, OTCQX-traded Nova Scotian firm Ucore Rare Metals; at Elk Creek, Nebraska, being developed by TSX-listed, OTCQX-traded NioCorp; and more. A Texas-based firm, Urban Mining Company, likewise, is develop-ing a domestic source for NdFeB rare earth permanent magnets.

Moving beyond the United States, Canada is a mining powerhouse, and it is also a key supplier of thirteen of the thirty-five minerals deemed critical by the United States. It is among the world's leading producers of battery materials, such as cobalt, graphite, and nickel, and hosts some of the largest lithium and rare earth reserves. In 2019, Canada was the world's largest producer of potash; second-largest producer of niobium and ur-anium; third-largest producer of diamonds and mined platinum-group metals; fourth-largest titanium and primary aluminum producer; fifth-largest producer of nickel and gold; seventh-largest producer of cobalt and molybdenum; eighth-largest producer of lithium, zinc, iron ore, and refined lead; and tenth-largest producer of graphite.

In June 2019, US president Donald Trump and Canadian prime minister Justin Trudeau agreed to develop reliable, integrated North American supply chains for critical minerals, with several bilateral Critical Minerals Working Group meetings held since. This was followed by the Geological Survey of Canada joining forces with Geoscience Australia and the US Geological Survey in the trinational Critical Minerals Mapping Initiative, which held its first meeting in Ottawa in December 2019 (USGS 2020). That same month, Canada and the United States also signed an international memorandum of understanding (MoU) confirming Canada's participation in the US-led Energy Resource Governance Initiative, which includes Australia, Botswana, Peru, Argentina, Brazil, Democratic Republic of the Congo, Namibia, Philippines, and Zambia. On 9 January 2020, Canada and the United States announced the finalization of the Canada-US Joint Action Plan on Critical Minerals Collaboration, covering various areas of co-operation, including securing critical minerals supply chains for strategic industries and defence, improving sharing of mineral resource information, enhancing private sector engagement, collaborating in multilateral forums, engaging in supply chain modelling, and increasing support for industry (Natural Resources Canada 2020).

In August 2020, the Government of Saskatchewan announced CAD$31 million in funding to create in the province Canada's first rare earth processing plant, a facility which is to be owned and operated by Saskatchewan Research Council (SRC) and become fully operational in late 2022 (Saskatchewan Research Council 2020). In September 2020, Cheetah Resources, a subsidiary of the ASX-listed, Sydney-headquartered Australian firm Vital Metals, signed a binding term sheet with SRC about building and operating a rare earth extraction plant—that produces a mixed rare earth and carbonate product—alongside SRC's facility, harnessing the complementarity of their technologies (Cameron 2020). In 2021, Vital commenced rare earths production at its Nechalacho project in the Northwest Territories, making it the first rare earth producer in Canada and, after Mountain Pass, the second in North America (Bohlsen

2021). Its plan is to upgrade the ores using an ore-sorting machine before upgrading the intermediary product at the REE plant in Saskatchewan and then shipping it to a Norway-based firm REEtac, with which it has a definitive offtake agreement (Lasley 2021).

Canada also has other players in the REE space, focused on projects, processes, and facilities, including TSXV-listed Geomega Resources, which states that it is building "the world's first sustainable rare earths recycling facility" and developing its 100 per cent–owned Montviel REE/ Niobium project in Quebec; the TSXV-listed, Vancouver-based Canadian firm Search Minerals, which owns 100 per cent of the properties (including Foxtrot and Deep Fox) within the Port Hope Simpson–St. Lewis Critical Rare Earth Elements (CREE) District in southeastern Labrador; the Vancouver-based Canadian firm Medallion Resources, which said it was looking for sites across North America to develop an extraction plant for rare earths; the TSXV- and FSE-listed, OTCQB-traded, Vancouver-headquartered Defense Metals Corporation's Wicheeda Rare Earth Elements Property, located near Prince George, British Columbia; and the TSX-listed, OTCQB-traded, and Toronto-headquartered Avalon Advanced Materials' Separation Rapids Lithium Project in Kenora, Ontario, and Nechalacho REE Project at Thor Lake, Northwest Territories. A TSXV-listed, OTCQX-traded Nova Scotian firm Ucore is also developing the Bokan Mountain Heavy Rare Earth Elements Project on Prince of Wales Island in southeast Alaska.

Like Canada, Australia is a global powerhouse when it comes to mining. The resource-rich country is the largest producer of lithium; among the top five producers of antimony, manganese, rare earths, ilmenite, and rutile; and has the world's largest nickel reserves and second-largest cobalt reserves (Canavan, Birmingham, and Reynolds 2019). The largest rare earths mining and processing company outside China is also Australian: Lynas Corporation, which has two major operations—a mining facility at Mount Weld in Australia and a processing plant at Kuantan in Malaysia. As of September 2019, the Australian government had identified fifteen rare earth and critical mineral projects it intended to promote as part of joint Australia-US efforts to reduce reliance on China for materials crucial to the defence and high-tech sectors. (Smyth 2019).

In February 2018, following US president Donald Trump's meeting with Australian prime minister Malcolm Turnbull in Washington, DC, the two countries agreed "to work together on strategic minerals exploration, extraction, processing and research, and development of rare earths and high performance metals" (US Embassy and Consulates in Australia 2018). In December 2018, Australian minister for resources and northern Australia Matt Canavan and US secretary of the interior Ryan Zinke signed a letter of intent committing Geoscience Australia and the US Geological Survey to collaborate on critical minerals (Australian Government 2019a). In September 2019, President Trump and Australian counterpart, Prime Minister Scott Morrison, agreed to develop a US-Australia Critical Minerals Action Plan to "improve the security and supply of rare earths and other critical minerals in the United States and Australia; increase US–Australia connectivity throughout the supply chain of critical minerals; and leverage the interest of other like-minded partners to improve the health of the global critical minerals supply chain" (Prime Minister of Australia 2019). The Australian Government also published a report identifying fifteen rare earth and critical minerals projects it aimed to highlight as part of joint Australia-US efforts and that required AU$5.7 billion to develop (Australian Government 2019b).

In October 2019, Austrade released its report *Critical Minerals Supply Chain in the United States: Mapping the Landscape for Australian Suppliers* to help Australian producers identify end users in the United States and facilitate commercial offtake and investment agreements with them (Australian Government 2019c). It noted, for instance, how, "following the issuing of an interim rule amending the *Defense Federal Acquisition Regulation Supplement* to implement a section of the National Defense Authorization Act for Fiscal Year 2019, the US Department of Defense is prohibited from purchasing devices that contain certain magnets or tungsten from North Korea, China, Russia and Iran" (2019c, 6), opening a window of opportunity for Australian companies. In November 2019, Australia and the United States formalized their partnership with a project agreement signed by Geoscience Australia and the US Geological Survey, building on the letter of intent signed earlier (Ministers for the Department of Industry, Science, Energy and Resources 2019). In December 2019, the Critical Minerals Mapping Initiative—a research collaboration between

Geological Survey of Canada, Geoscience Australia, and US Geological Survey to pool mineral resource information, develop scientific consensus, identify new sources of supply, and promote critical minerals discovery—held its inaugural meeting in Ottawa, as discussed earlier. Likewise, in 2019, the Australian Government joined the US-led Energy Resource Governance Initiative to promote sound governance of the mining sector and resilient energy mineral supply chains (Robinson 2020a). Australia also secured partnerships with Japan, the United States, India, and the EU, with discussions under way for bilateral arrangements with the United Kingdom and Korea. In November 2020, Australia was welcomed along with Canada as a member of the EU-US-Japan Trilateral on Raw Materials. These measures, as Jessica Robinson, former head of Australia's Critical Minerals Facilitation Office, observed, signalled Australia's interest in moving up in the value chain from exploration and extraction to processing, separation, refining, and niche manufacturing capabilities (Robinson 2020b).

As the firms in Greenland currently producing expand and those prospecting or exploring eventually commence production, Greenland is well placed to become one of the United Kingdom's leading import sources for a number of critical minerals, including rare earth elements. Many of these firms will rely on UK expertise and mining finance, as is already the case, and potentially also look to use or to develop processing and logistical operations in the United Kingdom, or to connect with rare earth permanent magnet producers and a range of end users there. In December 2020, the formerly ASX-listed and currently LSE-listed firm Pensana announced that it is looking to develop the United Kingdom's first rare earths processing plant in Hull, a site chosen also for the city's excellent port and infrastructure. If successful, Pensana states, the plant will be one of two major producers of rare earth oxides outside China (BBC News 2020). Although the plant is being set up to process materials from Pensana's Longonjo Rare Earths Project in Angola, the management recognizes its future potential as a multi-use facility. The ASX-listed firm Peak Resources, likewise, plans to construct a refinery at Teesside that would receive rare earth concentrate from its planned Ngualla Rare Earth Project in Tanzania to produce neodymium praseodymium oxide and other separated rare earth products, and become the second fully integrated producer of the former alloy outside China (*Mining Review Africa* 2021). Furthermore, Cheshire-based Less Common Metals—the only rare earth magnet alloy producer outside China and Japan—is exploring the possibility of establishing a fully integrated supply chain for rare earth permanent magnet production in the United Kingdom (Saklatvala 2020). On all counts, it is as much in the interest of the United Kingdom as that of Greenland to ensure these mineral resources can be imported into the United Kingdom on a tariff- and quota-free basis, as was the case under the EU-OCT (Overseas Countries and Territories) arrangement within the scope of which UK-Greenland trade fell while the United Kingdom was still an EU member state. The potential linkages between producers in Greenland and importers, processors, manufacturers, and end users in the United Kingdom could be crucial to the development of integrated North Atlantic, FVEY, and possibly also FVEY-EU-EEA supply chains.

Although companies from New Zealand do not appear to have been as active as their British, Canadian, American, and Australian counterparts in critical minerals projects in the wider North, New Zealand has an increasingly outward-looking mining sector and growing technical expertise in critical minerals research and would be a strategic partner in any FVEY Critical Minerals Alliance.

The Five Eyes Critical Minerals Alliance and Enhanced Partnership with Greenland

It is precisely as the FVEY allies—the United Kingdom, the United States, Canada, Australia, and New Zealand—and their European partners look to reduce their dependence on China for critical minerals, including rare earths, that Greenland grows so strategically important. When it comes to rare earths alone, Greenland is reported to hold 38.5 million tonnes of rare earth oxides and is believed to have enough rare earths to meet at least a quarter of global demand in the future (Harvey 2012).

The ASX-listed Australian firm Greenland Minerals, which holds a 100 per cent interest in the Kvanefjeld multi-element rare earths project in southern Greenland, sits on a rare earths resource of a billion tonnes in three zones in the Ilimaussaq complex—Kvanefjeld, Sørensen, and Zone 3. It has promoted the project as comprising the world's second-largest rare earth deposit and sixth-largest deposit of uranium: 11.1 million tonnes of rare earth oxide and 593 million pounds of uranium. Greenland Minerals is partly owned by the Shanghai-listed Chinese rare earths giant Shenghe Resources Holding Company Ltd. The project, thus, has been controversial for two main reasons—environmental concerns, relating to the risk of radioactive pollution and toxic waste and its implications for the local community, agriculture, and water quality in what is, rather exceptionally, an arable area within Greenland; and security concerns, relating to the implications of Chinese ownership and influence in a territory so strategically important to the United States and its allies. As discussed earlier, its fate is now uncertain due to the legislation introduced by the new government in Greenland banning uranium mining and the extraction of resources with a uranium content of 100 ppm.

The privately owned Australian firm Tanbreez holds licences to the Kringlerne project not far from Kvanefjeld in southern Greenland and is believed to sit on substantial reserves of rare earths as well. The company claims that it is probably "the largest rare earth deposit in the world especially of the heavy rare earths such as dysprosium." The project's major commodities include tantalum, niobium, rare earth elements, and zirconium, though the deposit will also produce hafnium, tungsten, arfvedsonite, and feldspar. Tanbreez's JORC reserves stand at 29 million tonnes of contained REE in some 4.7 billion tonnes. It has had fewer obstacles to overcome with respect to opposition from local communities and environmental groups than Greenland Minerals, as the deposit contains only background values of thorium and uranium in the eudialyte, so the final REE contains no radioactive elements. That would explain why Tanbreez has largely escaped controversy and received its exploitation licence in 2020.

The TSXV-listed Canadian firm Hudson Resources holds the licence to the Sarfartoq carbonatite exploration project, believed to be rich in neodymium and a high-grade niobium/tantalum. Hudson's Sarfartoq REE project is near the main international airport of Kangerlussuaq. It has been drilled out and has a 43-101-compliant resource that has outlined over 30 million kilograms of neodymium and praseodymium to date. It still has substantial upside to define more tonnes of high-grade REEs.

It has completed a preliminary economic assessment and is moving to pre-feasibility in 2022 with the objective of making a production decision in 2023.

The London-headquartered British company Stallion Resources presents itself as "the owner and developer of the largest undeveloped Niobium-Tantalum-Zirconium-Rare Earths Project in the world, the Motzfeldt Deposit in Southern Greenland," which has a substantial defined JORC mineral resource of 340 metric tonnes with a contained metal inventory of 1,564,000 tonnes of zirconium ($ZrO2$), 884,000 tonnes of total rare earth oxides (TREO), 629,000 tonnes of niobium ($Nb2O5$), and 41,000 tonnes of tantalum ($Ta2O5$) (Stallion Resources 2021).

In November 2021, the Perth-headquartered Australian firm Eclipse Metals announced that it had identified high-grade polymetallic rare earth mineralization at the Ivittuut Project in Greenland, returning results of 536.30 ppm total rare earth elements, 3.54 per cent tin, and 3,680 ppm tungsten, with uranium levels of ranging from 0.7 to 24.3 ppm, much lower than the maximum limit of 100 ppm introduced in the Government of Greenland's new legislation (Shields 2021).

Greenland's vast critical minerals reserves and the sheer number of British, Canadian, and Australian companies operating in Greenland make it a new frontier for FVEY, as well as FVEY-EU-EEA co-operation. While the FVEY intelligence alliance can trace its origins to the Atlantic Charter in 1941 and the 1943 British-US Communication Intelligence Agreement (later formalized as the United Kingdom–United States of America Agreement in 1946), it has evolved over the years—not least through the inclusion of Canada in 1948 and Australia and New Zealand in 1956, as well as co-operation with third-party partners, such as Norway, Denmark, Sweden, Belgium, the Netherlands, France, Germany, Spain, Singapore, and South Korea. The principal proposals, thus, are, first, to extend the framework of the FVEY alliance, from joint co-operation in signals, geo-spatial, defence, security, and human intelligence, to more comprehensive political, scientific, and economic co-operation on critical minerals, including resource intelligence, technical collaboration, major project financing, and supply chain integration for minerals and materials critically important to national and economic security. Second, the FVEY allies should explore avenues to strengthen critical minerals collaboration among themselves, and to build an enhanced partnership with Greenland, to develop integrated, secure, stable, sustainable, resilient, and reliable critical minerals supply chains, thus enhancing resource security and autonomy and reducing dependence on China.

Although the scope for FVEY and FVEY-Greenland co-operation in this regard is limitless, the following ten "First Steps" provide a road map and lay the foundation for realizing the vision in the near-term future:

1. The Five Eyes should develop their respective Critical Mineral Strategies (Australia and the United States have already) and a collective strategy (as the EU has) and appoint agencies/facilitation offices to serve as central focal points and to lead engagement and activities.

2. The Five Eyes should develop bilateral frameworks of co-operation, such as the Canada-US and Australia-US Joint Action Plans on Critical Minerals Collaboration as a whole or on topics such as permanent magnets, batteries, and electric vehicles.

3. The Five Eyes should design a new multilateral framework of co-operation—the FVEY Critical Minerals Alliance— akin to the EU's European Raw Material Alliance and ensure that it also provides an inclusive network for dialogue with industry and academia.

4. The United Kingdom and New Zealand should join the US-led Energy Resource Governance Initiative, which already includes the United States, Canada, and Australia, as well as Botswana, Peru, Argentina, Brazil, Democratic Republic of the Congo, Namibia, Philippines, and Zambia.

5. The British Geological Survey and GNS Science should sign MoUs with the US Geological Survey, Geological Survey of Canada, and Geoscience Australia to strengthen international geoscience collaboration on critical minerals and join the Critical Minerals Mapping Initiative.

6. The Five Eyes should develop a Critical Minerals Prospectus and Major Projects Inventory, building on the *Australian Critical Mineral Prospectus* and Canada's *Major Projects Inventory* and *Canadian Mining Assets* bulletin, to provide data about their capabilities, major projects, and overseas mining assets.

7. The Five Eyes should build on Australia's Major Projects Facilitation Agency to develop either individual or a FVEY-wide Major Projects Agency that serves as a single entry point for major project proponents seeking tailored information or support with navigating regulatory approvals.

8. The Five Eyes should bring together government and non-government financing mechanisms, including UK Export Finance, US EXIM Bank, Export Development Canada, Export Finance Australia, and NZ Export Credit Office, to co-operate on critical minerals project financing.

9. The National Technology and Industrial Base, the framework to integrate and leverage defence industrial capabilities in the United States, the United Kingdom, Canada, and Australia, should include New Zealand and be strengthened (even replicated) to develop integrated, secure, reliable critical minerals supply chains.

10. The Five Eyes should enter into an enhanced partnership with Greenland for critical minerals, strengthening geoscience and technical collaboration, financing major projects of strategic interest, developing processing capabilities, and integrating producers in Greenland in FVEY supply chains.

As this chapter has demonstrated, the Five Eyes Critical Minerals Alliance and its enhanced partnership with Greenland would enable closer collaboration among the Five Eyes partners on geoscience, resource intelligence, technical, and financing in, with, and beyond Greenland, and to benefit from integrated, secure, stable, sustainable, resilient, and reliable supply chains for minerals critical to their national and economic security.

This chapter builds on, but substantially expands and updates, an in-depth briefing produced by the author for the Centre for Historical Analysis and Conflict Research—"The British Army's Think Tank"—in October 2020 (Menezes 2020) and a report produced by the author for the Polar Research and Policy Initiative in March 2021 (Menezes 2021).

REFERENCES

Australian Government. 2019a. *Australia's Critical Minerals Strategy 2019*. https://apo.org. au/sites/default/files/resource-files/2019-03/apo-nid227646_1.pdf.

———. 2019b. *Outlook for Selected Critical Minerals: Australia, October 2019*. Canberra: Australian Department of Industry, Innovation and Science https://www.industry. gov.au/sites/default/files/2019-10/outlook-for-select-critical-minerals-in-australia-2019-report.pdf.

———. 2019c. *Critical Minerals Supply Chain in the United States: Mapping the Landscape for Australian Suppliers*. Canberra: Australian Trade and Investment Commission https://apo.org.au/sites/default/files/resource-files/2019-10/apo-nid261496.pdf.

BBC News. 2012. "What Are 'Rare Earths' Used For?" BBC New, 13 March 2012. https:// www.bbc.co.uk/news/world-17357863.

———. 2013. "Greenland Awards London Mining Huge Iron Ore Project." BBC News, 24 October 2013. https://www.bbc.co.uk/news/world-europe-24658756.

———. 2020. "First Rare Earth Plant in UK Proposed for Hull." BBC New, 7 December 2020. https://www.bbc.co.uk/news/uk-england-humber-55223571.

Birney, Matt. 2021. "Eclipse One to Watch as Greenland Govt Extends License." *Business News*, 25 May 2021. https://www.businessnews.com.au/article/Eclipse-one-to-watch-as-Greenland-Govt-extends-licence.

Bohlsen, Matthew. 2021. "Vital Metals Is Now the Second Rare Earths Concentrate Producer in North America." *InvestorIntel*, 23 September 2021. https:// investorintel.com/markets/technology-metals/technology-metals-intel/vital-metals-is-now-the-the-second-rare-earths-concentrate-producer-in-north-america/.

Bradsher, Keith. 2010. "Amid Tension, China Blocks Vital Resource to Japan." *New York Times*, 22 September 2010. https://www.nytimes.com/2010/09/23/business/global/23rare.html.

Breum, Martin. 2016. "Did Denmark's Prime Minister Stop a Chinese Firm from Buying an Abandoned Military Base in Greenland?" *Arctic Today*, 23 December 2016. https://www.arctictoday.com/did-denmarks-prime-minister-stop-a-chinese-firm-from-buying-an-abandoned-military-base-in-greenland/.

Cameron, Belinda. 2020. "Vital Metals (ASX:VML) Subsidiary Signs Rare Earth Plant Agreement." *Market Herald*, 22 September 2020. https://themarketherald.com.au/vital-metals-asxvml-subsidiary-signs-rare-earth-plant-agreement-2020-09-22/.

Canavan, Matthew, Simon Birmingham, and Linda Reynolds. 2019. "New Financing Measures to Help Build Critical Minerals Sector." Export Finance Australia, press release, 14 November 2019. https://www.exportfinance.gov.au/resources-news/news-events/government-news/2019/november/new-financing-measures-to-help-build-critical-minerals-sector/.

Defense Acquisition Regulations System, Department of Defense. 2019. Defense Federal Acquisition Regulation Supplement: Restriction on the Acquisition of Certain Magnets and Tungsten (DFARS Case 2019—D054), 84 Fed Reg 18156 (April 30, 2019), 48 CFR 212, 48 CFR 225, 48 CFR 252. https://www.federalregister.gov/documents/2019/04/30/2019-08485/defense-federal-acquisition-regulation-supplement-restriction-on-the-acquisition-of-certain-magnets.

Eclipse Metals. 2021. "Projects Overview." Eclipse Metals, accessed 11 August 2022. https://www.eclipsemetals.com.au/projects-overview/.

European Commission. 2020. *Critical Raw Materials Resilience: Charting a Path Towards Greater Security and Sustainability, Communication from the Commission to the European Parliament, the Council, the European Economic and Social Committee and the Committee of the Regions.* Brussels: European Commission. https://eur-lex.europa.eu/legal-content/EN/TXT/PDF/?uri=CELEX:52020DC0474&from=EN.

Grasso, Valerie Bailey. 2013. *Rare Earth Elements in National Defense: Background, Oversight Issues, and Options for Congress.* CRS Report 7-5700. Washington, DC: Congressional Research Service. https://fas.org/sgp/crs/natsec/R41744.pdf.

Harvey, Fiona. 2012. "The Rare Earth Riches Buried under Greenland's Vast Ice Sheet." *The Guardian*, 31 July 2012. https://www.theguardian.com/environment/2012/jul/31/rare-earth-greenland.

International Energy Agency. 2021. *The Role of Critical Minerals in Green Energy Transitions.* Paris: International Energy Agency. https://www.iea.org/reports/the-role-of-critical-minerals-in-clean-energy-transitions.

Koetsier, John. 2021. "US Needs 10X More Rare Earth Metals to Hit Biden's Electric Vehicle Goals." *Forbes*, 29 September 2021. https://www.forbes.com/sites/johnkoetsier/2021/09/29/us-needs-10x-more-rare-earth-metals-to-hit-bidens-electric-vehicle-goals/?sh=b71ffbd3e41d.

Kozak, Frederick. 2021. "MP Materials: It Is Rare Earths Déjà Vu All Over Again." *InvestorIntel*, 16 February 2021. https://investorintel.com/markets/technology-metals/technology-metals-intel/mp-materials-it-is-rare-earths-deja-vu-all-over-again/.

Lasley, Shane. 2021. "Vital REE Mining in Northwest Territories." *North of 60 Mining News*, 19 February 2021. https://www.miningnewsnorth.com/story/2021/02/19/news/vital-ree-mining-in-northwest-territories/6703.html.

Llinares Taboada, Jaime. 2021. "Prairie Mining Shares Climb on A$9 Mln Deal to Acquire Copper Project in Greenland." *MarketWatch*, 6 October 2021. https://www.marketwatch.com/story/prairie-mining-shares-climb-on-a-9-mln-deal-to-acquire-copper-project-in-greenland-271633505669.

Menezes, Dwayne Ryan. 2020. "Greenland: Security, Trade, Competition." Centre for Historical Analysis and Conflict Research, 26 October 2020. https://chacr.org.uk/2020/10/26/greenland-security-trade-competition/.

———. 2021. *The Case for a Five Eyes Critical Minerals Alliance: Focus on Greenland*. London: Polar Research and Policy Initiative. https://polarconnection.org/wp-content/uploads/2021/03/Report-The-Case-for-a-FVEY-CMA.pdf.

Menezes, Dwayne Ryan, and Heather N. Nicol, eds. 2019. *The North American Arctic: Themes in Regional Security*. London: UCL Press.

Mining Review Africa. 2021. "Peak Resources Secures Land for Its Teesside Refinery." *Mining Review Africa*, 28 May 2021. https://www.miningreview.com/speciality-minerals/peak-resources-secures-land-for-its-teesside-refinery/.

Mining Technology. 2021. "Greenland Cancels General Nice's Isua Iron-Ore Project License." *Mining Technology*, 23 November 2021. https://www.mining-technology.com/news/greenland-cancels-general-nice-isua-iron-ore-project-licence/.

Ministers for the Department of Industry, Science, Energy and Resources. 2019. "Australia, US Partnership on Critical Minerals Formalised." Australian Government, press release, 19 November 2019.

MP Materials. 2021a. "Our Story." MP Materials, accessed 11 August 2022. https://mpmaterials.com/about/.

———. 2021b. "MP Materials Announces Timing of Q4 and Fiscal Year 2020 Financial Results Release, Conference Call and Webcast." MP Materials, 8 February 2021. https://investors.mpmaterials.com/investor-news/news-details/2021/MP-Materials-Announces-Timing-of-Q4-and-Fiscal-Year-2020-Financial-Results-Release-Conference-Call-and-Webcast/default.aspx.

Naalakkersuisut/Government of Greenland. 2021. "List of Licensees and Partners as of February 2021." Mineral Resources Authority, accessed 14 January 2022. https://govmin.gl/wp-content/uploads/2021/02/List-of-Licensees-and-Partners-February-2021.pdf.

Natural Resources Canada. 2020. "Canada and US Finalise Joint Action Plan on Critical Minerals Collaboration." Government of Canada, news release, 9 January 2020. https://www.canada.ca/en/natural-resources-canada/news/2020/01/canada-and-us-finalize-joint-action-plan-on-critical-minerals-collaboration.html.

Newell, Elisha. 2021. "Greenland Minerals Considers Options for Kvanefjeld after Greenland Government Meeting." *Proactive Investors*, 19 December 2021. https://www.proactiveinvestors.com/companies/news/969674/greenland-minerals-considers-options-for-kvanefjeld-after-greenland-government-meeting-969674.html.

Northern Miner. 2001. "Greenland Drilling Uncovers Kimberlite Dyke." *Northern Miner*, 15 October 2001. https://www.northernminer.com/news/greenland-drilling-uncovers-kimberlite-dyke/1000109121/.

Pehora, Brian. 2016. "Greenland to Nunavut Electricity Exports? It Just Might Be Possible." *Nunatsiaq News*, 14 January 2016. https://nunatsiaq.com/stories/article/65674greenland_to_nunavut_hydro_exports_it_just_might_be_possible/.

Prime Minister of Australia. 2019. "Outcomes from White House Meetings." Prime Minister of Australia, press release, 20 September 2019. https://www.pm.gov.au/media/outcomes-white-house-meetings.

ResearchInChina. 2019. *Global and China Rare Earth Permanent Magnet Industry Report, 2018–2023*. Beijing: ResearchInChina. https://www.reportlinker.com/p05389598/Global-and-China-Rare-Earth-Permanent-Magnet-Industry-Report.html?utm_source=PRN.

Ritter, Stephen K. 2017. "A Whole New World for Rare Earths." *C&EN: Chemical & Engineering News*, 28 August 2017. https://cen.acs.org/articles/95/i34/whole-new-world-rare-earths.html.

Robinson, Jessica. 2020a. "Update from Jessica Robinson, Critical Minerals Facilitation Office: March 2020." Australian Government Department of Industry, Science, Energy and Resources, 23 March 2020. https://www.industry.gov.au/news/update-from-jessica-robinson-critical-minerals-facilitation-office-march-2020.

———. 2020b. "Rare Earths and Critical Minerals Provide Significant Opportunities for Australia." *Resourceful* 22 (December 2020). https://www.csiro.au/en/Research/MRF/Areas/Resourceful-magazine/Issue-22/Rare-earths-and-critical-minerals-provide-significant-opportunities-for-australia.

Rosen, Mark E., and Cara B. Thuringer. 2017. *Unconstrained Foreign Direct Investment: An Emerging Challenge to Arctic Security*. Arlington, VA: CNA. https://www.cna.org/cna_files/pdf/COP-2017-U-015944-1Rev.pdf.

Saklatvala, Ellie. 2020. "LCM to Assess Potential for UK RE Magnet Supply Chain." *Argus Media*, 10 November 2020. https://www.argusmedia.com/en/news/2158412-lcm-to-assess-potential-for-uk-re-magnet-supply-chain.

Saskatchewan Research Council. 2020. "Saskatchewan to Create Canada's First Rare Earth Processing Facility at SRC." *PR Newswire*, 28 August 2020. https://www.prnewswire.com/news-releases/saskatchewan-to-create-canadas-first-rare-earth-processing-facility-at-src-301120108.html.

Scheyder, Ernest. 2020. "U.S. Rare Earths Miner MP Materials to Go Public in $1.47 Billion Deal." Reuters, 15 July 2020. https://uk.reuters.com/article/us-mp-materials-ipo/u-s-rare-earths-miner-mp-materials-to-go-public-in-1-47-billion-deal-idUKKCN24G1WT.

Schøler, Mikkel. 2021. "Mining in Greenland Down, but Not Out." *Polar Connection*, 24 November 2021. https://polarconnection.org/mining-in-greenland/.

Shi, Mingming, and Marc Lantaigne. 2019. "A Cold Arena? Greenland as a Focus of Arctic Competition." *The Diplomat*, 10 June 2019. https://thediplomat.com/2019/06/a-cold-arena-greenland-as-a-focus-of-arctic-competition/.

Shields, Phoebe. 2021. "Eclipse Metals' Historic Samples from Ivittuut Project Return High-Grade Rare Earth Results." *Proactive Investors*, 14 November 2021. https://www.proactiveinvestors.com/companies/news/966164/eclipse-metals-historic-samples-from-ivittuut-project-return-high-grade-rare-earth-results-966164.html.

Smyth, Jamie. 2019. "Australia's 15 Projects Aim to Break China Rare Earths Dominance." *Financial Times*, 3 September 2019. https://www.ft.com/content/fc43a3c6-ce0f-11e9-99a4-b5ded7a7fe3f.

———. 2020a. "Industry Needs a Rare Earths Supply Chain Outside China." *Financial Times*, 28 July 2020. https://www.ft.com/content/fc368da6-1c86-454b-91ed-cb2727507661.

———. 2020b. "US-China: Washington Revives Plans for Its Rare Earths Industry." *Financial Times*, 14 September 2020. https://www.ft.com/content/5104d84d-a78f-4648-b695-bd7e14c135d6.

Stallion Resources. 2021. "Company Overview." Stallion Resources, accessed 11 August 2022. https://www.stallionresources.com.

Tang, Didi, and Catherine Philp. 2020. "China Threatens to Starve US of Key Defence Materials." *The Times*, 16 July 2020. https://www.thetimes.co.uk/article/china-threatens-to-starve-us-of-key-defence-materials-j38rms7rn.

US Embassy and Consulates in Australia. 2018. "The White House: Trump-Turnbull Meeting Strengthens the Alliance." Office of the Press Secretary, 23 February 2018. https://au.usembassy.gov/white-house-statement-trump-turnbull-meeting-strengthens-alliance/.

USGS (US Geological Survey). 2020. "Critical Cooperation: How Australia, Canada and the United States Are Working Together to Support Critical Mineral Discovery." USGS, 16 October 2020. https://www.usgs.gov/news/critical-cooperation-how-australia-canada-and-united-states-are-working-together-support.

Wu, Yuehe. 2019. "United States, Don't Underestimate China's Ability to Strike Back." *People's Daily*, 31 May 2019. http://en.people.cn/n3/2019/0531/c202936-9583292.html.

Yu, Sun, and Demetri Sevastopulo. 2021. "China Targets Rare Earth Export Curbs to Hobble US Defence Industry." *Financial Times*, 16 February 2021. https://www.ft.com/content/d3ed83f4-19bc-4d16-b510-415749c032c1.

PART II

Prologue: A Southern Perspective

A. J. (Tony) Press

Russia's illegal invasion of Ukraine in early 2022 will focus the thoughts of Antarctic observers, policy-makers, and scholars on the short- and long-term fallout from the dramatic actions of one of the original signatories to the 1959 Antarctic Treaty. As I write this prologue, the annual Antarctic Treaty Consultative Meeting is coming to a close in Berlin. Both Russia and Ukraine, as Antarctic Treaty Consultative Parties, participated in the meeting. Russia's invasion prompted an unprecedented démarche and walkout by twenty-five countries during an address to the meeting by the representative of Russia.

I will return to the potential consequence of these events later but have highlighted them here to emphasize that the Russia-Ukraine conflict is the biggest perturbation to the Antarctic Treaty System since the Antarctic Treaty came into force in 1961.

Antarctica is simultaneously distinct from, yet similar to, the Arctic. While the Arctic is an ocean surrounded by continents and islands, Antarctica is a continent surrounded by ocean and islands. Governance of Antarctica is chiefly achieved through the Antarctic Treaty System (ATS), a regime of international agreements stemming from the Antarctic Treaty. The Arctic, on the other hand, has layered governance: the laws of Arctic states are made with respect to their own countries; and rights to territorial seas, exclusive economic zones, and extended continental shelves are derived from the 1982 United Nations Convention on the Law of the Sea.

Only a small part of the Arctic Ocean and its seabed falls outside of some form of national government control. In contrast, through the operation of the Antarctic Treaty, the seven claimant states set aside overt application of their national domestic laws in the Antarctic Treaty area and apply them only to their own nationals.

In this discussion, I define the Antarctic, ecologically, as the ocean, islands, and continent south of the Antarctic Polar Front (also called the Antarctic Convergence). Geopolitically, the Antarctic Treaty applies to all areas below 60 degrees south latitude, while the related 1980 Convention on Conservation of Antarctic Marine Living Resources (the CAMLR Convention) applies to the Antarctic Treaty area, plus the ecosystems bounded by the Antarctic Polar Front.

The ATS consists of the Antarctic Treaty, subsequent legal instruments agreed by the parties to that treaty, and other laws, regulations, institutions, and decisions made within the system. The first international agreement after the Antarctic Treaty was the 1972 Convention for the Conservation of Antarctic Seals—an agreement that is moribund, but which was negotiated to cover the possibility of recommencing commercial sealing in Antarctica. Concern over the potential impacts of krill harvesting on the conservation of the great whales led to the negotiation of the CAMLR Convention. In the 1980s, the Antarctic Treaty Parties negotiated a pre-emptive agreement to manage future environmental impacts of mining in Antarctica. The 1988 Convention on the Regulation of Antarctic Mineral Resource Activities (the Minerals Convention) never entered into force, even though it was agreed, because Australia and France, followed by other countries, decided to not ratify it. Following the collapse of the Minerals Convention, the Antarctic Treaty Parties negotiated the Protocol on Environmental Protection to the Antarctic Treaty (the Environmental Protocol), which was signed in 1991, and which came into force in 1998. Besides providing a comprehensive regime to consider the environmental impacts of activities in the Antarctic Treaty area, the Environmental Protocol imposes an indefinite ban on mining in Antarctica.

The decision-making bodies of the ATS are the Antarctic Treaty Consultative Meeting (ATCM), established through the Antarctic Treaty; and the Commission for the Conservation of Marine Living Resources (CCAMLR). The ATCM usually meets annually "for the purpose of exchanging information, consulting together on matters pertaining Antarctica, and formulating and considering, and recommending to their governments, measures in furtherance of the principles and objectives of the Treaty" (Antarctic Treaty 1959). CCAMLR also meets annually and makes legally binding measures covering all aspects of the conservation of Antarctic marine living resources, including, but not limited to measures relating to harvesting.

The work of the ATCM is facilitated and supported by the Antarctic Treaty Secretariat, established in 2003 and based in Buenos Aires, Argentina. The CCAMLR Secretariat was established directly through the CAMLR Convention and is based in Hobart, Australia. The annual CCAMLR meetings are held in Hobart (except when held online in 2020 and 2021 due to the COVID-19 pandemic).

The Environmental Protocol established the Committee for Environmental Protection (CEP), which meets annually, usually in conjunction with the ATCM. The CEP's responsibilities are "to provide advice and formulate recommendations to the Parties in connection with the implementation of this Protocol . . . for consideration at Antarctic Treaty Consultative Meetings, and to perform such other functions as may be referred to it by the Antarctic Treaty Consultative Meetings" (Protocol on Environmental Protection to the Antarctic Treaty 1991). The ATCM receives the advice of the CEP and makes legally binding measures, and other decisions, based on that advice.

The CAMLR Convention established a Scientific Committee as a consultative body to the Commission. The Scientific Committee is "a forum for consultation and co-operation concerning the collection, study and exchange of information with respect to [Antarctic] marine living resources" (Convention on the Conservation of Antarctic Marine Living Resources 1980). The Scientific Committee provides advice to the Commission, which is then used in the formulation of legally binding conservation measures, among other decisions.

The Antarctic agreements and instruments, the ATCM, CCAMLR, CEP, Scientific Committee, all agreed measures, and the Secretariats constitute the ATS. The ATS also requests and receives advice from expert bodies such as the Scientific Committee on Antarctic Research.

The ATS falls outside of the United Nations system but is open to adherence by any of that body's member states. From the original 12 states that adopted the Antarctic Treaty in 1959, 43 additional countries have now joined. Of these, 29 are Antarctic Treaty Consultative Parties—that is, they have the right to participate in decision making in ATCMs. The Environmental Protocol has 42 state signatories. The CAMLR Convention has 25 states (plus the European Union) as signatories. As a product of the Cold War, the ATS has evolved from a response to potential conflict over territorial claims and the threats of 1950s superpower competition into a comprehensive regional governance regime, with participation of states across the globe. The emerging geopolitical challenges facing the ATS will be discussed below.

Antarctica, with its vast ice caps, holds about 90 per cent of the earth's ice and 70 per cent of its fresh water. The relentless impacts of climate change though atmospheric and oceanic warming will inevitably lead to the significant melting of the Antarctic ice cap and consequential global sea-level rise. Even though the Antarctic continent is surrounded by the cold Southern Ocean, the current extent and trajectory of greenhouse gas emissions ensures that the environmental changes now manifesting in the Antarctic will be locked in for many hundreds, if not thousands, of years to come. The global mean sea level is rising, and the contribution of Antarctica to this rise is accelerating.

Despite uncertainties surrounding future responses of the Antarctic ice cap to global climate change, global average sea-level rise of more than 0.8 metres above the 1950 average by the end of the century is projected. In the past decade Antarctica has been losing approximately 160 gigatons of its glacial ice per year due to the thinning of the ice sheet, and the loss of outlet glaciers in West Antarctica. This is the equivalent of about 0.5 millimetres per year of global sea-level rise (projected to a total contribution of 10 centimetres by 2100), a contribution that will continue well beyond the end of this century, and that will increase in rate annually. Sustained climate change will see significant irreversible instability of the ice sheet, and without mitigation of greenhouse gas emissions, Antarctica's future contribution to global sea-level rise will be measured in several metres, not fractions of a metre.

The Southern Ocean has warmed significantly, accounting for up to 50 per cent of heat gain in the upper two thousand metres of the global ocean in the past decade. The deep Southern Ocean is also warming.

While significant loss of sea ice is one of the clearest physical changes observed in the Arctic region, the behaviour of Antarctic sea ice has followed a different pattern. The annual changes in extent of Antarctic sea ice is one of the greatest natural events on earth. At its peak in the austral winter, Antarctic sea ice has an aerial extent of around nineteen million square kilometres, and at its nadir in summer this is reduced to around three million. Overall, Antarctic sea ice extent (as opposed to sea ice thickness) has not shown consistent significant trends, but there are distinct regional changes in sea ice extent in the Antarctic, with declines in the Amundsen Sea region and increased sea ice in the Ross Sea region.

Climate change has brought poleward shifts in the distribution of marine species in polar regions, as well as local changes to ecosystems in the Antarctic, including the appearance of invasive species from outside the Antarctic region. There is evidence of a southward shift in the distribution of Antarctic krill in the southern Atlantic Ocean, and changes in the distributions of some penguin species.

The Southern Ocean is a key global sink for the sequestration of atmospheric carbon dioxide, being responsible for 40 per cent of the global uptake by the oceans of carbon dioxide emissions. This in turn has led to the oceans becoming more acidic, with potentially great impacts on marine life and ecosystems. Current projections are that "business as usual" scenarios for global greenhouse gas emissions will see direct impacts of ocean acidification on some species of marine organisms by the end of this century.

Climate change is the greatest threat to the Antarctic, and the impact on the Antarctic climate will have major regional and global repercussions. Climate change may also have ramifications for Antarctic geopolitics, but these will most likely manifest differently than in the Arctic because of Antarctica's remoteness from human populations and international trade routes, and its unique international legal status.

The Antarctic does not have a permanent human population, although many of the Antarctic research stations are occupied year-round. The Antarctic Treaty designates Antarctica as a place for "peace and science," and the CAMLR Convention permits some regulated fisheries through its provision for "rational use." The largest "industry" in Antarctica is the combined input, support, and output of Antarctic science. Fisheries for toothfish, some other finfish, and krill are the major fisheries in the Antarctic. Biological prospecting for Antarctic genetic resources is also undertaken. Tourism is a growing industry, though recently it has been heavily impacted by the COVID-19 pandemic, and has the potential to grow well beyond the seventy thousand tourists who visited the Antarctic in 2019. The future trajectory of climate change *will* impact these human endeavours and related industries and put pressure on the stability of the ATS and its modes and norms.

The current Antarctic regime is deeply rooted in post–Second World War geopolitics. The twelve nations that participated in Antarctic research activities during the International Geophysical Year (1957–58) were invited to Washington by US president Dwight Eisenhower to negotiate an international agreement for Antarctic governance. Those countries were Argentina, Australia, Chile, Belgium, France, Japan, New Zealand, Norway, South Africa, the United Kingdom, the United States, and the Soviet Union. The claimant States—Argentina, Australia, Chile, France, New Zealand, Norway, and the United Kingdom—were then in the majority of the Treaty Parties. The United States and the Soviet Union each asserted historical rights to the basis of Antarctic claims. Japan, an original signatory to the treaty, was denied any right to an Antarctic territorial claim through the 1951 Treaty of Peace with Japan. The operation of the Antarctic Treaty's Article IV resolved the "problem" of Antarctic claims by neither confirming nor denying them, establishing that no new claims could be made, and that activities during the existence of the Treaty could not be used as the basis of future Antarctic claims.

The Treaty provides that military "manoeuvres" cannot be conducted in the Antarctic Treaty area, and that the testing of nuclear weapons and disposal of nuclear waste be prohibited. These prohibitions were further supported by the provision that allows any Antarctic Treaty Consultative Party to conduct unfettered inspections of facilities in Antarctica. Together, the non-militarization of Antarctica, and the setting aside of potential disputes over Antarctic claims, provided, and still provides, a stable regional governance arrangement that successfully diffuses active international belligerence in the region. The Soviet Union and the United States continued to participate in constructive Antarctic discussions during the height of the Cold War, as did the United Kingdom and Argentina during the Falklands/Malvinas armed conflict.

That is not to say that Antarctica is immune from the shifting forces of global power. There are now twenty-nine Antarctic Treaty law-making countries, and the claimants and the original signatories are no longer in the majority. The emergence of China as a global power, as well as various geopolitical developments in the Arctic, have in recent years seen an increasingly "militarized" discourse and commentary about Antarctic affairs. This discourse portrays the ATS as a historic artifact that is not "fit for purpose" to deal with the future geopolitical reality. These discussions are often centred on portrayals of "grey zone" activities, or the emergence of dual-use technologies deployed in the Antarctic (for example, telescopes and satellite ground stations such as the Chinese BeiDou system or Russia's GLONASS). Often, this discourse is linked to an assertion that the Antarctic Treaty "comes to an end" or is "open for amendment" in 2048— assertions that, while far too common, stem from a misunderstanding of the various agreements in the ATS (and a specific subject too long to go into here).

This discourse needs to be balanced against current Antarctic reality and the global interests and power of the vast majority of Antarctic Treaty parties. The non-militarization provisions of the Antarctic Treaty do not prohibit the use of military personnel or equipment for the conduct of science or other peaceful purposes in the Antarctic. The loose description of "dual use" technologies as potential breaches of these non-militarization provisions is also potentially misleading and fails to account for the reality that many similar systems (e.g., GPS) have operated in the Antarctic, without criticism, for decades. Much of the critically important Antarctic data that will be collected in the future by remotely operated autonomous marine and airborne systems may have potential military applications, even if not specifically collected for that purpose.

The protection that Antarctic Treaty Parties have against military activities in the Antarctic is through the inspection and reporting provisions of the Antarctic Treaty. As said above, Antarctic facilities can be inspected by any Party without notice. The Treaty allows for these inspections to be made by "aerial observation," and current and emerging technologies should also be used to verify compliance with non-militarization obligations. Just as Cold War tensions prompted the inclusion of an inspection regime in the Treaty, emerging global geopolitical tensions should stimulate the parties to the Antarctic Treaty to reinvigorate and modernize inspections—after all, mutual assurance can help to defuse tensions, thereby enhancing geopolitical stability.

Protection of the norms and modes of the ATS is also fundamental to the system's operation and to overall security in the region. Increasingly, Russia and China are using the consensus decision-making mechanisms of the ATS to stall or block progress on initiatives that are supported by the vast majority of Treaty Parties. This behaviour is most evident in the failure in recent years to declare additional Marine Protected Areas in the Antarctic. Both Russia and China have increasingly used novel interpretations of Antarctic law, or claimed that there is "not enough science," as reasons to not agree with the rest of the Antarctic community on these measures. More concerningly, Russia used its ability to block consensus to stop one of its fishing vessels being listed as in breach of a fisheries conservation measure; and it made the false claim of scientific uncertainty to depart from customary practice and to block a straightforward fisheries catch-limit measure.

The use of "failure of consensus" to pursue narrow national interests and to stall progress in decision-making in the ATS should be challenged by other Parties, not only within the confines of the decision-making forums themselves, but also individually and collectively outside these meetings through strong diplomatic engagement. Parties should use their collective efforts to promote and seek the consensus required to break these deadlocks.

The Treaty Parties have many "natural groupings," such as the claimants, original signatories, southern hemisphere states, South American states, Asian states, and so on. "External groupings" such as the Five Eyes, the Indo-Pacific Partnership, ANZUS, the Quad, and the newly formulated AUKUS also have some intersection with Antarctic affairs.

The consequences of Russia's illegal invasion of Ukraine—one Antarctic Treaty Party invading another—are yet to play out in the ATS. The earlier 1982 Falkland Islands/Islas Malvinas armed conflict occurred in the period between significant ATS meetings and was managed with a high degree of diplomatic nuance inside the ATS. But the Russian invasion of Ukraine has already seen this conflict discussed in the 2022 Berlin meeting, and has resulted a diplomatic shunning of Russia by the other Antarctic Treaty Parties.

Russia also continues a path of consensus blocking on critical Antarctic decisions, and with China, continues to erode long-established decision-making norms inside the ATS. Russia's investments in Antarctic activities are likely to decline because of the economic impacts of its invasion of Ukraine—as was the case in the 1990s after the collapse of the Soviet Union. But Russia will still likely continue to be a destabilizing influence inside the formal meetings of the ATS.

These emerging Antarctic challenges should be met with concerted, coordinated action by those countries that see the future stability of the Antarctic region as globally important. The future of the earth is intrinsically bound to the protection of the Antarctic environment, which in turn depends on protecting the ATS—the only viable mechanism for governance of the region.

REFERENCES

Antarctic Treaty. 1959. Adopted 1 December 1959, 402 UNTS (entered into force 23 June 1961).

Convention on the Conservation of Antarctic Marine Living Resources. 1980. Adopted 20 May 1980, UNTS 1329 (entered into force 7 April 1982).

Protocol on Environmental Protection to the Antarctic Treaty. 1991. Adopted 4 October 1991, 4921 UNTS (entered into force 14 January 1998).

5

Challenges and Opportunities for Southern Ocean and Antarctic Governance

Joanna Vince

Surrounding the vast Antarctic continent is the treacherous Southern Ocean, which is rich in marine life. The Antarctic region is governed by the Antarctic Treaty System (ATS), which is made up of international agreements that manage marine resources and protect the Antarctic environment. Governance of this marine space is further complicated by other regimes outside of the ATS, such as the United Nations Convention on the Law of the Sea (UNCLOS), which gives Antarctic Treaty claimant states the ability to assert claims to adjacent offshore areas. In Australia's case, the Australian Antarctic Territory and its adjacent exclusive economic zone are not recognized by all states involved in activities in the region. Consequently, these governance issues have resulted in political tensions for claimant states over maritime boundaries, the use of marine resources in the Southern Ocean, and the level of environmental protection.

This chapter analyzes these geopolitical tensions and the ongoing challenges faced by states involved in activities in the Southern Ocean. It also addresses the opportunities that these governance arrangements can provide in this era of environmental and political uncertainty. Although the Southern Ocean is small compared to other oceans, it is known for being "large" in other ways: it has the Antarctic Circumpolar Current, the largest ocean current; it is one of the world's largest sinks for atmospheric carbon dioxide; it has the largest waves on the planet; it is home to penguins, whales, seals, and numerous fish species; and it makes an important contribution to biological diversity (Johnson 2017). The Southern Ocean is healthy and supports several fisheries, including Antarctic krill, which is known as one of the remaining unexploited fish populations in the world's oceans (Brooks et al. 2020). The ecosystems of both the Antarctic continent and the Southern Ocean are intertwined, and as a result, the governance arrangements of the Southern Ocean cannot be examined in isolation. The international agreements that provide the framework for governance in the region—namely, through the ATS—regulate activities for both the Antarctic continent and the surrounding seas. Unlike the Artic, which is a sea surrounded by land, the Antarctic is a continent surrounded by an ocean, and therefore jurisdictional and geopolitical issues differ between the two regions. Many state and non-state actors (such as non-governmental organizations) have vested interests in Antarctic and Southern Ocean marine resources, and decision making is often influenced by politics related to the region and/or beyond in other contexts. It is because of this that oceans governance in the Southern polar region is unique and often complicated.

The ATS is known as one of the most successful global multilateral governing systems (Brady 2011) and includes a number of agreements that are pertinent to oceans governance and marine resources management in the Southern Ocean: the 1959 Antarctic Treaty, the 1972 Convention for the Conservation of Antarctic Seals, the 1980 Convention of the Conservation of Marine Living Resources (CCAMLR), and the 1991 Protocol on Environmental Protection to the Antarctic Treaty (the so-called Madrid Protocol). The Antarctic Treaty applies to the area 60 degrees south latitude and includes areas within the Southern Ocean. The Madrid Protocol extends it to associated ecosystems, and CCAMLR's ocean area is even larger.[1]

Outside of the ATS, other international agreements also contribute to the governance framework of the Southern Ocean. These include the Convention on Migratory Species of Wild Animals, the 1983 Convention on International Trade of Endangered Species Wild Flora and Flora, the 1946 International Convention for the Regulation of Whaling, the 1973/78 Convention for the Prevention of Pollution from Ships (MARPOL), the aforementioned UNCLOS, which is also known as the 1982 United Nations Law of the Sea Convention (LOSC), and other international environmental agreements. As a result, there is an emerging "regime complex" comprised of a number of regimes that interact with one another in a spatially defined area "in the sense that the operation of each affects the performance of others" (Young 2012, 394; see also Haward 2017; McGee and Haward 2019). LOSC outlines the basis for managing ocean space and provides definitions of key maritime zones for coastal states, based on the established baselines from which these zones are delimited (Haward and Vince 2008).

States involved in the Antarctic region and Southern Ocean are currently facing a multitude of issues and challenges; however, this chapter is limited to examining three of these challenges. The first arises from the legal maritime boundaries of claimant states (states that laid claim to territories on the Antarctic continent before the Antarctic Treaty came into force) and the political consequences of asserting new territorial claims. The second is the use of resources in the Southern Ocean. And the third is marine environmental protection. This chapter examines these from an Australian perspective to understand how a claimant state can address these challenges, and it suggests opportunities that can arise from oceans governance in the Antarctic region.

Governance of the Southern Ocean

Global oceans governance has been fraught with challenges for the last century, with states attempting to resolve tensions about delineating boundaries, regulating access to marine resources and fisheries, and, more recently, protecting the marine environment. The ATS and LOSC provide a legal framework for establishing maritime boundary claims and for regulating marine resource management activities.

The Antarctic Treaty System

The Antarctic Treaty is central to the ATS, and a prime example of good international relations based on the values of peace and scientific co-operation (Lord 2020), although geopolitics drives interactions between contracting parties (Haward 2017). The ATS bans military activity and is also a significant security instrument. Importantly, it incorporates commitments to scientific collaboration. There are fifty-three contracting parties to the treaty and twenty-nine Consultative Parties. The original claimant states are Australia, New Zealand, France, Norway, the United Kingdom, Argentina, and Chile. Article 4 of the Antarctic Treaty is known as an "agreement to disagree" (Hodgson-Johnston 2015; Scott 2013). It stops any conflicts over existing territorial claims and rights in the region by the original claimant states and disallows new claims from being made and existing claims from being enlarged (Haward 2017). The Antarctic Treaty permits claimant states to continue asserting their territorial claims under article 4 while allowing signatories to the treaty to maintain their positions regarding the status of these claims (Titterton and Haward 2022).

Australia has one of the longest records of Antarctic engagement. This reflects its geographical proximity to the continent and the regional connections it maintains with it through climate and the Southern Ocean. Australia claims 42 per cent of the Antarctic continent, an area known as the Australian Antarctic Territory, and it had a major role in negotiating capstone features of the Antarctic Treaty. The proclamation of the Australian Antarctic Territory stops at the coastline of the Antarctic continent, and maritime areas are dealt with through LOSC (Haward and Bergin 2010). Only four states—France, New Zealand, Norway, and the United Kingdom—recognize Australia's territorial claim. Other states see the Antarctic as a commons in "which no territorial sovereignty may be asserted and maritime zones claimed" (Hemmings and Stephens 2009, 4). This does not mean, however, that article 4 diminishes the existing territorial claims or sovereignty (Haward and Press 2010).

The Law of the Sea Convention

LOSC was negotiated between 1974 and 1982 and entered into force in 1994. This convention provides rights for coastal states and establishes a regime of maritime zones. These zones include the territorial sea and contiguous zone, the exclusive economic zone (EEZ; which extends two hundred nautical miles from coastal baselines), the continental shelf, and the high seas. Sixty-four per cent of the world's oceans are "high seas," or areas beyond national jurisdiction (ABNJ; the area beyond EEZs). LOSC does not directly address Antarctica but covers the maritime areas south

60 degrees south latitude (the Antarctic Treaty area). There are further complexities to consider in understanding the maritime boundaries in the Southern Ocean. According to Johnson (2017), due to the sovereignty situation and the operation of article 4, the Southern Ocean's ABNJ cannot be wholly identified (of which more below). Kaye and Rothwell (2002) have also argued that territorial sea baselines are difficult to determine in Antarctica because of uncertainty about what is land and what is ice. The sub-Antarctic islands (such as Australia's Heard Island)—under national jurisdiction and outside the treaty area—are not subject to article 4 of the Antarctic Treaty and can legitimately generate EEZs and continental shelves.

The unresolved issues and challenges centre on the extent to which claimant states can claim rights as "coastal states," or whether coastal states even exist in Antarctica given the particular status of Antarctic claims under the Antarctic Treaty. Antarctica was specifically excluded from discussions at the third and most lengthy United Nations Conference on the Law of the Sea (1973–1982) in order to keep Antarctic sovereignty issues separate from LOSC. Over time it has become an accepted view that claimants in Antarctica may make no new territorial claims but may create an adjacent EEZ or assert continental shelf rights (Sosin 2022). The establishment of EEZs has resulted in diplomatic tensions between Antarctic Treaty Parties, in particular states that do not acknowledge the territorial claims of the Antarctic continent or that see the Southern Ocean circumpolar waters as high seas rather coastal waters (Johnson 2017). Australia declared an EEZ of two hundred nautical miles adjacent to its Antarctic Territory in 1994.

Claims for Extending the Continental Shelf

Under article 76 of LOSC, claimant states can apply to the Commission on the Limits of the Continental Shelf (CLCS) to extend their legal continental shelf. Australia began this process in the 1990s, which raised the issue of new territorial claims in the Southern Ocean. Interestingly, the Madrid Protocol recognizes the status of claimants and the ability of states to request the extension of the continental shelf (Ferrada 2018). The United States has maintained that it does not recognize any territorial claims in Antarctica and the seabed and subsoil of ocean areas adjacent to and beyond Antarctica (United States of America 2004). This is consistent with its view of LOSC, which the United States has not ratified.

Recently, Australia's claim for an extended continental shelf adjacent to the Australian Antarctic Territory became a source of contention for other Antarctic Treaty Parties. Kaye (2015) argued that when claiming the continental shelf beyond two hundred nautical miles

> the Australian government faced a difficult decision. If the AAT [Australian Antarctic Territory] possessed a continental shelf, and Article IV of the Antarctic Treaty did not prevent the assertion of such a shelf, then Australia would potentially undermine its claim by taking no action in support of a claim. To distinguish Antarctic lands from the rest of Australia would be to indicate that Australian sovereignty over these lands was of some inferior form. (344)

If the data were submitted to the CLCS there would likely be protests from other Antarctic Treaty Parties as it would reopen the issue of sovereignty. In 2004, Australia lodged its submission to extend its continental shelf, but asked the CLCS not to place the data regarding the shelf adjacent to the Australian Antarctic Territory under its active consideration. In doing so, it was consistent with its obligations to LOSC, which imposed a time limit on the lodgement of the data. Australia was able to legally oblige without compromising how the data were used or the CLCS's decision (Sosin 2022). The following note to the secretary-general of the United Nations, which accompanied Australia's submission, stated the following:

> Australia recalls the principles and objectives shared by the Antarctic Treaty and UNCLOS, and the importance of the Antarctic system and UNCLOS working in harmony and thereby ensuring the continuing peaceful cooperation, security and stability in the Antarctic Area. (quoted in Haward and Bergin 2010, 615)

Australia recognized that most states consider the area subject to unresolved dispute, and Germany, India, Japan, the Netherlands, Russia, and the United States had a strong "diplomatic response" to Australia's extended continental shelf claim (Hemmings and Stephens 2009). These states expressed that they did not want the CLCS to consider Australia's data in the Southern Ocean. Others were grateful for Australia's request of the CLCS not to consider the shelf adjacent to the Australian territory. For instance, the United States stated that it "acknowledges with appreciation Australia's request to the commission that it not take any action on that portion of its submission" (United States of America 2004, 1).

Only half of the extended continental shelf that Australia requested in the Southern Ocean was approved by the CLCS (Hemmings and Stephens 2009). The approved areas were adjacent to the territory of Heard Island and the McDonald Islands, and to Macquarie Island, which lie outside the Antarctic Treaty area. It is important to note that "the area of continental shelf is not a territorial claim, it is an area where rights can be exercised because a territorial claim already exists on land" (Press 2012).

New Zealand, Argentina, Norway, and Chile have also made full or partial submissions to the CLCS. New Zealand, Norway, and the United Kingdom have indicated that they may make submissions later (Wehrmann 2018). By claiming extended continental shelves, states can have access to offshore hydrocarbon resources (Joyner 2011). This is a pressing issue for many Antarctic Treaty Parties. Nevertheless, in 2009 during the fiftieth anniversary of the Antarctic Treaty, through a ministerial declaration, Treaty Parties reaffirmed their commitment to article 4 of the treaty and article 7 of the Madrid Protocol, which prohibits mineral resource extraction (Joyner 2011).

Politics in Southern Ocean and Antarctic Governance

There is no doubt that politics has played a role in decisions regarding the Antarctic region. Individual states' political interests are often discussed at Antarctic Treaty Consultative Meetings, and they affect many decisions. However, political interests have also been addressed in other fora, such as the Scientific Committee on Antarctic Research (SCAR), which is otherwise intended to focus on issues of a non-political nature. SCAR was created in 1958 in order to provide "objective and independent scientific advice" during the meetings (SCAR n.d.). Ferrada (2018) has claimed that the focus on politics is a result of the influence of non-governmental organizations in meetings, particularly with regard to issues such as Antarctic tourism and climate change, where little regulation exists. The issues of sovereignty and maritime boundaries are a challenge for Antarctic Treaty Parties involved in Southern Ocean activities. Political decision making is a natural response to these issues. As long as the ATS remains unchanged, this challenge is unlikely to disappear.

Use of Marine Resources

CCAMLR and Fisheries

There will always be tension in the Antarctic region between how many and what types of resources should be exploited and what level of marine environmental protection is needed. The Southern Ocean has abundant fisheries and the potential for other activities such as seabed mining. Fishing in the Southern Ocean is risky and expensive, so the economic return for states has to be such that it justifies the effort. The krill and toothfish fisheries are growing and they are "of high dietary potential and high commercial value" (Ferrada 2018, 100). CCAMLR sets conservative catch limits on fish stocks and has put measures in place such as management areas to regulate fishing activities (Haward, Jabour, and Press 2012). CCAMLR was one of the first regional fisheries-management authorities to identify and address illegal fishing of Patagonian and Antarctic toothfish (Nilsson et al. 2016). Before 2000, illegal fishing in this region was conducted by large commercial vessels operating under flags of convenience (Warner 2018). This has now been reduced through the following measures: monitoring, control, and surveillance; illegal sighting reports; illegal vessel lists; recovery of illegal, unreported, and unregulated (IUU) fishing gear; port inspections; at-sea inspections; and compulsory vessel-monitoring systems (Nilsson et al. 2016). CCAMLR provides surveillance and prosecution support for its members. Its members participate in the Catch Documentation Scheme (CDS), which records toothfish catches at landing and then tracks them through the supply chain. By identifying the key players in the chain of custody, the CDS is a useful market-based tool to increase compliance with trade-related measures (Grilly et al. 2015). However, Grilly et al. (2015), who did an analysis of the CDS, found that there were more states involved in the toothfish trade than were reported by CCAMLR through the CDS. CCAMLR is also unable to regulate the Southern Ocean fishing activities of non-member states (Warner 2018). Further investigation is required to determine the level of legality in the reporting system and whether knowledge of global trade patterns can provide the essential economic information needed by management authorities to effectively manage the toothfish trade (Grilly et al. 2015).

CCAMLR is also limited in its effectiveness by its data-retrieval processes and institutional structure. For instance, the secretariat does not receive vessel-monitoring data directly, and must instead request it from member states. Where countries are reluctant to share, due to political goals, failure to control their vessels, or other factors, the CCAMLR Secretariat has little capacity to obtain vessel-monitoring data (Vince, Wilcox, and Hardesty 2021). Although there are sources for some information on vessels in the region, these do not provide comprehensive monitoring due to coverage, data-processing needs, or the voluntary nature of the data provision. This makes it difficult for the secretariat to discover behaviour that should be discussed in the commission, and to confirm issues that it suspects are occurring.

Co-operation between CCAMLR and its members has been essential in battling IUU fishing. CCAMLR and Australian surveillance patrols around the sub-Antarctic Australian islands have resulted in no instances of IUU fishing in Australia's southern EEZ since 2005 (Australian Government Department of Agriculture 2014). Australian legal toothfish operators have been a large part of this success through their involvement in the Coalition of Legal Toothfish Operators. Australia and France agreed to co-operative surveillance and enforcement in both the Australian and French EEZs in the Southern Ocean through the 2003 Treaty between the Government of Australia and the Government of the French Republic on Cooperation in the Maritime Areas adjacent to the French Southern and Antarctic Territories, Heard Island, and the McDonald Islands. This agreement

> provides for the exchange of information about the location, movements and other details of vessels suspected of fishing illegally to facilitate operational responses, logistical support in the conduct of hot pursuits and the undertaking

of cooperative research on marine living resources. There is also provision for surveillance of each party's maritime zones with the consent of the relevant coastal State. (Warner 2018, 15)

In 2007, Australia and France signed the Agreement on Cooperative Enforcement of Fisheries Laws between the Government of Australia and the Government of the French Republic in the Maritime Areas Adjacent to the French Southern and Antarctic Territories, Heard Island, and the McDonald Islands. This agreement allows each state to use law enforcement in each other's EEZs. This, too, has contributed to the decline of IUU fishing in the area (Australian Government Department of Agriculture 2014). In addition to reducing IUU fishing activities, collaborative efforts in the region between states and CCAMLR has decreased seabird mortality in the area (Österblom and Bodin 2012; Petrossian, de By, and Clarke 2016; Tuck, Polacheck, and Bulman 2003). It is important to note that not all states are in the same position as Australia and France, who can use surveillance and enforcement and are capable of bearing the large costs to monitor the Southern Ocean. Many are too busy with surveillance and enforcement in their own fishing zones to make any meaningful contribution to the high seas zone within CCAMLR's jurisdiction (Griggs and Lugten 2007). Despite the limitations of CCAMLR and member states, illegal fishing has decreased significantly in the Southern Ocean, but it has not been eliminated in areas outside of Australia's EEZ.

One of the factors that has made the elimination of IUU fishing difficult is that the high seas are governed by a principle of freedom. However, this "freedom" has required further definition and is often questioned when illegal activities occur. Negotiations are currently taking place under the auspices of the United Nations to establish a new internationally legally binding instrument for the conservation and sustainable use of the ABNJ (United Nations n.d.), known as the Marine Biodiversity Beyond National Jurisdiction Agreement (BBNJ). This agreement will focus on, inter alia, area-based management tools such as marine protected areas (MPAs), environmental impact assessments, and regulating biological prospecting and mineral resource exploitation.

Commercial Biological Prospecting

Commercial biological prospecting has been an area of concern for Antarctic Treaty Parties. According to Joyner (2011),

> Increasing scientific research on flora and fauna in and around Antarctica is being conducted with the aim of discovering commercially beneficial genetic and biochemical resources. Growing commercial interest in Antarctic genetic resources is evident, as indicated by the fact that products from Antarctic genetic resources are already being marketed by several companies, including nutraceuticals from krill oil, antifreeze proteins, anticancer drugs, enzymes, and compounds for cosmetic products. Much of this commercial activity focuses on the marine environment, in particular, the crustacean krill. Nearly 200 research organizations and companies from 27 states are undertaking research for commercial purposes in the Antarctic. Amongst the major sponsoring states are Japan, United States, Spain, United Kingdom, Korea, Canada, Sweden, Russia, China, Chile, New Zealand, France, Belgium, India, Denmark, the Netherlands, Germany, and Poland, all ATCPs [Antarctic Treaty Consultative Parties]. The most entries in the recently constructed Antarctic Bioprospecting Database originate from Japan and mainly focus on organisms in the marine environment, principally Antarctic krill. The second largest number of entries originate from United States, most of which also focus on marine biota, especially krill, bacteria, and fish. (98)

Bioprospecting will remain confined to discovery of new biological resources for now; however, the issues of commercial confidentiality and intellectual property rights and how they fit with the existing governance regime have not been addressed. The impact on the marine environment if large commercial operations are established will need to be further explored. No decision has been made during Antarctic Treaty Consultative Meetings regarding biological prospecting (Jabour 2013).

Marine Protection

Marine Protected Areas

The third challenge is to protect the Southern Ocean from the over-exploitation that has been wrought on other oceans. The Antarctic Treaty does not distinguish between terrestrial and marine living resources and neither do the Agreed Measures for the Conservation of Antarctic Fauna and Flora adopted in 1964 (Roura, Steenhuisen, and Bastmeijer 2018). Protection of marine species been addressed through the ATS as it has developed. Annex 5 to the Madrid Protocol provides for Antarctic Specially Protected Areas (ASPAs) and Antarctic Specially Managed Areas (ASMAs) to be designated in the Antarctic Treaty area. It states, "For the purposes set out in this Annex, any area, including any marine area, may be designated as an Antarctic Specially Protected Area or an Antarctic Specially Managed Area" (art. 2(1), annex 5), and that activities in those areas "shall be prohibited, restricted or managed in accordance with Management Plans adopted under the provisions of this Annex." According to Roura, Steenhuisen, and Bastmeijer (2018), eleven APSAs and three ASMAs contained a "marine component" and required approval by CCAMLR before they were adopted at Antarctic Treaty Consultative Meetings. Ten ASPAs and one ASMA that were not reviewed by CCAMLR also included a marine component, however they did not meet the criteria of Antarctic Treaty Consultative Meeting Decision 9 (2005). This decision stated that the areas that need prior approval by CCAMLR are those with harvesting potential or that may restrict CCAMLR-related activities.

Because the area of the Southern Ocean that is regulated by CCAMLR is even more extensive than the Antarctic Treaty area, it is widely recognized as covering a large ABNJ (De Santo 2018). The CCAMLR agreement is unique as it employs precautionary and ecosystem-based approaches to fisheries management. The commission includes members that are not parties to the Antarctic Treaty; however, these members must acknowledge the special obligations and responsibilities for the Antarctic Treaty Consultative Parties. The commission began discussing MPA management on the high seas in the 1990s. Over time this has become a politically contentious issue. CCAMLR requires full consensus on all decisions to be passed, rather than a majority, and this can be a cause of conflict and can undermine international co-operation (Brooks et al. 2020).

In 2009, the South Orkney Islands Southern Shelf MPA, the world's first high seas MPA, was adopted. This happened relatively quickly; however, the MPA had no evaluation criteria or management and monitoring plans for implementation (Brooks et al. 2020). The proposal for this "no-take" MPA met with little resistance because fisheries were not impacted (Smith, McGee, and Jabour 2016). After the adoption of Conservation Measure 91-04 in 2011, a legal framework for MPAs and proposals for MPAs in the Ross Sea and East Antarctica were submitted. Most of the opposition to both proposals came from Russia and China; consensus was in the end not reached. The Ross Sea MPA was negotiated over several years, with objections raised about scientific uncertainty, the impacts on fisheries, and the commission's legal status to establish MPAs. Brooks et al. argued that the MPA negotiations "had broken trust in CCAMLR—a powerful sentiment in a commission with a small number of total representatives" (2020, 6). Political tensions between Russia and the United States were also identified as being a major factor in influencing negotiations due to political tensions caused by the war in the Ukraine. The Ross Sea MPA was adopted by consensus in 2016; however, a sunset clause was included that outlined a thirty-five year "end date" for the MPA (Ferrada 2018).

Negotiations over CCAMLR's MPAs continued to be contentious. In 2012, Australia, France, and the European Union proposed a marine park in East Antarctica that would be a representative system of seven MPAs and cover 1.8 million square kilometres. Due to objections from Russia and China, the park's size was reduced in 2017 to a million square kilometres. For eight consecutive years, CCAMLR members were unable to reach consensus to establish the marine park (Readfearn 2019). China (CCAMLR's newest member) and Russia voiced concerns over the no-take zones, and the two countries' interests in the krill fishery may be a reason why they have reservations about the marine park. It is known that China intends to develop its krill fishery and is investing heavily in polar fisheries technology (Liu 2019). Liu and Brooks (2018) have argued that China may change its objections to the East Antarctic marine park if Australia, France, and the European Union "find economic levers of influence and diplomatic common ground" (Liu and Brooks 2018, 194). In addition to

China and Russia, Ukraine and Japan have also been critical of proposals for MPAs in the Southern Ocean (Smith, McGee, and Jabour 2016). During the 2013 CCAMLR meeting, Ukraine suggested that "CCAMLR should delegate responsibility for MPAs to the Madrid Protocol" (Smith, McGee, and Jabour 2016, 184), and this is something that has also been discussed by Antarctic Treaty Consultative Parties.

For instance, in 2018–19, discussions by the Committee for Environmental Protection (created under the Madrid Protocol) and Antarctic Treaty Consultative Parties centred on integrating the ATS instruments for the protection of the marine environment with CCAMLR MPAs. New Zealand led informal discussions on this matter; however, all committee members were not convinced this was a suitable way forward for marine protection. Roura, Steenhuisen, and Bastmeijer (2018) argued, however, that an integrated approach and more consistent application of annex 5 could provide stronger protection for marine mammals and seabirds. They went on to say, "harmonisation would also apply to other Antarctic activities relevant for both land and sea, including shipping, tourism and scientific research, and to land-based sources of marine pollution" (Roura, Steenhuisen, and Bastmeijer 2018, 311). However, delegates at the 42nd Antarctic Treaty Consultative Meeting were unable to come to an agreement on the harmonization initiative, demonstrating the roadblock created by consensus decision making (Gardiner 2020). This example supports "a commonly shared criticism that the ATS is increasingly unable to develop environmental policy apace with the rapidly changing Antarctic environment and subsequent conservation issues" (Gardiner 2020, 6).

Tourism

The human impact on the Antarctic environment also needs to be considered in the scope of environmental protection. More than fifty thousand people visit Antarctica each year, and this number is increasing. The vast majority arrive by ship, navigating the Southern Ocean to reach their destination. Their time on the continent is also limited, with most of it spent on the ship. Antarctic tourism is a self-regulated activity. The International Association of Antarctica Tour Operators monitors and manages tourism and reports annually at the Antarctic Treaty meetings each year. The association represents industry but is also recognized as being "mindful of the extraordinary responsibilities it carries for maintaining the integrity of the pristine Antarctic environment" (Haward, Jabour, and Press 2012, 603). However, due to the impact of the COVID-19 pandemic, it is anticipated that in the medium term (up to 2024), Antarctic tourism will be "severely" reduced and may even face collapse (Frame and Hemmings 2020).

Pollution from ships is also an important issue in the Australian Antarctic Territory; however, due to the pandemic, the of number of vessels in the Southern Ocean and the amount of pollution from these vessels are likely to decrease over the medium term (Frame and Hemmings 2020). The International Maritime Organization (IMO) already imposes strict regulation of shipping and pollution and a ban on heavy and intermediate fuel in the Antarctic Treaty area through MARPOL (see IMO Resolution 189(60), 26 March 2010). The increase of maritime activities in the future, once COVID-19 subsides, needs to be closely monitored to protect the marine environment. Human impact in Antarctica is an extensive topic that cannot be addressed in detail in this chapter; however, it is an important aspect of marine protection.

Climate Change

Melting sea ice is already changing the Antarctic land and marine environments and the species living within them (McGee and Haward 2019). The impact of climate change has been evidenced in the polar regions more than any other place in the world, in fact, and CCAMLR members and Antarctic Treaty Parties who are already discussing this issue will find that the topic of climate change will continue to arise in future meetings. Climate change also has the potential of creating new political tensions between states (McGee and Liu 2019). McGee and Haward (2019) have argued that the ATS has been reluctant to engage with other international institutions in the Antarctic regime complex, and that will be a challenge ATS must face when attempting to address issues such as climate change.

Plastic Pollution

Plastic has been found in the Southern Ocean and the polar regions since the 1960s (Masura et al. 2015; Suaria et al. 2020). CCAMLR has recognized ship-sourced pollution as an issue, and it has put strict measures in place to reduce such occurrences. For instance, there is a mandatory requirement for fishers in the Southern Ocean to report gear loss to the CCAMLR Scientific Committee (CCAMLR 2015). However, land-based plastics are the most concerning type, and these have already made their way to the Southern Ocean. The 42nd Antarctic Treaty Consultative Meeting adopted a resolution aimed at "Reducing Plastic Pollution in Antarctica and the Southern Ocean" (Secretariat of the Antarctic Treaty 2019). It states that there is a "current lack of plastics monitoring data to inform decision-making," and acknowledges that "the majority of plastic found in Antarctica originates from outside of Antarctica" (Secretariat of the Antarctic Treaty 2019). The resolution also recommends that SCAR members engage in studies to help quantify the amount of plastic pollution in the Antarctic region (Zhang, Haward, and McGee 2020). It is anticipated that this issue will continue to grow in significance for the ATS. In 2022, the United Nations Environment Assembly announced the development of a new, legally binding global plastics treaty (UNEP 2022). The regime complex in the Antarctic region may expand to include this new treaty. The solution to plastic pollution will require extensive coordination with other international organizations, states, and NGOs so that holistic solutions can reduce plastic pollution in the Antarctic region, and indeed in all the world's oceans (Vince and Hardesty 2018). This may also be an opportunity for the ATS to evolve.

The Future and Opportunities

There is an array of research that addresses the future of the Antarctic region. Some authors defend the ATS's adaptability to new pressures (see, for example, Haward, Jabour, and Press 2012), while others have argued that the current governance framework will be unable to cope with present challenges (Chown et al. 2012). Ferrada (2018) outlined five future scenarios to be contemplated in Antarctica. These include political-legal implications: heterogeneity among states that participate in this international regime; pressure to internationalize Antarctic governance; the unresolved topic of sovereignty; the growing politicization of Antarctic technical and scientific discussions; and finally, the probable necessity of exploiting Antarctic resources more intensively. With respect to the Southern Ocean, while all of these will have an impact, it is the exploitation of marine resources that will continue to cause political tensions. Access to fisheries and restrictions through MPAs are important concerns for many states. While Australia remains a claimant state and the Antarctic Treaty remains unchanged, Australia will continue, along with the other claimant states, to influence the governance of the Antarctic region (Ferrada 2018). Australia's roles in CCAMLR in combating illegal fishing, support of MPAs, and other interests in the Southern Ocean are a strength and opportunity.

The year 2048 will mark the point at which a conference could be called to review the Madrid Protocol, the key environmental protection instrument in the ATS. However, this can only occur if a number of complex conditions are met (Ferrada 2018). Many states may take the opportunity to revisit the issue of mining in the Antarctic region. Other measures that are used for environmental protection may also be reviewed. An integrated approach to marine resource protection within the ATS would be favourable, but it will be difficult to achieve. The forthcoming BBNJ Agreement may affect marine protection in the Southern Ocean, and its relationship to CCAMLR will need to be further explored.

Conclusion

Governance of the Southern Ocean cannot be examined in isolation. This chapter focused on sovereignty in relation to the creation of EEZs and the claiming of extended continental shelves, and the challenge of resolving tensions between resource use and protection. These challenges can be overcome if current diplomatic efforts and peaceful coexistence continues. The governance of the Southern Ocean will be impacted by broader decisions about sovereignty and security; however, it is an area of the world that we can claim is rather well managed compared to others. CCAMLR will continue to be instrumental in achieving resource sustainability in the Southern Ocean, and consensus decision making can be an advantage as much as a disadvantage, allowing meaningful decisions to be made despite being driven by geopolitics. The governance of the Antarctic region is inherently political. The way these politics are managed is what strengthens the regime. Protecting the region from over-exploitation and continuing the sustainable use of resources will be a challenge, but one that can be achieved.

NOTE

1   This region, as stated by CCAMLR, consists of all waters bounded by the Antarctic continent to the south, and to the north by a line starting at lat. 50°S, long. 50°W; thence due east to long. 30°E; thence due north to lat. 45°S; thence due east to long. 80°E; thence due south to lat. 55°S; thence due east to long. 150°E; thence due south to lat. 60°S; thence due east to long. 50°W; thence due north to the starting point.

REFERENCES

Australian Government Department of Agriculture. 2014. Australia's Second National Plan of Action to Prevent, Deter and Eliminate Illegal, Unreported and Unregulated Fishing. Canberra: Commonwealth of Australia.

Brady, Anne-Marie. 2011. "Science Diplomacy: Antarctica, Science, and the Governance of International Spaces." *Polar Journal* 1 (2): 301–2. DOI: 10.1080/2154896X.2011.626645.

Brooks, Cassandra M., Larry B. Crowder, Henrik Österblom, and Aaron L. Strong. 2020. "Reaching Consensus for Conserving the Global Commons: The Case of the Ross Sea, Antarctica." *Conservation Letters* 13 (1): 1–10. https://doi.org/10.1111/conl.12676.

CCAMLR (Convention of the Conservation of Marine Living Resources). 2015. "Conservation Measure 26-01." Adopted at CCAMLR-XXXIV, 19–30 October 2015.

Chown, Steven L., Jennifer E. Lee, Kevin A. Hughes, Jim Barnes, P. J. Barrett, Dana M. Bergstrom, Peter Convey, Don A. Cowan, Kim Crosbie, and G. Dyer. 2012. "Challenges to the Future Conservation of the Antarctic." *Science* 337 (6091): 158–59. DOI: 10.1126/science.1222821.

De Santo, Elizabeth M. 2018. "Implementation Challenges of Area-Based Management Tools (ABMTs) for Biodiversity beyond National Jurisdiction (BBNJ)." *Marine Policy* 97:34–43. https://doi.org/10.1016/j.marpol.2018.08.034.

Ferrada, Luis Valentín. 2018. "Five Factors that Will Decide the Future of Antarctica." *Polar Journal* 8 (1): 84–109. https://doi.org/10.1080/2154896X.2018.1468623.

Frame, Bob, and Alan D. Hemmings. 2020. "Coronavirus at the End of the World: Antarctica Matters." *Social Sciences & Humanities Open* 2 (1): 100054. https://doi.org/10.1016/j.ssaho.2020.100054.

Gardiner, Natasha B. 2020. "Marine Protected Areas in the Southern Ocean: Is the Antarctic Treaty System Ready to Co-exist with a New United Nations Instrument for Areas beyond National Jurisdiction?" *Marine Policy* 122:104212. https://doi.org/10.1016/j.marpol.2020.104212.

Griggs, Lynden, and Gail Lugten. 2007. "Veil over the Nets (Unravelling Corporate Liability for IUU Fishing Offences)." *Marine Policy* 31 (2): 159–68. https://doi.org/10.1016/j.marpol.2006.05.015.

Grilly, Emily, Keith Reid, Sarah Lenel, and Julia Jabour. 2015. "The Price of Fish: A Global Trade Analysis of Patagonian (Dissostichus eleginoides) and Antarctic Toothfish (Dissostichus mawsoni)." *Marine Policy* 60:186–96. https://doi.org/10.1016/j. marpol.2015.06.006.

Haward, Marcus. 2017. "Contemporary Challenges to the Antarctic Treaty and Antarctic Treaty System: Australian Interests, Interplay and the Evolution of a Regime Complex." *Australian Journal of Maritime & Ocean Affairs* 9 (1): 21–24. https://doi. org/10.1080/18366503.2016.1245380.

Haward, Marcus, and Anthony Bergin. 2010. "Vision Not Vigilantism: Reply to Dodds and Hemmings." *Australian Journal of Politics & History* 56 (4): 612–16. https://doi. org/10.1111/j.1467-8497.2010.01574.x.

Haward, Marcus, Julia Jabour, and A. J. Press. 2012. "Antarctic Treaty System Ready for a Challenge." *Science* 338 (6107): 603. DOI: 10.1126/science.338.6107.603.

Haward, Marcus, and Tony Press. 2010. "Australia, the Antarctic Treaty and the Law of the Sea." *Australian Journal of Maritime & Ocean Affairs* 2 (1): 32–33. https://doi.org/10 .1080/18366503.2010.10815653.

Haward, Marcus G., and Joanna Vince. 2008. *Oceans Governance in the Twenty-First Century: Managing the Blue Planet.* Cheltenham, UK: Edward Elgar Publishing.

Hemmings, Alan D., and Tim Stephens. 2009. "Australia's Extended Continental Shelf: What Implications for Antarctica?" *Public Law Review* 20 (1): 9–16.

Hodgson-Johnston, Indi. 2015. "Australian Politics and Antarctic Sovereignty: Themes, Protagonists and Antagonists." *Australian Journal of Maritime & Ocean Affairs* 7 (3): 183–202. https://doi.org/10.1080/18366503.2015.1101811.

Jabour, Julia. 2013. "Biological Prospecting in the Antarctic: Fair Game." In *The Emerging Politics of Antarctica*, edited by Anne-Marie Brady, 242–58. Abingdon, UK: Routledge.

Johnson, Constance M. 2017. "The Relevance of the Southern Ocean to the Development of a Global Regime for Marine Areas beyond National Jurisdiction—an Uncommon Commons." *International Journal of Marine and Coastal Law* 32 (4): 709–32. https://doi.org/10.1163/15718085-13204026.

Joyner, Christopher C. 2011. "Potential Challenges to the Antarctic Treaty." In *Science Diplomacy: Antarctica, Science, and the Governance of International Spaces*, edited by Paul Arthur Berkman, Michael A. Lang, David W. H. Walton, and Oran Young, 97–102. Washington, DC: Smithsonian Institute.

Kaye, Stuart. 2015. "Australian Practice in Respect of the Continental Shelf beyond 200 Nautical Miles." *Marine Policy* 51:339–46. https://doi.org/10.1016/j. marpol.2014.09.016.

Kaye, Stuart B., and Donald R. Rothwell. 2002. "Southern Ocean Boundaries and Maritime Claims: Another Antarctic Challenge for the Law of the Sea?" *Ocean Development & International Law* 33 (3–4): 359–89. https://doi. org/10.1080/00908320290054828.

Liu, Nengye. 2019. "The Rise of China and the Antarctic Treaty System?" *Australian Journal of Maritime & Ocean Affairs* 11 (2): 120–31. https://doi.org/10.1080/183665 03.2019.1589897.

Liu, Nengye, and Cassandra M. Brooks. 2018. "China's Changing Position towards Marine Protected Areas in the Southern Ocean: Implications for Future Antarctic Governance." *Marine Policy* 94:189–95. https://doi.org/10.1016/j. marpol.2018.05.011.

Lord, Thomas. 2020. "The Antarctic Treaty System and the Peaceful Governance of Antarctica: The Role of the ATS in Promoting Peace at the Margins of the World." *Polar Journal*:1–19. https://doi.org/10.1080/2154896X.2020.1757821.

Masura, Julie, Joel E. Baker, Gregory Foster, Courtney Arthur, and Carlie Herring. 2015. Laboratory Methods for the Analysis of Microplastics in the Marine Environment: Recommendations for Quantifying Synthetic Particles in Waters and Sediments. Silver Springs, MD: US Department of Commerce, National Oceanic and Atmospheric Administration, [National Ocean Service], NOAA Marine Debris Program.

McGee, Jeffrey, and Marcus Haward. 2019. "Antarctic Governance in a Climate Changed World." *Australian Journal of Maritime & Ocean Affairs* 11 (2): 78–93. https://doi.or g/10.1080/18366503.2019.1637679.

McGee, Jeffrey, and Nengye Liu. 2019. "The Challenges for Antarctic Governance in the Early Twenty-First Century." *Australian Journal of Maritime & Ocean Affairs* 11 (2): 73–77. https://doi.org/10.1080/18366503.2019.1634940.

Nilsson, Jessica A., Elizabeth A. Fulton, Marcus Haward, and Craig Johnson. 2016. "Consensus Management in Antarctica's High Seas—Past Success and Current Challenges." *Marine Policy* 73:172–80. https://doi.org/https://doi.org/10.1016/j. marpol.2016.08.005.

Österblom, Henrik, and Örjan Bodin. 2012. "Global Cooperation among Diverse Organizations to Reduce Illegal Fishing in the Southern Ocean." *Conservation Biology* 26 (4): 638–48. https://doi.org/10.1111/j.1523-1739.2012.01850.x.

Petrossian, Gohar A., Rolf A. de By, and Ronald V. Clarke. 2016. "Illegal Long-Line Fishing and Albatross Extinction Risk." *Oryx* 52 (2): 336–45. https://doi.org/10.1017/ S0030605316000818.

Press, Tony. 2012. "Explainer: Australia's Extended Continental Shelf and Antarctica." *The Conversation*, 30 May 2012. https://theconversation.com/explainer-australias-extended-continental-shelf-and-antarctica-7298.

Readfearn, Graham. 2019. "Antarctic Marine Park: Conservationists Frustrated after Protection Bid Fails for Eighth Time." *The Guardian*, 2 November 2019. https:// www.theguardian.com/environment/2019/nov/02/antarctic-marine-park-conservationists-frustrated-after-protection-bid-fails-for-eight-time.

Roura, Ricardo M., Frits Steenhuisen, and Kees Bastmeijer. 2018. "The Shore Is the Limit: Marine Spatial Protection in Antarctica under Annex V of the Environmental Protocol to the Antarctic Treaty." *Polar Journal* 8 (2): 289–314. https://doi.org/10.10 80/2154896X.2018.1541549.

SCAR (Scientific Committee on Antarctic Research). n.d. "Welcome to the Scientific Committee on Antarctic Research." Scientific Committee on Antarctic Research, accessed 22 August 2022. https://www.scar.org/.

Scott, Shirley V. 2013. "The Evolving Antarctic Treaty System: Implications of Accommodating Developments in the Law of the Sea." In *The Law of the Sea and the Polar Regions*, edited by Erik. J. Molenaar, Alex. G. Oude Elferink, and Donald R. Rothwell, 17–34. Leiden, NL: Brill Nijhoff.

Secretariat of the Antarctic Treaty. 2019. "Resolution 5 (2019)—ATCM XLII—CEP XXII, Prague: Reducing Plastic Pollution in Antarctica and the Southern Ocean." Secretariat of the Antarctic Treaty, accessed 28 July 2022. https://www.ats.aq/devAS/Meetings/Measure/705.

Smith, Danielle, Jeffrey McGee, and Julia Jabour. 2016. "Marine Protected Areas: A Spark for Contestation over 'Rational Use' of Antarctic Marine Living Resources in the Southern Ocean?" *Australian Journal of Maritime & Ocean Affairs* 8 (3): 180–98. https://doi.org/10.1080/18366503.2016.1229398.

Sosin, Claudia. 2022. "Continental Shelves in the Antarctic Region: Implications for Resource Management." *Polar Journal* 12:1–26. https://doi.org/10.1080/2154896X.2022.2062559.

Suaria, Giuseppe, Vonica Perold, Jasmine R. Lee, Fabrice Lebouard, Stefano Aliani, and Peter G. Ryan. 2020. "Floating Macro- and Microplastics around the Southern Ocean: Results from the Antarctic Circumnavigation Expedition." *Environment International* 136:105494. https://doi.org/10.1016/j.envint.2020.105494.

Titterton, Haydn, and Marcus Haward. 2022. "The Kerguelen Plateau: Interactions between the Law of the Sea and the Antarctic Treaty." *Marine Policy* 138:104993.

Tuck, Geoffrey N., Tom Polacheck, and Cathy M. Bulman. 2003. "Spatio-Temporal Trends of Longline Fishing Effort in the Southern Ocean and Implications for Seabird Bycatch." *Biological Conservation* 114 (1): 1–27. https://doi.org/10.1016/S0006-3207(02)00378-6.

UNEP (United Nations Environment Programme). 2022. Draft Resolution: End Plastic Pollution: Towards an International Legally Binding Instrument (UNEP/EA.5/L.23/Rev.1). https://wedocs.unep.org/bitstream/handle/20.500.11822/38522/k2200647_-_unep-ea-5-l-23-rev-1_-_advance.pdf?sequence=1&isAllowed=y.

United Nations. n.d. "United Nations Intergovernmental Conference on Marine Biodiversity of Areas beyond National Jurisdiction." United Nations, accessed 22 August 2022. https://www.un.org/bbnj/.

United States of America. 2004. "Diplomatic Note to the United Nations Secretary-General, 3 December 2004." https://www.un.org/depts/los/clcs_new/submissions_files/aus04/clcs_03_2004_los_usatext.pdf.

Vince, Joanna, and Britta D. Hardesty. 2018. "Governance Solutions to the Tragedy of the Commons that Marine Plastics Have Become." *Frontiers in Marine Science* 5 (214). https://doi.org/10.3389/fmars.2018.00214.

Vince, Joanna, Chris Wilcox, and Britta D. Hardesty. 2021. "Progress and Challenges in Eliminating Illegal Fishing." *Fish and Fisheries* 22 (3). https://doi.org/10.1111/faf.12532.

Warner, Robin M. 2018. "The Australian and Antarctic Perspective on Global Ocean Governance." In *The IMLI Treatise on Global Ocean Governance*. Vol. 1, *UN and Global Ocean Governance*, edited by David Attard, David M. Ong, and Dino Kritsiotis, 301–23. Oxford: Oxford University Press.

Wehrmann, Dorothea. 2018. Critical Geopolitics of the Polar Regions: An Inter-American Perspective. London: Routledge.

Young, Oran R. 2012. "Building an International Regime Complex for the Arctic: Current Status and Next Steps." *Polar Journal* 2 (2): 391–407. https://doi.org/10.1080/215489 6X.2012.735047.

Zhang, Mengzhu, Marcus Haward, and Jeffrey McGee. 2020. "Marine Plastic Pollution in the Polar South: Responses from Antarctic Treaty System." *Polar Record* 56:1–7.

6

Australia's East Antarctic Geostrategic Futures: Nirvana or Doom Inbound?

Peter Layton

Antarctic issues are becoming fashionable once more.[1] There was a long stagnation that began when the Cold War ended, easing geostrategic pressures and making Antarctica less salient to the governments of the world. Circumstances have changed, however, and an increasing number of states are again becoming deeply engaged. With this reawakened interest, Antarctica's future is becoming increasingly fluid and uncertain. This concerns Australia, for Antarctica is its closest southern neighbour; the country also claims almost half the frozen continent, a territorial declaration regarding an area equal to some 80 per cent of Australia itself.[2]

Australia's claim and those of six other nations have, however, been deliberately set aside. This has created the unusual situation according to which, in an international system apparently completely divided into individual sovereign states, Antarctica is not deemed anyone's territory. Antarctica is instead managed multilaterally through international committees based on mutually decided treaties and agreements. An increasing number of states now want to influence these treaties and agreements.

Antarctica's isolation and inhospitableness have allowed it to remain largely unaffected by humans. The resulting pristine natural environment makes Antarctica an ideal laboratory for a range of scientific activities and has led to science becoming the defining feature of contemporary

Antarctica operations. In turn, this primacy has shaped the strategic arrangements that guide interactions between the interested states.

The hallmarks of the Antarctic Treaty System (ATS) that has developed over the last sixty years are science, environmental protection, and avoiding militarization. The ATS regulates activities south of the 60 degrees south latitude, an area within which lie the Antarctica land mass, associated islands, and significant ice shelves (Secretariat of the Antarctic Treaty 1959, article 6; CCAMLR 1980, article 1). The four agreements that comprise the ATS, and their supporting institutions, have been instrumental in maintaining a stable, rules-based order in Antarctica despite the presence of multiple geostrategic changes elsewhere. It is considered to be an "unprecedented success in international law and diplomacy" (Fogarty 2011, 15).

The central institutional pillar of the ATS is the Antarctic Treaty, signed by 12 states in Washington at the height of the Cold War, in December 1959. Today, there are 54 parties to the Antarctic Treaty made up of 29 Consultative Parties, those states conducting "substantial research activity" in Antarctica and with decision-making rights within the system, and 25 Non-consultative Parties, states that are invited to observe but do not have decision-making rights. The Antarctic Treaty is unique because it is "a peace treaty not to stop hostilities but to prevent them" (Bergin et al. 2013, 5).

Three articles establish the ATS's key features. Article 1 begins with a clear statement of intent: "Antarctica shall be used for peaceful purposes only." The article goes on to prohibit "measures of a military nature," but not the use of military force for peaceful purposes. Article 2 establishes the principle of scientific freedom and co-operation, which remains the cornerstone of international involvement in the region. Article 4 freezes disputes over territorial claims. The treaty acknowledges that some states have laid claim to Antarctic territory, but neither supports nor denies these claims. Further, it prohibits the making of new claims to territory. This article of the treaty has proved resilient in the face of growing interest in Antarctica. There are only seven states with Antarctic claims, but twenty-nine states operate research bases on the continent.

Not all fifty-three Antarctic Treaty parties have signed the other three agreements that comprise the ATS: the 1972 Convention for the Conservation of Antarctic Seals, the 1980 Convention on the Conservation of Antarctic Marine Living Resources (CCAMLR), and the 1991 Protocol on Environmental Protection to the Antarctic Treaty (the Madrid Protocol). Despite the smaller number of parties being formally bound by these three agreements, they are generally abided by.

The two agreements of concern to Australia are the CCAMLR and the Madrid Protocol. The CCAMLR is the primary mechanism for managing the Southern Ocean's under-exploited fishery resources. Various conservation measures have been adopted by the CCAMLR that cover both contracting parties and non-parties to the convention.

In contrast, the Madrid Protocol designates "Antarctica as a natural reserve, devoted to peace and science." The key clause, article 7, simply states that "Any activity relating to mineral resources, other than scientific research, shall be prohibited." If at sea, sustainable fishing is allowed; onshore, exploitation is banned.

Away from making rules in distant capitals, there is increasing activity by states on the ground in Antarctica. The big wave of accession by states to the Antarctica Treaty was during the late Cold War, in the 1980s, with others less hurriedly joining in the decades after that. Over the last fifteen years, many nations have moved beyond simply attending international meetings to building and maintaining bases on the continent.

Old, refurbished, and new Antarctic bases are now seen as allowing the participating states to be much better able to influence the development of the future rules governing Antarctica. For many of these states, the bases have a further perceived benefit in ensuring their countries are well positioned to undertake marine, genetic, and mineral resource exploitation when and if this is allowed. Lastly, for a small group of states, there is the intangible lure of national prestige, a factor most attractive to new great powers like China, India, and Brazil. There are now some eighty separate facilities open in Antarctica, with more under construction.

This chapter initially examines Antarctica today with a focus on activities in the East Antarctic region Australia claims. This is then used to look beyond twenty years to discuss four plausible geostrategic futures. The future of the Antarctic is uncertain but seems to lie within definable boundaries; a range of possible alternative futures appears discernible. It is important to note that this chapter simply discusses future possible geostrategic environments and does not develop any strategy intended to shape the future in any particular, desired direction.

East Antarctica Today

In broad terms, Antarctica comprises three major areas: the Antarctic Peninsula, which snakes up toward South America and is an extension of the Andes; the small West Antarctica region, which is relatively low in elevation; and the much larger East Antarctic region, which is mostly a very high plateau. West and East Antarctica are separated by the 3,000-kilometre-long, 4,000-metre-high Transantarctic Mountain range. The range is punctuated by volcanoes, with the best known, Mount Erebus, still active (Talalay 2014, 5–8).

Although Antarctica is almost totally covered by glacial ice, this is not a single sheet. The East Antarctic glacial ice sheet flowing east is much larger, thicker, and older than the West Antarctic glacial ice sheet flowing west. This ice cover ensures Antarctica has the highest average surface elevation of any continent at around 2,000 metres above sea level, albeit with distinct differences between West and East Antarctica. In West Antarctica, the average elevation is 1,300 metres; in East Antarctica it averages 2,200 metres. Inland East Antarctica's ice is very thick; at Dome A the surface elevation is more than 4,000 metres. As these figures suggest, in East Antarctica the low-lying coastal area is very narrow with the ice sheet rising steeply from it (Press 2018, 129–32).

East Antarctica, by global standards, is very cold and very dry. Staff at Russia's inland Vostok Station recorded –89.2 degrees Celsius with recent satellite-collected data revealing a temperature of –93.2 degrees Celsius in some small valleys elsewhere in the East Antarctic plateau (Fischetti 2013). Australia's East Antarctic territory is almost completely covered in thick, permanent ice with only some small ice- and snow-free coastal areas. While 0.4 per cent of the Antarctic is free of ice and snow, almost all of this is outside Australia's claimed area, mainly in the Antarctic Peninsula (Australian Government 2021). Being ice free on land does not mean sea ice is not present, only that the land areas are very dry. Sea ice forms seasonally around Antarctica, which means ship access to the coast is only possible during two or three months of summer.

Within the territory that Australia claims there are several bases operated by a range of countries. The most active new participant in East Antarctica base development is China.

China in East Antarctica

China initially joined the ATS in 1983, became a Consultative Party in 1985, signed the Madrid Protocol in 1998, and agreed to the CCAMLR in 2007. Today, China has undertaken some thirty-eight national Antarctic expeditions and runs five research stations in Antarctica; the newest is on Inexpressible Island, within New Zealand's claimed Antarctic territory, and was completed in 2022 (Lei 2021).

In 2005 China's top polar scientist advocated for his country to become a "polar great power"—that is, a power strong in military, scientific, and economic terms in both the North and South Polar regions (Brady 2017, 3). President Xi Jinping first publicly embraced this idea when visiting Hobart in 2014, giving the polar great power expression his imprimatur and consequently wide Chinese public usage. The president further outlined that the guiding principles for Chinese polar activities should be "understand, protect, and use" (Liu 2019, 126).

In this, the ATS has some real advantages for great powers. Any country with the requisite economic strength can have unfettered access across the whole of the Antarctic landmass and littoral without having to consider other nations' rights. With such access, great powers can assess the continent's resources, locate important natural assets, and develop the latent capabilities to extract them when circumstances change. In 2017, Chinese vice-premier Zhang Gaoli noted there was a "need for a proper balance between the protection and utilization of Antarctica in order to achieve green and sustainable development of the continent and unleash its potential and value" (EFE-EPA 2017).

In the Chinese political system, polar affairs are part of maritime affairs, thus, becoming a polar great power falls within the ambit of China's maritime strategy. The State Oceanic Administration informally distributed China's first white paper on Antarctic matters in May 2017 during the fortieth Antarctic Treaty Consultative Meeting in Beijing. Titled "China's Antarctic Activities," the white paper noted that China had made "significant progress in its Antarctic activities in terms of integrated logistic support" (Liu 2019, 123).

In the last ten years, China has worked to extend its presence over a relatively narrow triangular area of East Antarctica. Three of China's Antarctic bases, three of its airfields, and two field camps are in this sector. China's main East Antarctic base, Zhongshan, opened in 1989 near Russia's older Progress facility. Zhongshan has doubled in size in recent years, and is now a medium-sized, year-round base that acts as both a research facility and a coastal support base for activities further inland. It can support twenty-five staff in winter and sixty in summer.

Inland Taishan was opened in 2014 and is a summer-only base that supports the much further inland Kunlun facility, together with expeditions into the nearby Grove Mountains. Opened in 2009, the summer-only Kunlun Station is the second-southernmost research base in Antarctica, behind only the United States' South Pole Station. Taishan and Kunlun have 600-metre ice runways and can accommodate twenty and twenty-eight staff, respectively, over summer. Illustrating the protracted nature of building infrastructure in the harsh Antarctica environment, automatic meteorological stations began operating at Taishan and Kunlun in December 2021, some five and nine years, respectively, after building commenced on each station (Global Times 2021).

Kunlun, being well inland and at high altitude (some 4,000 metres), has excellent clear air and dark sky qualities, perfect for imaging telescopes used for astronomical observations and space debris monitoring. The latter is becoming increasingly important for a nation's civilian and military space operations as near-earth orbits become more crowded (Layton 2019, 33–36). Maintaining the complex equipment needed for space situational awareness across winter would be difficult and require Kunlun becoming a year-round facility, but the location is nearly perfect for polar orbiting satellite and debris detection.

China previously used Russian airfields as part of the logistical support of its Antarctic activities. In recent years, however, China has begun developing its own air hub infrastructure. In 2014 it built an ice runway at the Zhongshan base, and then in 2016 it operated its first fixed-wing aircraft from there. In 2018, China announced plans to build a more permanent

1,500-metre airstrip of compacted snow on a glacier some 28 kilometres from Zhongshan.

Given its length, initially the only aircraft based there will be China's sole Basler BT-67, a turboprop-powered DC-3 specially modified in Canada for Antarctic research operations. Renamed as the Xue Ying 601 (Snow Eagle), the BT-67 is operated by Kenn Borek Air, a Canadian air charter company, and used for summer air operations supporting the two inland bases and various research expeditions within 1,300 kilometres of Zhongshan. The BT-67 deploys in summer to Zhongshan through South America and a multi-base hop across Antarctica.

The new airfield will take several years to become operational but will give China experience in a polar airfield's construction and maintenance, ground support, airspace management, and navigation aids. China's official *Science and Technology Daily* noted that the airbase "will provide a foundation for operating large aircraft, creating multiplane services, and building an Antarctic air traffic network in the future . . . and [allow] China [to] have a say in the international management of Antarctic air space" (Zhen 2018).

China's base expansion has created two specific concerns. First, China has developed the BeiDou multi-satellite navigation system, broadly similar in function to the US Global Positioning System, the European Galileo, and the Russian GLONASS. BeiDou ground-receiving and reference stations have been installed at Zhongshan and Kunlun, and, while very useful for Antarctic operations, will apparently also improve the overall global performance of the system, particularly in terms of locational accuracy. The dual-use nature of BeiDou has led to worries about the militarization of Antarctica. Similar concerns were raised when Norway built the Trollsat Satellite Station at its Antarctic station. Trollsat supports Galileo and is Norway's main contribution to this major European project.

Second, concerns have been raised about China's proposal for a new Antarctic Specially Managed Area (ASMA) at Kunlun. ASMAs assist co-operation in busy areas and are managed by a single country or group of countries. There are several ASMAs across Antarctica, including at the United States' South Pole Station. Some see geopolitics behind China's proposal, with the University of Canterbury's Anne-Marie Brady believing the ASMA is seen by China as a "soft presence . . . [a] subtle way for [the] state to control territory" (2017, 10). Lacking an international endorsement for its ASMA proposal, China attempted to get multi-national agreement to a code of conduct for the area, but this also failed (Gothe-Snape 2019).

Russia in East Antarctica

While many bases closed after the Soviet Union's collapse, in recent years Russia has embarked on a reconstruction and reconstitution program. In East Antarctica, the country now operates two small summer-only bases (Druzhnaya 4 and Molodezhnaya), a small year-round base (Vostok), a medium-sized, year-round base (Progress 2), and a large year-round base (Mirny). Vostok is well inland, whereas the others are coastal facilities. Mirny is by a significant margin the largest base of any nation in East Antarctica; it can accommodate 60 staff during winter and 169 during summer. Of note is that Russia's old Novo airbase in Queen Maud Land, just outside of Australia's East Antarctic claim, has returned to life as a major airhead used by some eleven nations. In mid-2020 the Russian government approved an action plan to build new wintering facilities at Vostok and Mirny; construction commenced at Vostok in 2021 (Wenger 2022).

Two concerns have been frequently raised about Russia's bases. The first relates to Russia's seeming deep interest in resource exploitation. Russia's ten-year Antarctic Strategy, formally approved in 2020 but not publicly released, apparently aims to "strengthen the economic capacity of Russia . . . through complex investigations of the Antarctic mineral, hydrocarbon, and other natural resources" (Boyd 2019; see also Buchanan 2021). The second is again the issue of navigation satellite systems, with Russia installing GLONASS equipment at Progress and Mirny.

New problems have now arisen with Russia's invasion of the Ukraine. Russia is deeply involved in the Dronning Maud Land Air Network (DROMLAN). The network has been operating for some two decades and involves Belgium, Finland, Germany, India, Japan, Norway, Russia, South Africa, Sweden, the Netherlands, and the United Kingdom. DROMLAN uses services provided by the South African company Antarctic Logistics Center International for the intercontinental link flown by Russian Il-76 transport aircraft from Cape Town to the Novo ice runway airfield and

Kenn Borek Air ski-equipped aircraft for the intra-continental air services that fan out from Novo (Colombo 2019).

Many of the DROMLAN participating nations actively oppose Russia's war and have introduced significant economic and business sanctions against the nation. It is unlikely that DROMLAN can continue in its present form, while Canadian company Kenn Borek Air may no longer be permitted to use the Novo airfield. A related matter is the renovation of the inland Vostok base in East Antarctica. The project is partially sponsored by the now war-sanctioned Russian oligarch Leonid Mikhelson, the major shareholder of gas producer Novatek. Reportedly, Mikhelson is providing about $60 million of the project's cost (Walters 2022).

Other National Facilities in East Antarctica

Larseman Hills Stations

Four nations have stations clustered closely together, within roughly a couple of kilometres of each other, in the ice-free Prydz Bay area. Along with Russia's Progress Station and China's Zhongshan (both already noted), India and Romania also have research stations. India's Bharati is a medium-size, year-round base and is the country's second active Antarctic research facility. Bharati was established in 2012 and can support twenty-four staff during winter and forty-seven in summer. Romania's Law-Racovita summer-only station opened in 2006. It was Australia's Law Station, originally constructed in 1986 and now rebuilt. The station can accommodate up to thirteen staff.

France/Italy

The Concordia Research Station opened in 2005 and is a medium-size, year-round facility established—like China's Kunlun and Russia's Vostok—well inland on the high Antarctic Plateau. Located at an elevation of some 3,200 metres, the station can support fifteen staff during winter and sixty staff in summer. Concordia has a 1,500-metre ice runway (Mekarnia and Frenot 2013, 178–80).

Belarus

The Vechernyaya summer-only station opened in 2016 some twenty-seven kilometres from Russia's also summer-only Molodezhnaya base. The coastal station can accommodate up to ten staff.

United States

Just outside East Antarctica, at the geographic South Pole, the United States maintains a very large, year-round facility that dates to 1957. The Amundsen-Scott South Pole Station has a surrounding ASMA and includes the Jack F. Paulus Skiway, a 3,500-metre-long snow runway.

Australia's Antarctica

The United Kingdom first claimed territory in Antarctica in 1841. In 1933, these claims were transferred to Australia under the Australian Antarctic Territory Acceptance Act. In 1954, Australia's first continental research facility, Mawson Station, was established; it is now the longest continuously operating station south of the Antarctic Circle.

Since then, Australia has built another two permanent scientific research stations in the Australian Antarctic Territory. All contribute to an internationally significant, ongoing scientific research program. The Department of Agriculture, Water and the Environment, through its Australian Antarctic Division (AAD), leads, coordinates, and delivers the Australian Antarctic program and administers the Australian Antarctic Territory.

In 2014, the Australian Government commissioned former AAD head Anthony Press to provide recommendations concerning future national Antarctic policies. The resulting report warned that "Australia's standing in Antarctic affairs is eroding because of historical under-investment at a time when new players are emerging in Antarctica" (Press 2014, 2). Acting on this, and after considering recommendations of a Senate inquiry, the Australian Government in 2016 released the *Australian Antarctic Strategy and 20 Action Year Plan* (Australian Government 2016). This document, in setting out the vision and the policy intentions for Australia's future Antarctic engagement, described Australia's national interests as follows:

- maintain Antarctica's freedom from strategic and/or political confrontation;

- preserve our sovereignty over the Australian Antarctic Territory, including our sovereign rights over adjacent offshore areas;

- support a strong and effective Antarctic Treaty System;

- conduct world-class scientific research consistent with national priorities;

- protect the Antarctic environment, having regard to its special qualities and effects on our region;

- be informed about and able to influence developments in a region geographically proximate to Australia; and

- foster economic opportunities arising from Antarctica and the Southern Ocean, consistent with our Antarctic Treaty System obligations, including the ban on mining and oil drilling. (Australian Government 2016, 17)

There are some seeming incompatibilities between the various interests, especially between preserving Australian sovereignty and supporting the ATS. The ATS sets aside Australia's claim, so it does not preserve Australia's sovereignty but instead disregards it. Indeed, under the ATS, Australia's claim seems somewhat anachronistic.

The counter-argument is that while the ATS continues, no nation can make a counterclaim to Australia's. From this perspective, the ATS keeps Australia's claim safe, and, crucially, achieves another key Australian objective: keeping Antarctica free from strategic conflict.

Supporting this position is the fact that the ATS is now sixty years old. It has succeeded not just in constraining geostrategic tensions in Antarctica, but also in encouraging rivals—such as the United States and the USSR during the Cold War—to collaborate in scientific research. The ATS has provided a durable framework for co-operative internationalism, allowing governments, including Australia's, to advance the idealistic notion that their primary Antarctic objective is gaining scientific know-ledge that is then made available to all.

Even so, the ATS may at some stage fade away under rising geostrategic tensions or intense resource exploitation demands. In such an eventuality, Australia's claim could become a useful diplomatic tool in negotiating a new Antarctic regime. The claim then becomes an important strategic asset. Daniel Bray has written that

> Preserving Australia's claim can . . . be seen as a hedge against the collapse of the ATS—a situation where histori-cal claims would give Australia a strong diplomatic position in constructing a new regime and in any formal resolution of sovereignty claims. But perhaps most importantly, Aus-tralia's claim helps to deny sovereignty to other states by ensuring that its referent territory will always be a contest-ed space should any other state seek sovereignty rights or exclusive access to Antarctic resources in the future. (2016, 268–69)

The obvious tensions between claiming sovereignty and strongly supporting the ATS, which disregards sovereignty, suggest a strong bi-focal approach in Australian Antarctica strategic policy (Haward and Cooper 2014). Such an apparent incoherence provides a usefully flexible strategic stance in a somewhat uncertain Antarctica future. To achieve its various interlocking policy objectives, Australia has made considerable investments in Antarctic bases, supporting infrastructure and ongoing activities.

Australia's East Antarctic Operations

Australia has three medium-sized, year-round bases spread out along the East Antarctic coast, principally supported logistically and admin-istratively from Hobart, Australia's most southerly state capital. In East Antarctic terms, Australia's three bases are a significant presence, particu-larly as they are year-round facilities. However, there is a sharp distinc-tion between these coastal stations and the inland, high-altitude facilities built on the high East Antarctic Plateau with its average elevation of some

3,000 metres. Australia is re-acquiring an Antarctic overland traverse capability but has no inland bases, as China, Russia, France, and Italy do, even if some are summer-only facilities.

The Australian bases are logistically supported using air and sea transport, with shipping providing the logistical backbone. For some three decades, this involved the *Aurora Australis*, an 8,400-tonne, multi-purpose research and resupply icebreaker. The ship provided essential fuel and supplies to the three Australian stations, undertook personnel transfer, and was used for marine scientific research. Its Romanian-built replacement, the *Nuyina*, at 25,500 tonnes displacement, is significantly larger than the *Aurora Australis* and has much greater cargo and fuel-carrying capacity. After sea trials, the *Nuyina* arrived in Hobart in October 2021 and commenced Antarctic operations in the 2021–22 summer season, completing a thirty-nine-day voyage to resupply the Davis and Casey Stations.

Air operations are increasingly important, especially for personnel movement. Mawson has a summer ski runway constructed either on nearby sea ice (if present), or more often inland about 10 kilometres from Mawson at Rumdoodle. Davis station in the ice-free Vestfold Hills uses a ski runway on the Davis Plateau some 40 kilometres from the station and reconstructed each year on snow.

Casey's principal airfield is Wilkins, some 70 kilometres inland and sited 700 metres above sea level. The Wilkins runway has a foundation of natural glacial ice, which after annual surface grooming can accept wheeled, large transport aircraft. Wilkins is operational between October and March each year but closes for about six weeks in the middle of summer as warmer temperatures cause subsurface melting that undermines runway strength and creates blisters. This midsummer melt issue is likely to worsen as global warming intensifies.

Air operations can be usefully divided into inter- and intra-continental. Since 2007, the AAD has operated an intercontinental air link using wheeled A319CJ passenger jet aircraft flying between Hobart and Wilkins airfield carrying personnel and high-priority, lighter-weight cargo. Since 2016, Royal Australian Air Force C-17A heavy-lift aircraft also fly into Wilkins to deliver high-priority outsize cargo.

Since 2010, the AAD has contracted to Kenn Borek Air for intra-continental services using Basler BT-67 and DHC-6 Twin Otter aircraft, and to a Tasmanian company, Helicopter Resources, for Squirrel helicopter support. The fixed-wing aircraft provide services from the Wilkins entry point to the other Australian stations, Mawson, and Davis, as well as supporting distant inland expeditions. The Squirrels are sea- and land-based. When operating at sea, the helicopters undertake ship-to-shore carriage of expeditioners and cargo. Two or three Squirrels are also typically land-based at Davis during summer supporting numerous scientific programs and deploying, supporting, and retrieving field parties.

The 2016 Strategy and Action Plan announced an intention to develop a paved year-round runway in a rare ice-free area near Davis station to be capable of supporting intercontinental flights. There are no paved runways in East Antarctica, although on the other side of the continent, at the northernmost tip of the Antarctica Peninsula, there is a small airbase operated year-round by Argentina. However, the climatic conditions, variable weather, the ability to work only in summer, and the great distance from Australia all combine to make building a runway in East Antarctica a very difficult task. The planned airfield was unlikely to be in service until the late 2030s. In November 2021, the project was cancelled on cost and environmental grounds.

The Antarctic Region in Twenty Years' Time

Intuitively we know the future is always uncertain; our predictions may or may not eventuate. A way around this dilemma is through using an alternative futures approach. This approach tries to make use of the certainty of uncertainty, initially by being more specific about what uncertainty is. The type of uncertainty encountered in a problem may be conceptually classified as follows:

- **Level 1.** The residual uncertainty is irrelevant to making strategic decisions as robust analysis shows only a single possible future with change linear and evolutionary.

- **Level 2.** The future will be one of two or three discrete scenarios.

- **Level 3.** Although there are only a few uncertain dimensions, analysis is unable to reduce the future to a limited number of discrete scenarios. A range of futures along a continuum for each identified dimension can be identified. Uncertainty is bounded.

- **Level 4.** The numerous dimensions of uncertainty interact, making it impossible to determine a range of potential outcomes or scenarios, or to identify the relevant variables that will define the future. The uncertainty is unbounded. (Courtney 2001, 15–38)

In applying these uncertainty levels to the future of East Antarctica it is apparent that level 1 is too simplistic as there are many possible futures, not just one. Level 2 is similarly afflicted in that the future, being non-linear and subject to "butterfly" effects, cannot be reduced to only two or three tightly scripted alternatives. However, the chaotic vision of level 4 also seems inappropriate as there are certain dimensions or parameters from the present that carry on into the future. The future will build on the past; it is not totally unbounded.

Level 3 seems the relevant type of uncertainty when considering how East Antarctica may change. This level of uncertainty means little can be accurately predicted based on past events, but it is possible to examine the present and discern important existing trends and emerging drivers. A bounded range of possible futures can be determined, although which specific scenario will eventuate is unable to be ascertained.

Antarctic Alternative Futures

In broad terms, there seems to be some fundamental uncertainties when thinking about Antarctica's future. Twenty-nine states unquestionably want a say in how the ATS evolves. They are already conducting substantial and expensive research activity within Antarctica as part of ensuring they possess ATS decision-making powers. These states all have different agendas and objectives they wish to advance but these will not all be easy to reconcile, and some will probably be in conflict. The ATS governance mechanism will evolve in the future, but how that eventuates is not certain.

The greatest emerging tension seems to be between states that wish to keep Antarctica a pristine wilderness for scientific research and those that wish to exploit its marine, genetic, and mineral resources. The eventual future balance that will be achieved between these competing interests is uncertain.

Antarctica does not exist in a political void. The twenty-nine states deeply involved in the ATS bring their national ambitions and international relationships with them. Geostrategic stresses affect the Antarctic even as the ATS tries to limit their more harmful aspects. Antarctica's particular uncertainties in relation to governance and resource exploitation are themselves set within the context of the wider international system and its own uncertainties.

Future uncertainties are important, but they are not the whole picture. In thinking about Antarctica's future, distinct continuities, strong trends, and certain assumptions appear evident. In terms of continuities, in the future Antarctica will remain a tough place to get to, work in, and survive in, especially during the winter. Decisions relating to human engagement in Antarctica will take time to be implemented. In general, most activities can only happen during summer months, slowing progress down. Furthermore, such activities are costly, making decision making to fund them usually protracted.

The ATS involves many states, so achieving agreement on new initiatives takes time and patience. In some cases, this is deliberate and institutionalized. The Madrid Protocol, for example, puts off even debating changing Antarctica's resource-exploitation regime until 2048. Of course, states can just ignore the protocol, or flaunt it, but such steps in themselves would impose friction, constraints, and delays. In general, changes in how humans relate to Antarctica or the ATS will remain slow and, for people used to the twenty-first century's frenetic pace, surprisingly seasonal.

Considering trends, the dominant one in the current era is climate change. In this there is no uncertainty: Antarctica will be affected by climate change in all alternative futures. Access for large vessels that are not ice-strengthened is likely to become easier, but sea ice movements may be less predictable and more frequently trap vessels. The easier access combined with a longer summer season will allow more time to undertake scientific research or tourism, but Antarctica's unique flora and fauna will decline as other warmer-weather species move in. In this, the effects of climate change are happening much faster in West Antarctica, where they are being measured in years. So far, the visible pace of change is slower in East Antarctica, with its much thicker ice sheet, being measured in decades.

More broadly, across the globe there will be a progressive increase in weather variability. Food production will become more difficult through longer droughts and changed temperature patterns. There may be associated population movements, wars, and epidemics. Accordingly, some states may shift their interest and research funding away from costly Antarctic science, with its slow rate of return, toward more pressing, greater-payoff initiatives. The Antarctic may become a less important investment to states as climate change deepens.

The various uncertainties, continuities, trends, and assumptions can be usefully combined using the scenario matrix planning methodology. This uses two selected key uncertainties axes to derive four quadrants, each an alternative future qualitatively different from the others in a logical, non-random way.

Such an endeavour has recently been undertaken in a seminal New Zealand study about Antarctica's futures (Liggett et al. 2017). The axes devised were appropriate for the specific study but have some shortcomings in being particular to Antarctica and so less able to be extended into comparative examinations of Arctic alternative futures. Moreover, they only tangentially situate the future of Antarctica within the wider international system.

Given this chapter's geostrategic thrust, it is useful to place the alternative futures the wide-ranging New Zealand study created within a broadly strategic studies-related framework. To achieve this, a futures framework originally developed to provide strategic insights for the Netherlands and since adopted by the Australian and UK defence forces is useful (Netherlands Ministry of Defence 2010; Department of Defence 2016; UK Ministry of Defence 2018) In this futures framework, the two axes were, first, states having more or less power in the international system and, second, states being co-operative or competitive toward each other. The two axes in crossing create four quadrants: co-operative/less state power, co-operative/more state power, competitive/less state power, and competitive/more state power.

The four alternative futures derived from the New Zealand study have been somewhat modified and then mapped using a geostrategic futures

Table 6.1. Antarctic Alternative Futures

Alternative future	Quadrant	Description
Networked	Co-operative/less state power	ATS becomes regime for the collaborative management of resource exploitation. Focus on technology development and testing to support responsible exploitation. Commercial operators regulated. NGOs become partners in regulation development. Marine resource exploitation expanding, diversification into marine bioprospecting and aquaculture. Tourism declining.
Multilateral	Co-operative/more state power	Maintain ATS governance arrangements. Ongoing national investment in Antarctic science. Highest priorities environmental management and scientific research. Sustainable marine resource exploitation. Fisheries maintained within CCAMLR targets. Marine protected areas established across Southern Ocean. Sustainable tourism but not expanding.
Fragmented	Competitive/less state power	ATS collapsing. Declining national interest in Antarctica with falling investment. States acting independently driven by commercial imperatives. Private investment favoured. Privately owned facilities researching alternative uses for Antarctic resources. Illegal, unreported, and unregulated fishing significantly increases. Land-based niche tourism.
Multipolar	Competitive/more state power	ATS increasingly ignored. States driven by their competing national interests. Focus on technology development to improve exploitation. States make bilateral agreements to assist exploitation. States support commercial ventures and privately owned facilities. Environmental standards only of secondary interest. Tourism expanding with rapid diversification, including developing land-based facilities.

framework onto the four quadrants. This creates four alternative futures, labelled for ease as Networked, Multilateral, Fragmented, and Multipolar. Each alternative future is described in table 6.1 above and in more detail in the text following. Each world is different, although it is possible to imagine how particular current trends when extrapolated might possibly lead to each world in twenty years' time.

None of these four futures is necessarily expected to emerge. Instead, the hope is that the future is broadly captured somewhere within the wide span of possibilities all four worlds cover. Ideally, these four alternative futures bracket the range of future strategic environments that may eventuate. Importantly, no one world is considered more likely than the others. The futures are so developed to both allow the differences between them to be explored and to form the basis for later development of strategies that might try to shape the future in a desired direction.

Multilateral Future

In this alternative future, globalization is ongoing. States are the most important actors in the international system and are focused on making absolute gains through co-operation. States are deeply engaged in strong regional and global multilateral institutions, with the UN playing a particularly important role in global governance. There is a growing sense of global community with foreign aid, foreign direct investment, and subsidies seen as preferred ways to help less-developed countries. The emphasis on co-operation, though, means that to address problems there is a need to build consensus, which can be both difficult and time consuming.

In terms of Antarctica, this future world is essentially a better today. In it, states uphold and strengthen the ATS with scientific research remaining the highest priority. The ATS deepens through better funding of the Antarctic Treaty Secretariat and the development of a wide-ranging co-operative work program among the Antarctic Treaty parties. Sustainable marine resource exploitation continues with krill and finfish catches maintained within CCAMLR targets; a series of marine protected areas is established across the Southern Ocean. The global importance of Antarctic science is increasingly publicly recognized, leading governments to invest more in national and international research initiatives. A mature relationship develops with the tourism industry, thereby enhancing research opportunities and including citizen science activities. Tourism focuses on sustainability, peaks around 2030, and then plateaus.

Networked Future

In the networked alternative future, globalization is deepening, with non-state actors and states working together to make absolute gains. There are strong regional and global multilateral institutions, including a powerful UN. However, the participants are diverse and dissimilar, ranging across states, large commercial organizations, civil society groups, and non-governmental organizations (NGOs). There is a broadly based global governance regime, a strong sense of global community, and a desire to solve problems through consensus.

This future world envisages states, commercial entities, and non-state actors continuing to support the ATS but with all shifting to a more utilitarian perspective. The ATS is perceived as a regime for the collaborative management of resource exploitation. It is strengthened through increased membership and the negotiation of additional resource-management agreements, including the return of the Antarctic mineral resource convention and negotiation of a convention to regulate bioprospecting. Marine exploitation is expanding on broadly sustainable terms, with diversification into marine bioprospecting and aquaculture. NGOs join the ATS to contribute through a partnership approach to the new sustainable exploitation regulations.

Research activities are increasingly moving to focus on developing the technology appropriate to sustainable resource exploitation. An international association, the Council of Managers of National Antarctic Program, adjusts its focus from coordinating scientific research toward providing education to new commercially oriented operators, together with coordinating safety management and search and rescue activities. Tourism is in decline as the wilderness aspects of Antarctica decline, but some niche and extreme tourism remains.

Fragmented Future

In the fragmented alternative future, globalization is declining. Conflict is persistent and widespread, with non-state actors and states actively competing against other non-state actors and states. All see advantage in working with other states and non-state actors to advance their aims. The catch cry is "the enemy of my enemy is my friend," with short-term, continually shifting alliances of convenience common.

This future world envisages Antarctica and Antarctic science becoming increasingly irrelevant to governments globally. With the consequent decreasing political and financial investment, the ATS is steadily collapsing. Environmental NGOs continue to advocate for conservation but gain little traction. There is a reduced public awareness of Antarctic issues as the media lose interest in the Antarctic and political commitment to the region becomes largely symbolic.

Reduced funding means international collaboration becomes hard to achieve. Science projects are now small-scale, short-term, and disparate, with many states encouraging national Antarctic programs to seek private investment to support their research. State-owned Antarctic research bases struggle to justify their continuance, become more commercially focused, and are complemented or replaced by private facilities investigating resource-exploitation options. Harvesting of Southern Ocean resources continues, but diminishing international co-operation means the level of illegal, unreported, and unregulated fishing is significantly increasing. As regulation evaporates, tourism moves into land-based facilities offering niche opportunities.

Multipolar Future

In the multipolar world, globalization is splintering, shaped by intense great power competition. Seeking security, small states and middle powers now cluster around these great powers in various types of blocs and alliance structures. The great powers are focused on improving their bloc's relative power, strength, and influence. The great powers may then at times offer military, economic, and diplomatic inducements to attract lesser states to leave existing blocs and join theirs.

In this alternative future, the ATS becomes progressively irrelevant and ignored. States shift from being part of the multilateral governance of scientific research toward making bilateral agreements with others about exploiting mutually beneficial commercial opportunities. States are now focusing on their own individual national or bloc interests and are supporting private ventures and privately owned facilities in the competition for resources. Environmental standards are of only secondary interest to the companies and states active in Antarctica.

The main research thrust is now on technology for better resource exploitation. The public interest in Antarctica has also become focused on the commercial benefits possible and a range of new entrepreneurial ventures has emerged. Tourism reflects this with a less regulated, more competitive industry that has diversified into land-based hotels and visitor facilities.

Conclusion

The four worlds are all different in particular ways, whether in ATS governance or the emphasis on resource exploitation or scientific research. Only one alternative future is like today.

An important aspect of using alternative futures for thinking is that no single world is more likely than another. Even so, it is interesting to speculate that the world could be moving from our contemporary multi-lateral, rules-based structure toward one where globalization seemingly splinters and a multipolar world then emerges. Some, sensing the rise of China and the relative decline of the United States, might be tempted to seize on this perspective. On the other hand, as climate change becomes more pronounced and more challenging, it is quite plausible that interest in expensive, long-payoff Antarctic science could markedly decline. Antarctica's future might then be the fragmented world of retrenchment and decline, although for different reasons than postulated in that world's earlier description.

In some respects, such changes have happened before. In the Cold War era, geostrategic imperatives saw "boom times" in Antarctica with relatively liberal funding by many parties involved. This period ended with the drawdown of the Cold War, shifting the justification for Antarctic involvement principally to scientific research payoffs. Today's emerging emphasis on great power competition may lead again to boom times that might be once again truncated, this time by climate change.

There are four possible alternative Antarctic futures, but they will not happen by accident. States and non-state actors can consciously choose their desired future and actively try to make it happen. If they decide not to be activist in this way, then either fate or, most likely, other states and non-state actors will choose their future for them. In this, the four alternative futures discussed provide a backdrop against which strategies can be devised that allow states and non-state actors to achieve their Antarctic ambitions.

NOTES

1   This chapter draws on Layton, Hallen, and Bishop (2019).

2   Antarctica covers some 14.2 million square kilometres, Australia some 7.6 million square kilometres. Australia's Antarctic claim is 6.0 million square kilometres.

REFERENCES

Australian Government. 2016. *Australian Antarctic Strategy and 20 Year Action Plan.* Hobart: Australian Antarctic Division. http://www.antarctica.gov.au/__data/ assets/pdf_file/0008/180827/20YearStrategy_final.pdf.

———. 2021. "Ice Sheets." Australian Antarctic Program, 9 September 2021. https://www. antarctica.gov.au/about-antarctica/ice-and-atmosphere/ice-sheet/.

Bergin, Anthony, Peter Jennings, Marcus Haward, Andrew Jackson, Anthony Press, Sam Bateman, Julia Jabour, Stephen Nicol, Patrick G. Quilty, and Lyn Goldsworthy. 2013. *Cold Calculations: Australia's Antarctic Challenges.* Canberra: Australian Strategic Policy Institute. https://www.aspi.org.au/report/strategic-insights-66-cold-calculations-australias-antarctic-challenges.

Boyd, Alan. 2019. "Cold War Chill Settles over Antarctica." *AsiaTimes,* 7 March 2019. https://www.asiatimes.com/2019/03/article/cold-war-chill-settles-over-antarctica/.

Brady, Anne-Marie. 2017. *China's Expanding Antarctic Interests: Implications for New Zealand.* Christchurch: University of Canterbury. https://www.canterbury.ac.nz/ media/documents/research/China's-expanding-Antarctic-interests.pdf.

Bray, Daniel. 2016. "The Geopolitics of Antarctic Governance: Sovereignty and Strategic Denial in Australia's Antarctic Policy." *Australian Journal of International Affairs* 70 (3): 268–69. https://doi.org/10.1080/10357718.2015.1135871.

Buchanan, Elizabeth. 2021. "Russia's 2021 National Security Strategy: Cool Change Forecasted for the Polar Regions." *RUSI: Commentary,* 14 July 2021. https://rusi. org/explore-our-research/publications/commentary/russias-2021-national-security-strategy-cool-change-forecasted-polar-regions.

CCAMLR (Commission for the Conservation of Antarctic Marine Living Resources). 1980. *Convention on the Conservation of Antarctic Marine Living Resources.* https:// www.ccamlr.org/en/organisation/camlr-convention-text#I.

Colombo, Andrea. 2019. "International Co-operation in Antarctica: The Influence of Regional Groups." *Polar Journal* 9 (1): 180–81. https://doi.org/10.1080/215489 6X.2019.1618555.

Courtney, Hugh. 2001. *20/20 Foresight: Crafting Strategy in an Uncertain World*. Boston: Harvard Business School Press.

Department of Defence. 2016. *Future Operating Environment: 2035*. Canberra: Commonwealth of Australia. https://defence.gov.au/vcdf/forceexploration/_ Master/docs/Future-Operating-Environment-2035.pdf.

EFE-EPA. 2017. "China Urges Balanced, Sustainable Development in Antarctica." Agencia EFE, 23 May 2017. https://www.efe.com/efe/english/world/china-urges-balanced-sustainable-development-in-antarctica/50000262-3274279.

Fischetti, Michael. 2013. "Found: The Coldest Place on Earth." *Scientific American*, 10 December 2013. https://blogs.scientificamerican.com/observations/found-the-coldest-place-on-earth/.

Fogarty, Ellie. 2011. *Antarctica: Assessing and Protecting Australia's Interests*. Sydney: Lowy Institute for International Policy. https://www.lowyinstitute.org/sites/default/files/pubfiles/Fogarty%2C_Antarctica_web_1.pdf.

Global Times. 2021. "China's Kunlun and Taishan Meteorological Stations Put into Operation in Antarctic." *Global Times*, 1 December 2021. https://www.globaltimes.cn/page/202112/1240396.shtml.

Gothe-Snape, Jackson. 2019. "Australia Declares China's Plan for Antarctic Conduct Has 'No Formal Standing.' " ABC News, 30 July 2019. https://www.abc.net.au/news/2019-07-30/antarctica-china-code-of-conduct-dome-a/11318646?nw=0.

Haward, Marcus, and Nicolas Cooper. 2014. "Australian Interests, Bifocalism, Bipartisanship, and the Antarctic Treaty System." *Polar Record* 50 (1): 60–71. https://doi.org/10.1017/S0032247412000459.

Layton, Peter. 2019. "Sustainable Middle Power Military Space Operations." In *Project Asteria 2019: Space Debris, Space Traffic Management and Space Sustainability*, ed. Michael Spencer, 31–44. Canberra: Air Power Development Centre.

Layton, Peter, Travis Hallen, and Lauren Bishop. 2019. *Australia's Antarctica National Air Power Futures*. Canberra: Air Power Development Centre.

Lei, Zhao. 2021. "Icebreaker Leaves for New Antarctic Expedition." *China Daily*, 5 November 2021. https://www.chinadaily.com.cn/a/202111/05/WS6184d40da310cdd39bc73990.html.

Liggett, Daniela, Bob Frame, Neil Gilbert, and Fraser Morgan. 2017. "Is It All Going South? Four Future Scenarios for Antarctica." *Polar Record* 53 (5): 459–78. https://doi.org/10.1017/S0032247417000390.

Liu, Nengye. 2019. "The Rise of China and the Antarctic Treaty System?" *Australian Journal of Maritime & Ocean Affairs* 11 (2): 120–31. https://doi.org/10.1080/18366503.2019.1589897.

Mekarnia, Djamel, and Yves Frenot. 2013. "The French-Italian Concordia Station." *Proceedings of the International Astronomical Union* 8 (S288): 178–85. https://doi.org/10.1017/S1743921312016845.

Netherlands Ministry of Defence. 2010. *Future Policy Survey: A New Foundation for the Netherlands Armed Forces*. https://www.files.ethz.ch/isn/157125/Netherlands%202008%20Future%20policy%20survey.pdf.

Press, A. J. 2014. *20 Year Australian Antarctic Strategic Plan.* Hobart: Australian Antarctic Division. http://www.antarctica.gov.au/__data/assets/pdf_file/0008/178595/20-Year-Plan_Press-Report.pdf.

Press, Anthony. 2018. "Australia's Most Southern Shores: The Strategic Geography of Antarctica and the Southern Ocean." In *Australian Contributions to Strategic and Military Geography*, ed. Stuart Pearson, Jane L. Holloway, and Richard Thackway, 129–41. Cham, SE: Springer.

Secretariat of the Antarctic Treaty. 1959. *Antarctic Treaty.* https://documents.ats.aq/keydocs/vol_1/vol1_2_AT_Antarctic_Treaty_e.pdf.

Talalay, Pavel G. 2014. "Exploration of Gamburtsev Subglacial Mountains (East Antarctica): Background and Plans for the Near Future." *Geography, Environment, Sustainability* 7 (1): 5–15. https://doi.org/10.24057/2071-9388-2014-7-1-5-15.

UK Ministry of Defence. 2018. *Global Strategic Trends: The Future Starts Today.* 6th ed. https://assets.publishing.service.gov.uk/government/uploads/system/uploads/attachment_data/file/1065623/20181008-dcdc_futures_GST_future_starts_today.pdf.

Walters, Tiara. 2022. "Russian Polar Vessel Arrives in Cape Town as Pact Aims to Quell Tensions." *Daily Maverick*, 18 May 2022. https://www.dailymaverick.co.za/article/2022-05-18-russian-polar-vessel-arrives-in-cape-town-as-pact-aims-to-quell-tensions/.

Wenger, Michael. 2022. "Construction Start of New Russian Vostok Station in Antarctica." *Polar Journal*, 24 January 2022. https://polarjournal.ch/en/2022/01/24/construction-start-of-new-russian-vostok-station-in-antarctica/.

Zhen, Liu, 2018. "China to Begin Building First Permanent Airfield in Antarctica." *South China Morning Post*, 29 October 2018. https://www.scmp.com/news/china/diplomacy/article/2170735/china-begin-building-first-permanent-airfield-antarctica.

Antarctic Environmental Security: Status and Challenges

Robin Warner

Antarctica represents one of the most pristine and environmentally sensitive habitats in the world and hosts a variety of threatened species. The sparse and periodic human habitation and limited range of human activities to date has reinforced the innate environmental value of this remote area. With the steady increase in human activities in Antarctica and external threats such as climate change, the need for effective environmental protection has become even more urgent. The law and policy framework for environmental protection in Antarctica has evolved through the constellation of international law instruments in the Antarctic Treaty System (ATS). This chapter discusses the development of some key principles and approaches in the global environmental law framework, including the principle of sustainable development, ecosystem-based management, the precautionary principle, and environmental impact assessment, and their application to Antarctica, particularly the marine environment including the Southern Ocean. It analyzes how these principles and approaches have been incorporated in Antarctic governance regimes through the ATS and points to future challenges for the Antarctic environmental protection regime.

Global Law and Policy Framework for Environmental Protection

The Principle of Sustainable Development

Developments in international environmental law and policy over recent decades have promoted an integrated approach to environmental protection, which aligns environmental protection objectives with social and economic goals. The relationship between environmental protection and economic development was recognized in the 1972 Stockholm Declaration on the Human Environment, but it was not until the 1980s that a series of environmental declarations and reports initiated by the International Union for Conservation of Nature and the General Assembly of the United Nations (UNGA) attempted to synthesize these two factors in the concept of sustainable development (Stockholm Report 1972, 1,4; IUCN, WWF, and UNEP 1980; Resolution 37/7 1982, 17). In its 1987 report, *Our Common Future* (i.e., the Brundtland Report), the World Commission on Environment and Development defined sustainable development as "development that meets the needs of the present without compromising the ability of future generations to meet their own needs" (WCED 1987, 43). On a practical level, sustainable development entailed finding a balance between economic and social development goals and the protection of the environment for present and future generations (44–45). The Brundtland Report's findings on oceans, which have particular resonance for the poles, demonstrated that the ecological resilience of the oceans was under threat from "over exploitation, pollution and land based development" (263). Noting the underlying unity of the oceans and the interdependence of marine ecosystems, it emphasized the need for global and regional co-operation in oceans management if sustainable development was to be realized (264–65). For the high seas, as with other parts of the planet that fell outside national jurisdiction, the Brundtland Report concluded that sustainable development could only be secured through "international cooperation and agreed regimes for surveillance, development and management in the common interest" (261). The report assessed that the sum of the multiple conventions and programs in place did not represent an adequate management regime either for ocean space within national jurisdiction or for extraterritorial ocean space (265; see also Curtis 1993, 188).

In the early 1990s, the Preparatory Commission meetings for the United Nations Conference on Environment and Development (UNCED) began to analyze the practical implications of sustainable development and to devise an action plan for implementing sustainable development across the whole spectrum of human interactions with the environment. Of the products of UNCED, the Rio Declaration and Agenda 21 have the most relevance for the subsequent development of environmental protection at the poles and elsewhere (United Nations 1993; Rio Declaration 1992). The Rio Declaration contains twenty-seven basic principles to guide states and the international community in their efforts to achieve sustainable development (Grubb et al. 1993, xv). These principles reiterated some of the basic tenets of the Stockholm Declaration and incorporated new concepts such as the precautionary approach and the common but differentiated responsibility of developed and developing states in a series of carefully worded political compromises (86). Agenda 21 was a wide-ranging action plan that addressed the integration of environment and development concerns from different angles and recommended global, regional, and national measures to achieve sustainable development in particular program areas (Robinson 1992, xxvi). Chapter 17 of Agenda 21 was devoted to the protection of the oceans (United Nations 1993, 238).

The World Summit on Sustainable Development (WSSD), held in Johannesburg in 2002, reaffirmed the commitment of the international community to the principle of sustainable development. The fundamental theme of many of the recommendations contained in the WSSD Plan of Implementation (WSSD Plan) was a call for states to make existing global and regional instruments work more effectively to protect the environment and its biodiversity, rather than a call for the creation of new multilateral instruments or institutions. In relation to the oceans, the WSSD Plan notes that oceans form an integrated and essential component of the earth's ecosystem, which is critical for global food security and economic prosperity (United Nations 2002). The key to ensuring sustainable development of the oceans is identified as the effective coordination and co-operation of relevant bodies at the global and regional levels (United Nations 2002, annex para. 30). The 1982 United Nations Convention on the Law of the Sea (UNCLOS 1982) is endorsed as providing the overall framework for oceans activities. The oceans chapter of Agenda 21 and the Jakarta Mandate on Marine and Coastal Biodiversity (COP CBD 1995), adopted by the parties to the 1992 Convention on Biological Diversity (CBD 1992), are recognized as providing the program of action for achieving the related objectives of sustainable development of oceans and the conservation of marine biodiversity (United Nations 2002, para. 30(a–b), para. 32(b)). Some of the actions recommended in the WSSD Plan include the maintenance of the productivity and biodiversity of important marine areas within and beyond national jurisdiction, the development and application of the ecosystem approach in fisheries conservation and management by 2010, the elimination of destructive fisheries practices, the establishment of marine protected areas, including representative networks of such areas, by 2012, and time/area closures for the protection of nursery fishing grounds (para. 30(d), para. 32(a), para. 32(c)). The plan emphasizes the critical importance of coordination and co-operation measures in oceans management, encouraging states to develop regional and international programs for halting the loss of marine biodiversity (para. 32(d)).

Member states of the UN reaffirmed their commitment to sustainable development at the Rio+20 Conference in 2012. In the outcomes document from that conference, *The Future We Want*, they acknowledged "the need to further mainstream sustainable development at all levels, integrating economic, social and environmental aspects and recognizing their interlinkages, so as to achieve sustainable development in all its dimensions" (Resolution 66/288 2012, clause 3).

In 2015, member states of the UN adopted the 2030 Agenda for Sustainable Development and its seventeen Sustainable Development Goals (SDGs) (Resolution 70/1 2015). The SDGs entered into force on 1 January 2016 and are to be implemented over the ensuing fifteen years. SDGs 13, 14, and 15 on climate change, oceans and biodiversity, and forests and desertification, respectively, are especially relevant to environmental protection at the poles. SDG 13 exhorts states to take urgent action to combat climate change and its impacts, and includes among its targets the following:

13.1   Strengthen resilience and adaptive capacity to climate-related hazards and natural disasters in all countries

13.2   Integrate climate change measures into national policies, strategies, and planning

13.3   Improve education, awareness-raising and human and institutional capacity on climate change mitigation, adaptation, impact reduction and early warning

SDG 14 on the oceans exhorts states to conserve and sustainably use the oceans, seas, and marine resources, and includes the following:

14.1   By 2025, prevent and significantly reduce marine pollution of all kinds, in particular from land-based activities, including marine debris and nutrient pollution

14.2   By 2020, sustainably manage and protect marine and coastal ecosystems to avoid significant adverse impacts, including by strengthening their resilience, and take action for their restoration in order to achieve healthy and productive oceans

14.3   Minimize and address the impacts of ocean acidification, including through enhanced scientific cooperation at all levels

14.4   By 2020, effectively regulate harvesting and end overfishing, illegal, unreported, and unregulated fishing and destructive fishing practices and implement science-based management plans, in order to restore fish stocks in the shortest time feasible, at least to levels that can produce maximum sustainable yield as determined by their biological characteristics

14.5   By 2020, conserve at least 10 percent of coastal and marine areas, consistent with national and international law and based on the best available scientific information

Finally, the biodiversity component of SDG 15 exhorts states to halt biodiversity loss:

15.5   Take urgent and significant action to reduce the degradation of natural habitats, halt the loss of biodiversity and, by 2020, protect and prevent the extinction of threatened species

15.9   By 2020, integrate ecosystem and biodiversity values into national and local planning, development processes, poverty reduction strategies and accounts

These global goals and their associated targets provide additional impetus for the ongoing environmental protection initiatives being taken in Antarctica through the ATS.

Ecosystem-Based Management

The concept of ecosystem-based management has developed in parallel with the principle of sustainable development. This concept promotes a more integrated approach to conservation and management of the environment, considering species, habitats, and their interconnections rather than concentrating on the protection of single species. An early signpost to the subsequent development of ecosystem-based management in the marine environment can be found in article 194(5) of UNCLOS, which imposes obligations on states' parties to protect and preserve rare or fragile ecosystems as well as the habitat of depleted, threatened, or endangered species and other forms of marine life. The 1992 Rio Declaration provides in principle 7 that "States shall cooperate in a spirit of global partnership to conserve, protect and restore the health and integrity of the Earth's ecosystem." The action program emerging from Agenda 21 also reflected a movement toward ecosystem-based management of the marine environment in chapter 17 on the oceans, with references to the "protection and restoration of endangered marine species" and the "preservation of their habitats and other ecologically sensitive areas" (United Nations 1993, 252).

The CBD further developed the ecosystem-based management approach to environmental protection through the concept of biodiversity. Biological diversity is a comprehensive term defined in article 2 of the CBD as "the variability among living organisms from all sources including, *inter alia*, terrestrial, marine and other aquatic ecosystems and the ecological complexes of which they are part" and including "diversity within species, between species and of ecosystems." In the context of the marine environment, the concept of biodiversity was allied to the notion of large marine ecosystems forming an interconnecting web of marine living resources and their habitats (Joyner 1995, 637). This comprehensive approach added new dimensions to the protection of the marine environment, which previously had been largely based on pollution control and the conservation of single species (637). The conservation of marine biodiversity entailed protection of a range of components of biodiversity in the marine environment including species, habitats, ecosystems, and genetic material (646). This inclusive form of protection also considered the social, economic, and political factors affecting the various components of marine biodiversity (644). The framework provisions of the CBD provide some guidance for the contracting parties in implementing biodiversity protection measures, including article 7 on identifying the components of biodiversity within their national jurisdictions and article 14 on environmental impact assessment (EIA). These framework provisions have been supplemented by the ongoing decisions of the Conference of the Parties (COP). The CBD COP occurs biennially and is advised by the scientific advisory body for the convention, the Subsidiary Body on Scientific, Technical and Technological Advice. The contracting parties also concluded the Jakarta Mandate on Marine and Coastal Biodiversity in 1995 (COP CBD 1995, note 16). At the COP CBD meeting in Bratislava in 1998, the contracting parties adopted a decision (IV/5) on conservation and sustainable use of marine and coastal biological diversity, including a multi-year program of work on marine and coastal biological diversity (COP CBD 1998). The work program was founded on six basic principles, including the ecosystem approach, the precautionary principle, and the importance of science. The five key program elements of the Jakarta Mandate Work Programme are

- integrated marine and coastal area management (IMCAM)

- marine and coastal living resources (MCLR)

- marine and coastal protected areas (MCPA)

- mariculture

- alien species and genotypes (COP CBD 1998, para. 14)

Many decisions taken under each of these programs over the past twenty years relate directly to ecosystem-based management of the marine environment and are implemented through the contracting parties. These include the identification of ecologically and biologically significant areas in marine environments within and beyond national jurisdiction (COP CBD 2008, annex) and the development of Voluntary Guidelines for the Consideration of Biodiversity in EIAs and SEAs for marine areas (Secretariat of the Convention of Biological Diversity 2015).

The Precautionary Principle

The UNCED process had the effect of catalyzing the formation of a body of emerging international environmental law principles, including the precautionary principle or approach. Although different versions of the precautionary approach had been contained in other regional and global instruments prior to UNCED, its inclusion in principle 15 of the Rio Declaration was a major step in its emergence as a principle of customary international law (Birnie and Boyle 2002, 116; Birnie 1997, 51; Kaye 2001, 171–72; Freestone 1994, 216). The principle 15 formulation of the precautionary approach specifies that "where there are threats of serious or irreversible damage to the environment, lack of full scientific certainty shall not be used as a reason for postponing cost-effective measures to prevent environmental degradation" (Rio Declaration 1992). For the poles and their marine areas, the precautionary principle is particularly relevant because of the still-developing state of scientific knowledge on the poles and most aspects of their marine environments. This developing state of scientific knowledge arguably imposes an even greater responsibility on states to adopt precautionary strategies to protect this part of the global environment. The introduction to chapter 17 of Agenda 21 also emphasizes the need for fresh approaches to marine and coastal management at the various levels of oceans governance, specifying that such approaches should be "integrated in content" and "precautionary and anticipatory in ambit" (United Nations 1993, 238).

Many of the international environmental law principles contained in the oceans chapter of Agenda 21, including the precautionary principle or approach, were directly incorporated into subsequent international law instruments applicable to the marine environment and its resources, such as the 1995 UN Fish Stocks Agreement. A key benefit of the UN Fish Stocks Agreement was its translation of these general conservation principles into practical recommendations for co-operative action by states, either directly or through sub-regional or regional fisheries-management organizations. Article 6 of the agreement contains a very comprehensive description of how the precautionary approach can be interpreted and applied in the conservation of straddling and highly migratory fish stocks. The measures prescribed, although consistent with a precautionary approach, can also be related to other conservation norms, including sustainable development, use of best scientific evidence, EIA, and ecosystem-based management. The article 6(2) formulation of the precautionary approach in the UN Fish Stocks Agreement sets the threshold for the application of the approach a little lower than that specified in the Rio Declaration. States are urged to "be more cautious when information is uncertain, unreliable or inadequate," and article 6 further provides that "the absence of adequate scientific information is not to be used as a reason for postponing or failing to take conservation and management measures." The remaining provisions in article 6 specify a range of measures to implement the precautionary approach. States are required to improve decision making for fishery resource conservation and management by obtaining and sharing the best scientific information available and implementing improved techniques for dealing with risk and uncertainty (Agreement Relating to Fish Stocks 1995, art. 6.3(a)). On the basis of the best scientific evidence available, states must determine stock-specific reference points that constrain harvesting of fish stocks within safe biological limits that will allow the stocks to produce their maximum sustainable yield. These precautionary reference points are also to be used to develop management strategies to prevent stocks falling below sustainable levels (art. 6.3(b), annex 2). The precautionary principle or approach has also been incorporated into different aspects of the Antarctic governance regimes discussed in later sections of this chapter.

Environmental Impact Assessment

The process of EIA is one of the fundamental means by which states can implement a range of international environmental law principles and approaches. EIA plays a fundamental role in discharging states' obligations to prevent trans-boundary harm, adopt a precautionary approach, and promote sustainable development (Craik 2008, 54, 77, 224). The well-established process of EIA, with its recognized stages of screening, scoping, and public consultation, is critical to minimizing adverse human impacts on these areas and developing suitable mitigation measures for the duration of such activities and beyond. EIA can alert states to the potential for trans-boundary harm from certain activities in marine areas, and in many cases requires states to notify and consult other states where risks to marine areas under their jurisdiction emerge. EIA is an integral component of a precautionary approach to human activities with the potential for adverse effects on the marine environment. Undertaking prior EIA and ongoing monitoring of activities with the potential for adverse effects on the marine environment is also vital in incorporating environmental concerns into the development process and facilitating sustainable development. The fundamental importance of EIA as an environmental protection obligation is recognized in a range of binding and non-binding international instruments, including article 206 of UNCLOS, article 41 of the CBD, and principle 17 of the Rio Declaration. The customary international law status of the obligation on states to conduct EIA of activities with the potential to significantly affect the environment, including its marine components, has been steadily emerging in the recent jurisprudence of the International Court of Justice (ICJ) and the International Tribunal for the Law of the Sea (ITLOS). In the *Gabčíkovo-Nagymaros* case, the court considered assessment, notification, and consultation—effectively the elements of an EIA process—to be a necessary step in a state's implementation of the duty to prevent trans-boundary harm and the concept of sustainable development (case concerning Gabčíkovo-Nagymaros Project 1997, 7 para. 141; Boyle 1997, 18; Craik 2008, 114). In the *Pulp Mills* case, the ICJ found that

> it may now be considered a requirement under general international law to undertake an environmental impact assessment where there is a risk that the proposed industrial activity may have a significant adverse impact in a trans-boundary context, in particular, on a shared resource (*Case Concerning Pulp Mills* 2006, 113 para. 204).

In the *MOX Plant* case, ITLOS ordered the parties, Ireland and the United Kingdom, to improve their trans-boundary environmental co-operation, including by carrying out an adequate assessment of the potential impacts of a nuclear fuel reprocessing plant in Cumbria on the marine environment of the Irish Sea (ITLOS 2001, para. 82; Boyle 2007, 377). The advisory opinion of the Seabed Disputes Chamber of the ITLOS on the *Responsibilities and Obligations of States Sponsoring Persons and Entities with Respect to Activities in the Area* also acknowledged the customary international law status of the obligation to conduct EIA of activities with the potential for significant impacts on the marine environment, including for areas beyond national jurisdiction, specifically the deep seabed beyond national jurisdiction (ITLOS 2011).

International Environmental Law Principles and Antarctic Governance Regimes

Ecosystem-Based Management in the Antarctic

The parties to the Antarctic Treaty (United Nations 1961) have co-operated in the development of a comprehensive environmental protection regime that applies to the terrestrial and marine areas of the Antarctic Treaty area south of 60 degrees south latitude and, in the case of the Convention on the Conservation of Antarctic Marine Living Resources (United Nations 1980), marine areas south of the Antarctic Convergence. The 1991 Madrid Protocol was the first comprehensive environmental protection instrument to apply to the whole of the Antarctic Treaty area, including the land mass and sea (Madrid Protocol 1991, art. 2). Although the protocol was adopted prior to the negotiation of the CBD, it does contain elements that reflect a similar integrated approach to the protection of the Antarctic environment. The interdependence of Antarctic ecosystems is recognized in article 2, which commits the parties to the comprehensive protection of the Antarctic environment and dependent and associated ecosystems. The Committee for Environmental Protection (CEP) was created under the protocol (art. 11). It provides advice to the parties on implementation of the protocol, but key decisions on environmental protection are still the province of the Antarctic Treaty Consultative Meeting (ATCM), which occurs annually (art. 12; Cordonnery 1998, 29). Parties are required to undertake regular and effective monitoring of the impact of ongoing activities on the Antarctic marine environment and dependent and associated ecosystems (Madrid Protocol 1991, art. 3(2)(d); Bastmeijer and Roura 2008, 191). They must also submit annual reports on their implementation of the protocol to the CEP (Madrid Protocol 1991, art. 17; Vidas 2000, 55). The collaborative nature of activities in the Antarctic Treaty area is emphasized in article 6 of the protocol, which requires parties

- to cooperate in programs to protect the marine environment

- to undertake joint expeditions and share facilities

- to avoid the cumulative effect of multiple human activities in any location

- to assist each other with environmental impact assessments of proposed activities. (Madrid Protocol 1991, art. 6)

The principal objective of the CAMLR Convention is to conserve and manage all marine living resources, except whales and seals, in the area south of 60 degrees south latitude and in the area between 60 degrees south latitude and the Antarctic Convergence.[1] The vast majority of this area lies beyond national jurisdiction except for offshore maritime zones adjacent to the territorial claims of some Antarctic Treaty partners on the Antarctic continent and waters within the offshore maritime zones of some sub-Antarctic islands in the Southern Ocean claimed by Australia, France, South Africa, and the United Kingdom.[2] The Commission on the Conservation of Antarctic Marine Living Resources (CCAMLR) conservation and management responsibilities extend beyond fish species to molluscs, crustaceans, and birds found south of the Antarctic Convergence (United Nations 1980, art. 1(2)). The convention explicitly adopts a precautionary and ecosystem-based approach to the management of marine living resources, one that recognizes the complex interconnections between all parts of the Antarctic ecosystem (art. 2(3); Miller, Sabourenkov, and Ramm 2004, 319; Kaye 2001, 368). Its conservation and management objectives were ambitious portents of environmental protection principles endorsed by the international community over a decade later in the oceans chapter of Agenda 21. Article 2(3) of the convention sets out the various elements of CCAMLR's conservation and management approach, which allows for rational use of marine living resources in accordance with strict conservation principles. The three key conservation principles that apply to harvesting of marine living resources and associated activities are

a) prevention of decrease in the size of any harvested population to levels below those which ensure its stable recruitment. For this purpose, its size should not be allowed to fall below a level close to that which ensures the greatest net annual increment;

b) maintenance of the ecological relationships between harvested, dependent, and related populations of Antarctic marine living resources and the restoration of depleted populations to the levels defined in sub-paragraph (a) above; and

c) prevention of changes or minimization of the risk of changes in the marine ecosystem which are not potentially reversible over three or two decades, taking into account the state of available knowledge of the direct and indirect impact of harvesting, the effect of the introduction of alien species, the effects of associated activities on the marine ecosystem and of the effects of environmental changes, with the aim of making possible the sustained conservation of Antarctic marine living resources. (United Nations 1980, art. 2(3))

The CCAMLR members have adopted a variety of innovative measures to implement the convention's ecosystem-based approach to conservation. These include banning destructive fisheries practices, such as bottom trawling for particular fish species in the CCAMLR area, mandating measures to reduce incidental seabird mortality caused by baited hooks in longline fishing, monitoring the effects of fishing on non-target species by collection of data on CCAMLR member state fishing vessels, and prohibiting fishing for certain species by CCAMLR member state fishing vessels where the risk to by-catch species is thought to be too great (Miller, Sabourenkov, and Ramm 2004, 323–44).

Marine protected areas (MPAs) may also be designated by CCAMLR for the purposes of scientific study or conservation (United Nations 1980, art. 9(2)(f)(g)). CCAMLR Conservation Measure 91-04 (2011) provides a general framework for establishing CCAMLR MPAs. MPAs must be adopted based on best available scientific evidence and consistent with UNCLOS, for the achievement of the following objectives:

- The protection of representative examples of marine ecosystems, biodiversity, and habitats at an appropriate scale to maintain their viability and integrity in the long term.

- The protection of key ecosystem processes habitats and species, including populations and life history stages.

- The establishment of scientific reference areas for monitoring natural variability and long-term change or for monitoring the effects of harvesting and other human activities on marine living resources and on the ecosystems of which they form part.

- The protection of areas vulnerable to impact by human activities, including unique, rare, or highly biodiverse habitats and features.

- The protection of areas critical to the functioning of local ecosystems.

- The protection of areas to maintain resilience or the ability to adapt to the effects of climate change. (CCAMLR 2011)

As a first step in creating a network of MPAs in the CAMLR Convention area, CCAMLR established an MPA covering the South Orkney Island's southern shelf in 2009 (CCAMLR 2009). This was followed by the creation in 2016 of the world's largest MPA beyond national jurisdiction in the Ross Sea, covering a total area of 1.55 million square kilometres (CCAMLR 2016). Over the past eight years, CCAMLR has been considering other extensive proposals for MPAs in the Antarctic Treaty area, including a proposal by Australia, France, and the European Union for an MPA to protect 1.2 million square kilometres of East Antarctic waters (CCAMLR 2018, 24–27 paras. 6.17–6.28). Their proposal would allow for exploratory and research activities within the MPA if they were consistent with the maintenance of the MPA's objectives. As yet, consensus has not been reached on the designation of any of these areas (24–27 paras. 6.17–6.28).

Environmental Impact Assessment in Antarctica

Prior EIA of human activities with the potential for significant impacts on the species, habitats, and ecosystems of the Antarctic continent and the surrounding marine areas is an important component of the Antarctic governance regime. The general obligation to conduct EIA of such activities appears in a variety of global and regional instruments applicable to Antarctic marine areas, including UNCLOS, the UN Fish Stocks Agreement, and the CBD. In addition, the Madrid Protocol provides a multi-level system of EIA for activities conducted by parties in the Antarctic Treaty area. There are also detailed EIA provisions applicable to fisheries activities in the marine areas of the Antarctic in CCAMLR. The interaction of these global, regional, and sector-specific regimes, as well as their relationship to national law and policy on environmental assessment, is complex. This section examines how overarching provisions in UNCLOS and other global instruments such as the CBD apply to EIA in Antarctica and its surrounding marine areas. The development of EIA regimes for sectoral activities such as fisheries at the global and regional level and their relevance for Antarctica will also be discussed. The evolution of more detailed EIA instruments and policies for Antarctica will be reviewed, as will regional instruments specific to particular sectors of activity or sub-regions in the poles. A detailed analysis of national approaches to EIA in Antarctica is beyond the scope of this chapter, but linkages between the global, regional, and sectoral environmental assessment regimes and national environmental assessment will be identified. The overall efficacy of EIA in the marine areas of Antarctica will be discussed from a number of perspectives: whether all sectoral activities are covered by the current mix of global, regional, and sectoral environmental assessment instruments and arrangements applicable to Antarctica; whether trans-boundary impacts of activities are adequately covered by global, regional, and sectoral environmental assessment instruments and arrangements for Antarctica; and whether activities affecting marine areas beyond national jurisdiction are covered by such regimes.

EIA in the Antarctic

The test applied for screening activities for EIA under the Madrid Protocol is more complex and multi-layered than the EIA provisions of many other international instruments. The screening process has three levels: the preliminary assessment level, the initial environmental evaluation (IEE) level, and the comprehensive environmental evaluation (CEE) level. A preliminary assessment is carried out at the national level for all activities subject to the protocol with less than a minor or transitory impact (Madrid Protocol 1991, annex 1 art. 1(1)). If an activity has no more than a minor or transitory impact, an IEE must be carried out, and if it has more than a minor or transitory impact, a CEE must be carried out (annex 1 arts. 2(1), 3(1)). All activities, both governmental and non-governmental, in the Antarctic Treaty area are subject to these provisions, except for fishing, sealing, whaling, and emergency operations (art. 8(1)).

An IEE under the Madrid Protocol must contain:

- a description of the proposed activity, including its purpose, location, duration, and intensity; and

- consideration of alternatives to the proposed activity and any impacts that the activity may have, including consideration of cumulative impacts in light of existing and known planned activities. (annex 1 art. 2(2))

Activities having more than a minor or transitory impact are subject to a more in-depth assessment in keeping with the pristine and sensitive nature of the Antarctic environment and the lack of scientific understanding of potential impacts. A CEE has a more extensive list of components, including

- a description of the proposed activity, including its purpose, location, duration, and intensity, and possible alternatives to the activity, including the alternative of not proceeding and the consequences of those alternatives;

- an estimation of the nature, extent, duration, and intensity of the likely direct impacts of the proposed activity;

- a description of the initial environmental reference state with which predicted changes are to be compared and a prediction of the future environment reference state in the absence of the proposed activity;

- a description of the methods and data used to forecast the impacts of the proposed activity;

- consideration of cumulative impacts of the proposed activity in light of existing activities and other known planned activities; and

- identification of measures, including monitoring programs that could be taken to minimize or mitigate impacts of the proposed activity and to detect unforeseen impacts and that could provide early warning of any adverse effects of the activity. (annex 1 art. 3(2))

In undertaking environmental assessment of activities in the Antarctic Treaty area, the Antarctic Treaty Consultative Meeting has prescribed that particular values, identified in article 3(1) of the Madrid Protocol, be taken into account. These include

> the protection of the Antarctic environment and dependent and associated ecosystems and the intrinsic value of Antarctica, including its wilderness and aesthetic values and its value as an area for the conduct of scientific research, in particular research essential to understanding the global environment. (Secretariat of the Antarctic Treaty 1996, 26 para. 135)

Post-project monitoring is a discretionary component under the provisions relating to IEE but is a compulsory component under the provisions relating to CEE of activities having more than a minor or transitory impact on the environment. Article 5 of annex 1 to the Madrid Protocol provides that

> Procedures shall be put in place, including appropriate monitoring of key environmental indicators, to assess and verify the impact of any activity that proceeds following the completion of a CEE.
> The procedures referred to in paragraph 1 above . . . shall be designed to provide a regular and verifiable record of the impacts of the activity in order to:

> d) enable assessments to be made of the extent to which such impacts are consistent with the protocol; and

> e) provide information useful for minimizing or mitigating impacts, and where appropriate, information on the

need for suspension, cancellation, or modification of the activity.

Any significant information obtained, or procedures put in place, as a result of monitoring must be circulated to parties to the Madrid Protocol, forwarded to the CEP and made publicly available. The responsibility for monitoring under these provisions, however, still falls on parties individually with no prescribed enforcement or auditing role for the CEP or the ATCM. The Antarctic Treaty parties have agreed on a range of supplementary guidelines that assist them in implementing the Madrid Protocol, including non-binding guidelines on EIA (Secretariat of the Antarctic Treaty, n.d.). These guidelines elaborate EIA requirements under the protocol specifying the physical, chemical, and biological elements that need to be taken into account in conducting an EIA, the environmental baseline information to be gathered, the direct and cumulative impacts of the proposed activity to be evaluated, the potential alternatives that need to be considered, monitoring programs, mitigation and remediation measures, and the gaps in knowledge to be identified (Secretariat of the Antarctic Treaty, n.d.). The guidelines also provide practical information on the content and format of an environmental impact statement.

In addition to the Madrid Protocol, some environmental assessment of fisheries impacts on Antarctic marine areas takes place under the CCAMLR regime. An important aspect of the implementation of the CCAMLR conservation objectives has been the assessment of new fisheries to be undertaken in the convention area, such as those for Patagonian toothfish (Constable et al. 2000, 785–6). Preliminary assessment of new fisheries allows the Scientific Committee of CCAMLR to introduce measures that satisfy the conservation objectives of CCAMLR while permitting reasonable levels of fishing (786). This involves the submission of information to the Scientific Committee on the state of fish stocks in the areas proposed to be fished and subsequent survey activities before fishing is allowed to proceed. Measures for new fisheries have included catch limits to avoid over-exploitation of localized stocks and ongoing surveys of recruitment and growth of stocks in newly fished areas (786).

Notwithstanding the integrated nature of the EIA regime contained in the Madrid Protocol, there are some significant deficiencies in its coverage of current and potential activities in the marine areas of the Antarctic. In the two decades since its entry into force, there have been no CEEs of activities in the marine areas of the Antarctic Treaty area (Secretariat of the Antarctic Treaty 2021; Hemmings and Kriwoken 2010, 194–95). As the number of cruising and other vessels traversing these areas has increased significantly over this period, this would appear to be a significant omission in the protocol's coverage. Hemmings and Kriwoken have also expressed concern that no activities subject to CEEs have been substantially modified or prevented from proceeding despite the potential for serious adverse impacts on the sensitive Antarctic environment (2010, 187).

Conclusion

This chapter has reviewed the development of four interrelated international environmental law principles or approaches that have become embedded in global environmental practice and management over the past four decades, and examples of implementation in the Antarctic and its surrounding marine areas. The principle of sustainable development draws together the twin goals of environmental protection and economic development and aspires to create a balance between the two. The related approach of ecosystem-based management recognizes the links and interactions between species and their habitats and the need to conserve and manage the various components of natural environments in a more integrated manner. The precautionary principle emphasizes the need for a risk-based approach to certain activities where the threats to the natural environment and human health are as yet uncertain. The established process of EIA is fundamental to implementing all three of these principles or approaches. Environmental protection is a central feature of the Antarctic governance regime, and the four principles and approaches discussed in this chapter are integral to the environmental objectives of key instruments within the ATS, particularly the Madrid Protocol and CCAMLR. The protection of the Antarctic environment has been a prominent feature in the evolution of the ATS. It has developed in a more integrated way owing to the existence of a treaty system that considers the whole of the Antarctic region, and which is empowered to introduce conservation and management measures on a more holistic basis. While slow to emerge in a consensus-based, decision-making regime, the implementation of the ecosystem-based management approach in the conservation and management of the Antarctic's marine living resources is now becoming evident in measures such as the designation of the Ross Sea Marine Protected Area. With the threats posed by climate change, the associated impacts of ocean acidification, and increased human activities in Antarctica, the ongoing implementation of international environmental law principles and approaches will continue to be challenging in this remote but critical region.

NOTES

1   The Antarctic Convergence is also known as the Antarctic Polar Front and is situated at about 50 degrees south latitude, where the colder, fresher waters flowing north from the Antarctic meet the warmer, saltier waters flowing south from the Atlantic and Pacific Oceans. Whales and seals are covered by the 1946 International Convention for the Regulation of Whaling and the 1972 Convention for the Conservation of Antarctic Seals (United Nations 1980, art. 1(1)).

2   These islands include Heard and McDonald Islands belonging to Australia, Kerguelen and Crozet Islands belonging to France, Prince Edward and Marion Islands belonging to South Africa, and South Sandwich Islands and Shag Rocks belonging to the United Kingdom. These islands have been exempted from the application of CCAMLR (Rayfuse 2000, 261).

REFERENCES

Agreement Relating to Fish Stocks. 1995. *Agreement for the Implementation of the Provision of the United Nations Convention on the Law of the Sea of 10 December 1982 Relating to the Conservation and Management of Straddling Fish Stocks and Highly Migratory Fish Stocks*, opened for signature 4 December 1995, 2167 UNTS 3 (entered into force 11 December 2001). https://www.un.org/depts/los/convention_agreements/convention_overview_fish_stocks.htm.

Bastmeijer, Kees, and Ricardo Roura. 2008. "Environmental Impact Assessment in Antarctica." In *Theory and Practice of Transboundary Environmental Impact Assessment*, edited by Kees Bastmeijer and Timo Koivurova, 175–219. Leiden, NL: Martinus Nijhoff Publishers.

Birnie, Patricia. 1997. "The Status of Environmental 'Soft Law': Trends and Examples with Special Focus on IMO Norms." In *Competing Norms in the Law of the Marine Environmental Protection*, edited by Henrik Ringbom, 31–43. London: Kluwer Law International.

Birnie, Patricia, and Alan Boyle. 2002. *International Law and the Environment.* 2nd ed. Oxford: Oxford University Press.

Boyle, Alan. 1997. "The Gabčíkovo-Nagymaros Case: New Law in Old Bottles." *Yearbook of International Environmental Law* 8 (1): 13.

———. 2007. "The Environmental Jurisprudence of the International Tribunal for the Law of the Sea." *International Journal of Marine and Coastal Law* 22 (3): 369–81.

Case Concerning Pulp Mills on the River Uruguay (Argentina v Uruguay)—Provisional Measures. 2006. ICJ case 135.

Case Concerning the Gabčíkovo-Nagymaros Project (Hungary v Slovakia). 1997. ICJ case 92.

CBD (Convention on Biological Diversity). 1992. Opened for signature 5 June 1992, 1760 UNTS 79 (entered into force 29 December 1993).

CCAMLR (Convention on the Conservation of Antarctic Marine Living Resources). 2009. Conservation Measure 91-03 (2009), *Protection of the South Orkney Islands Southern Shelf.* https://www.ccamlr.org/en/measure-91-03-2009.

———. 2011. Conservation Measure 91-04 (2011), *General Framework for the Establishment of the CCAMLR Marine Protected Areas.* https://www.ccamlr.org/en/measure-91-04-2011.

———. 2016. Conservation Measure 91-05.(2016), *Ross Sea Region Marine Protected Area.* https://www.ccamlr.org/en/measure-91-05-2016.

———. 2018. *Report of the Thirty-Seventh Meeting of the Commission.* https://www.ccamlr.org/en/system/files/e-cc-xxxvii.pdf.

Constable, Andrew, William de la Mare, David M. Agnew, Inigo Everson, and Denzil Miller. 2000. "Managing Fisheries to Conserve the Antarctic Marine Ecosystem: Practical Implementation of the Convention on the Conservation of Antarctic Marine Living Resources (CCAMLR)." *ICES Journal of Marine Science* 57 (3): 778–91.

COP CBD (Conference of the Parties to the Convention on Biological Diversity). 1995. Decision II/10: *Conservation and Sustainable Use of Marine and Coastal Biological Diversity.* https://www.cbd.int/decisions/cop/2/10.

———. 1998. Decision IV/5: *Conservation and Sustainable Use of Marine and Coastal Biological Diversity, including a Program of Work.* https://www.cbd.int/decisions/cop/4/5/A1.

———. 2008. Decision IX/20: *Marine and Coastal Biodiversity.* https://wedocs.unep.org/bitstream/handle/20.500.11822/12355/CBD_and_UNEP_Regional_Seas.pdf?sequence=1&isAllowed=y.

Cordonnery, Laurence. 1998. "Environmental Protection in Antarctica: Drawing Lessons from the CCAMLR Model for the Implementation of the Madrid Protocol." *Ocean Development and International Law* 29 (2): 125–46.

Craik, Neil. 2008. *The International Law of Environmental Impact Assessment.* Cambridge: Cambridge University Press.

Curtis, C. E. 1993. "International Ocean Protection Agreements. What Is Needed?" In *Freedom for the Seas in the 21st Century,* edited by Jon M. Van Dyke, Durwood Zaelke, and Grant Hewison, 187–97. Washington, DC: Island Press.

Freestone, David. 1994. "The Road from Rio: International Environmental Law after the Earth Summit." *Journal of Environmental Law* 6 (2): 193–218.

Grubb, Michael, Matthias Koch, Koy Thomson, Abby Munson, and Francis Sullivan. 1993. *The "Earth Summit Agreements": A Guide and Assessment*. London: Earthscan Publications.

Hemmings, Alan, and Lorne Kriwoken. 2010. "High Level Antarctic EIA under the Madrid Protocol: State Practice and the Effectiveness of the Comprehensive Environmental Evaluation Process." *International Environmental Agreements: Politics, Law and Economics* 10 (3): 187–208.

ITLOS (International Tribunal for the Law of the Sea). 2001. "MOX Plant Case (Ireland v. United Kingdom), Provisional Measures." https://www.itlos.org/en/main/cases/list-of-cases/case-no-10/.

———. 2011. "Responsibilities and Obligations of States Sponsoring Persons and Entities with Respect to Activities in the Area (Request for Advisory Opinion submitted to the Seabed Disputes Chamber)." https://www.itlos.org/en/main/cases/list-of-cases/case-no-17/.

IUCN (International Union for Conservation of Nature and Natural Resources), WWF (World Wildlife Fund), and UNEP (United Nations Environment Programme). 1980. *World Conservation Strategy*. New York: UN.

Joyner, Christopher. 1995. "Biodiversity in the Marine Environment: Resource Implications for the Law of the Sea." *Vanderbilt Journal of Transnational Law* 28 (4): 635–87.

Kaye, Stuart. 2001. *International Fisheries Management*. The Hague: Kluwer Law International.

Madrid Protocol. 1991. Protocol on Environmental Protection of the Antarctic, opened for signature 4 October 1991, 2941 UNTS 3 (entered into force 14 January 1998).

Miller, Denzil, Eugene Sabourenkov, and David Ramm. 2004. "Managing Antarctic Marine Living Resources: The CCAMLR Approach." *International Journal of Marine and Coastal Law* 19 (3): 317–63.

Rayfuse, Rosemary. 2000. "The United Nations Agreement on Straddling and Highly Migratory Fish Stocks as an Objective Regime: A Case of Wishful Thinking?" *Australian Yearbook of International Law* 20 (1): 253–78.

Resolution 37/7. 1982. UN General Assembly, 48th plenary mtg. (28 October 1982). UN Doc A/37/51 22 ILM 455 (*World Charter for Nature*). https://digitallibrary.un.org/record/39295?ln=en.

Resolution 66/288. 2012. UN General Assembly, 123rd plenary mtg. (27 July 2012). UN Doc A/Res/66/288 (*The Future We Want*). https://www.un.org/en/development/desa/population/migration/generalassembly/docs/globalcompact/A_RES_66_288.pdf.

Resolution 70/1. 2015. UN General Assembly, 70th session (25 September 2015). UN Doc A/Res/70/1. (*Transforming Our World: The 2030 Agenda for Sustainable Development*). https://www.un.org/en/development/desa/population/migration/generalassembly/docs/globalcompact/A_RES_70_1_E.pdf.

Rio Declaration, UN Conference on Environment and Development. 1992. UN Doc A/
CONF.151/PC/WG.III/L.33/Rev.1. https://www.un.org/en/development/desa/
population/migration/generalassembly/docs/globalcompact/A_CONF.151_26_
Vol.I_Declaration.pdf.

Robinson, Nicholas A., ed. 1992. *Agenda 21 and the UNCED Proceedings*. New York:
Oceana.

Secretariat of the Antarctic Treaty. 1996. *Final Report of the Twentieth Antarctic Treaty
Consultative Meeting.* https://documents.ats.aq/ATCM20/fr/ATCM20_fr001_e.pdf.

———. 2021. "EIA Database." Secretariat of the Antarctic Treaty, accessed 9 August 2022.
https://www.ats.aq/devAS/EP/EIAList?lang=e.

———. n.d. "Guidelines for Environmental Impact Assessment in the Antarctic."
Secretariat of the Antarctic Treaty, accessed 9 August 2022. www.ats.aq/
documents/recatt/att266_e.pdf.

Secretariat of the Convention on Biological Diversity. 2015. "CBD Voluntary Guidelines
for the Consideration of Biodiversity in Environmental Impact Assessments (EIAs)
and Strategic Environmental Assessments (SEAs) in Marine Areas." Secretariat of
the Convention on Biological Diversity, accessed 9 August 2022. https://www.cbd.
int/doc/meetings/mar/mcbws-2015-01/other/mcbws-2015-01-cbd-03-en.pdf.

Stockholm Report. 1972. UN Conference on the Human Environment. UN
Doc A/CONF.48/41 11 ILM 1416. https://wedocs.unep.org/bitstream/
handle/20.500.11822/29567/ELGP1StockD.pdf?sequence=1&isAllowed=y.

UNCLOS (UN Convention on the Law of the Sea). 1982. Opened for signature 10
December 1982, 1833 UNTS 397 (entered into force 16 November 1994). https://
www.un.org/depts/los/convention_agreements/texts/unclos/unclos_e.pdf.

United Nations. 1961. *Antarctic Treaty*. https://treaties.un.org/doc/Publication/UNTS/
volume%20402/volume-402-I-5778-English.pdf.

———. 1980. *Convention on the Conservation of Antarctic Marine Living Resources*, opened
for signature 20 May 1980, 1329 UNTS 47 (entered into force 1981). https://treaties.
un.org/doc/Publication/UNTS/Volume%201329/volume-1329-I-22301-English.
pdf.

———. 1993. *Agenda 21, UN Conference on Environment and Development*. UN Doc A/
CONF.151/26 https://www.un.org/esa/dsd/agenda21/Agenda%2021.pdf.

———. 2002. United Nations General Assembly (UNGA), *Report of the World Summit on
Sustainable Development*, UN Doc A/CONF.199/20 (4 September 2002), Annex,
[30] [WSSD Plan].

Vidas, Davor. 2000. "Protecting the Polar Marine Environment: Interplay of Regulatory
Frameworks." In *Protecting the Polar Marine Environment: Law and Policy
for Pollution Prevention*, edited by Davor Vidas, 3–16. Cambridge: Cambridge
University Press.

WCED (World Commission on Environment and Development). 1987. *Our Common
Future* (Brundtland Report). Oxford: Oxford University Press.

8

New Zealand's Foreign and Security Policy in Antarctica: Small States, Shelter Seeking, and the Changing Polar Landscape

Joe Burton

New Zealand is one of the southernmost nations in the world. In winter, icebergs have been known to float off the South Island, and Antarctic weather fronts blanket the Southern Alps with snow. Commercial flights leave Christchurch to take tourists to see the Southern Borealis, and the city itself, the largest in the South Island, has become a major hub for Antarctic expeditions, with regular flights to Scott Base, New Zealand's Antarctic research station. New Zealand has strong economic, research, and security interests in the Antarctic region, and this is reflected in recent government policy. But the direction of New Zealand's policy in the Antarctic has become increasingly fraught with risk and contention, especially as China and other powers become more assertive in pursuing their Antarctic interests.

This chapter provides an overview of New Zealand's engagement in Antarctica, and how the government is seeking to manage its interests in an international environment characterized by increasing great power competition in the polar regions and the accelerating effects of climate change. Drawing on small states international relations theory, the chapter highlights how New Zealand's policy toward Antarctica is changing and becoming more contentious domestically and internationally. The chapter analyzes the range of scholarly and policy perspectives about New Zealand's role in the Antarctic, how Antarctica is reflected and prioritized in New Zealand defence and security policy, and growing concerns in New Zealand about great power competition in the region. The chapter also provides a reflection on how small states in both polar regions can advance their interests through "shelter seeking" in international forums and by building co-operative, human, and environmental security narratives and policies.

The chapter is divided into four parts. First, it introduces a theoretical framework for understanding how small states manage the challenges of being small in an international system characterized by the resurgence of great power competition and conflict (this framework is based on other work by the author on small states and cyber security; see Burton 2013). This section makes the argument that small states face difficult choices about how to engage in contested regions, and that alliance building, international norms, and international institutions present opportunities for states to pursue their interests and seek shelter from the turbulence of twenty-first-century international politics. The second section explores the history of New Zealand's involvement in the Antarctic region, contextualizing New Zealand's current challenges. Third, the chapter examines recent policy documents and scholarly opinions, which suggest increasing security concerns and a firm commitment to protect New Zealand's territorial claim in the Antarctic, including through enhanced defence and intelligence co-operation. The chapter concludes with a summation of key issues and interests for New Zealand in the region and by making the argument that New Zealand and other small states have an opportunity to go beyond shelter seeking and be pivotal advocates for rules-based polar regions that will guard against revisionism and the erosion of existing polar norms.

Shelter from the Storm: Small States' Foreign Policy

New Zealand is a small state. Its population is only 4.5 million people, and while it is a relatively affluent, prosperous, and developed nation, its international, diplomatic, economic, and security footprint is tiny relative to its much larger and more powerful Five Eyes partners. Smallness is not an insignificant concept in international relations. Many scholars have sought to analyze how being smaller (generally based on population, gross domestic product, geography, and self-perception) affects nations' foreign and security policies. Indeed, the major approaches to international relations offer divergent perspectives on how small states should approach theory security, especially as the great powers now appear to be aggressively asserting their interests in international affairs, and as international security norms, including those relating to contested polar regions, seem to be eroding.

According to the realist framework, smaller states seek to enhance their security in international affairs (and ameliorate their lack of power) by entering formal or informal alliance relationships with larger states. To illustrate, New Zealand's entry, with the United States and Australia, into the ANZUS alliance in 1951 was predicated on enjoying the security benefits of being allied with the United States during a period in which New Zealand officials feared the spread of communism in the Asia Pacific, and particularly Southeast Asia. The ANZUS alliance gave New Zealand an assurance that if it, or its close Australian partners, were attacked by any hostile power (as indeed Australia had been in the Second World War), it would benefit from the defence capabilities of the world's democratic superpower, the United States. Alliances provide many benefits for small states, and the pattern of alignment is repeated elsewhere in the world; the small states on NATO's eastern flank are obvious examples. Conversely, alliances entail costs for small states too. They may become entrapped in conflicts involving larger partners (New Zealand's involvement in the Vietnam and Korean Wars could be seen in this context) and may experience a lesser degree of political autonomy. New Zealand left the ANZUS alliance in 1984 arguably for this reason: it wanted to chart an anti-nuclear international foreign policy that did not align with the interests of the United States, and which led to the United States suspending its alliance commitment (and most intelligence sharing) with the government in Wellington.

A more liberal internationalist and institutionalist assessment of the role of small states in international affairs involves small states looking to international institutions to provide for their security—most notably toward the United Nations (New Zealand was a prominent founding member and argued for the rights of small states within the UN system), and other regional and sectoral organizations (Association of Southeast Asian Nations, the International Monetary Fund, Organization for Security and Co-operation in Europe, etc.). Small liberal states like New Zealand have invested in the creation of international forums in the hope that co-operation and mediation at the international level will help to mitigate the more unilateralist tendencies of the larger, more powerful states, and that dialogue and negotiation can lead to compromise and peaceful relations, even when states are confronted with difficult international issues. The importance that New Zealand and other small states have accorded the regional co-operative mechanism governing relations in the polar regions, including the Arctic Council in the North and the Antarctic Treaty in the South, is an example of this. Smaller states arguably have even greater incentives for the creation of these forums than do the more powerful countries, who more often have the means and capabilities to follow their interests unilaterally.

Although alliances and institutions have been vital international mechanisms for small states to achieve security, small states have also been involved in the negotiation and creation of international norms, broadly defined here as expectations of behaviour. Small states have often acted as "norm entrepreneurs" (Finnemore and Sikkink 1998)—the advocacy by small Scandinavian states for bans on cluster munitions and landmines, for example, has been prominent. International norms exist in many different domains, including the polar regions and in maritime security; the United Nations Convention on the Law of the Sea creates legal norms to which most states adhere concerning the rights of nations in the open seas and in their littoral zones. The norms that govern Antarctica, again created through international mechanisms, have been treated for the most part with respect—that the region would not be militarized, and that it would be used for peaceful scientific purposes. International norms relating to maritime territories are increasingly under pressure, however. Chinese attempts to militarize the South and East China Seas; the erosion of maritime norms, including freedom of navigation in international waters; and norms protecting territorial integrity of other states that have been broken (such as in the Ukraine, for example) are among many issue areas in which established norms are being contested and eroded. The challenge for small states will be to challenge this behaviour and maintain the norms that protect their interests and security.

Perhaps the most prominent analyst of small states in international affairs, Baldur Thorhallsson (2019), has argued that through alliances, institutions, and norms, small states exhibit shelter-seeking behaviour. Shelter-seeking theory suggests that small states take certain actions in international relations due to their size and corresponding vulnerability. This involves the reduction of risk in the face of possible crises, help from other states in absorbing international and systemic shocks, and assistance in the aftermath of crises. As Thorhallsson has argued, "small states are dependent on the economic, political, and societal shelter provided by large states, as well as regional and international organizations" (2019, 1).

In its pursuit of Antarctic security, New Zealand has utilized its alliances, leaned on international institutions, and tried to bolster international norms of behaviour. Although these aspects of New Zealand foreign policy do not always work together seamlessly (New Zealand allies, including the United States, have been responsible for eroding international norms too), this conceptual model helps us understand the country's role and foreign and security policy in this region. When analyzing New Zealand's historic role in the Antarctic, shelter-seeking behaviour (through alliances, institutions, and the promotion of norms) is clearly in evidence, as the chapter will now demonstrate.

New Zealand's Historical Engagement in the Antarctic

New Zealand has a long history of exploration in the Antarctic. According to recent research, Māori explorers may have visited Antarctic waters and even viewed the continent as early as the seventh century, and Māori were part of a number of European-led missions there in the 1800s (Wehi et al. 2021, 3). In the more modern era, New Zealand's official engagement in the Antarctic stretches back to 1923, when the New Zealand government co-operated with the United Kingdom on expeditions, and when the Ross Dependency was proclaimed by the British government and entrusted to New Zealand. In this sense, New Zealand's territorial claims to the Antarctic emerged from its Indigenous connections to the region dating back centuries, but also to New Zealand's colonial and alliance relationship with the United Kingdom. New Zealand maintains a right of sovereignty over the Ross Dependency, which includes the Ross Ice Shelf, the Balleny Islands, Scott Island, and other adjacent islands.

In 1957, Sir Edmund Hillary established Scott Base, and New Zealand took over the running of the research station, which is still widely used today for a variety of leading polar research. This was followed by the signing of the Antarctic Treaty in 1959. The treaty aims to ensure that Antarctica is used exclusively for scientific and other peaceful purposes and doesn't become the focus of international conflict. New Zealand was one of the original twelve signatories and was the only country to argue that states should surrender their territorial claims in Antarctica (this is evidence of the lengths small states will go to promote norms and international co-operation; Roberts 2012). The treaty, which prohibits military activity and nuclear testing in the Antarctic, was signed at an important juncture for New Zealand, with the country having joined the ANZUS treaty system with Australia and the United States earlier in the decade and having fought in the Korean War alongside American and Australian forces. In this sense, the treaty was part of a wider context of New Zealand's alignment and evolving security relationship with the United States, a country that had previously expressed a preference for using the Antarctic to test nuclear weapons. The treaty also formed part of a wider pattern of advocacy by New Zealand for international norms of disarmament and denuclearization, including the negotiation of the Treaty of Rarotonga, which established a nuclear-free zone in the South Pacific.

During the Cold War, New Zealand engaged in the Antarctic regularly, including through scientific and exploratory missions and tourism. Since 1965, The New Zealand Defence Force (NZDF) has helped New Zealand safeguard the region, and New Zealand has hosted meetings of the Consultative Parties to the Antarctic Treaty. This now includes providing support to the United States Antarctic Program, including search and rescue support, air transport, terminal operations at Harewood (Christchurch) and McMurdo (the US Antarctic base), Scott Base ship offload operations, and support personnel. Now that New Zealand's Provincial Reconstruction Team mission in Afghanistan has ended, the

NZDF's Antarctic missions are the country's largest, involving up to 220 personnel (New Zealand Army n.d.).

In the post–Cold War era, the focus on Antarctica shifted in New Zealand's foreign policy away from geopolitical competition to a more environmental normative outlook. This was because of the waning interest of the former USSR in Antarctica and the reduction in global military footprint on the US side. New Zealand during this period became a more prominent player in advocating for new environmental protections, which, at least for a time, displaced geopolitical concerns. This extended to New Zealand's own territorial claim and to the wider region and included a role in negotiating the Protocol on Environmental Protection to the Antarctic Treaty (1991). As the associate minister for foreign affairs said at the time,

> New Zealand has been at the forefront of work within the Treaty to prepare for the implementation of the Protocol. We took a strong lead at the Christchurch Consultative Meeting last May in proposing new management plans for areas in the Ross Dependency that require special environmental protection. We have set in place a robust framework and guidelines for the management of activities by all New Zealand visitors to the Ross Dependency. We will continue to show strong leadership and demonstrate the highest standards of environmental stewardship in this most important region of Antarctica. (New Zealand Government 1998)

In 1996, New Zealand recognized the strategic importance of Antarctica, and established Antarctica New Zealand, which coordinates the government's activities in the region and reports to the Ministry of Foreign Affairs Antarctic Policy Unit and the minister of foreign affairs. The agency is housed in the Antarctic Centre in Christchurch, which also hosts the US and Italian Antarctic programs. In more recent years, as the impacts of environmental factors have arguably worsened, including the effects of climate change and overfishing in the region, as well as deteriorating relations between the great powers, New Zealand policy appears to have taken another shift.

Antarctic Crisis? New Zealand Policy-Maker and Scholarly Views of the Antarctic

New Zealand's security environment is changing. This is a multi-faceted challenge for policy makers in Wellington. First, China is becoming a more active player in the South Pacific. Most recently, this has manifested in a tour by the Chinese foreign minister to Pacific Island nations in May 2022 with a view to securing further economic, political, and security linkages, including with the Solomon Islands (which has caused particular political controversy and concern in Wellington). While Pacific Island leaders subsequently rebuffed a "Common Development Vision" proposed by Beijing, which would have led to increased ties with ten Pacific nations, there is a growing political vacuum in the South Pacific that New Zealand and Australia, as well as the United States, will need to close (McClure 2022). This is not unrelated to the Antarctic region—precedents set in China's relations in the Pacific could affect how China seeks to pursue its interests in the Antarctic too, as well as how Antarctic states respond.

Second, on top of the increasing geopolitical contest in the Pacific, the effects of climate change are posing new challenges to New Zealand's interests and role in the region. In this respect, geopolitical change is combining with environmental change in new and novel ways—the need for the Pacific Islands to secure foreign investments to aid their climate resilience efforts is an obvious example.

Third, and relatedly, regional security dynamics are evolving in a way that may lead to further separation between Wellington and its key allies. Jacinda Ardern, and her governing Labour Party, has placed a premium on Pacific and Antarctic engagement, including a plan to invest in enhanced maritime patrol aircraft and vessels (Greener 2022), which will no doubt benefit regional collective security, but New Zealand has also been on the sidelines of some major developments in regional defence dynamics, including the formation of the trilateral AUKUS defence grouping involving Australia, the United Kingdom, and the United States. As Robert Ayson has recently argued,

> In comparison to Australia, there is less tendency to rely on military influence. Instead, New Zealand presents itself as a

small state with a special understanding of the worldviews of its even smaller neighbours. Rather than a preoccupation with great power competition, which Wellington knows is not the uppermost challenge for many of its Pacific Island partners, that means a focus on other problems, not the least of which is climate change. (2022)

There is increased recognition in New Zealand foreign and security policy of the risks posed by increased great power competition in the South Pacific and Southern Ocean. Alongside the accelerating influence of climate change on New Zealand defence and security missions, this challenge features strongly in recent strategic thinking in New Zealand.

Two of New Zealand's most significant policy statements/frameworks released by the NZDF indicate a strong commitment to maintain capabilities and commitments in the region and present further evidence of New Zealand's shelter-seeking behaviour. *Defence Capability Plan 2019* refers directly to New Zealand's activity in the region, including the "priority placed on the Defence Force's ability to operate in the South Pacific to the same level as New Zealand's territory, the Southern Ocean and Antarctic," noting that "New Zealand has strong ties to Antarctica" and is committed to "maintaining our claim in the region" (New Zealand Government 2019, 9). In practical terms, the plan commits to the delivery of a specialized Southern Ocean patrol vessel with the ability to refuel at sea from HMS *Aotearoa*, with a particular emphasis on patrolling fisheries. The vessel will have minimal military capabilities but will enable missions that are longer in duration with a broader patrol area and will support scientific missions. This follows the decision in 2018 to procure four P-8A Poseidon maritime patrol aircraft to retain a common strategic air surveillance capability with partners. Recent plans also include investment in space-based capabilities to enhance maritime and Southern Ocean situational awareness, with New Zealand being one of the smallest nations in the world to invest in such a capability.

Increased investment in Antarctic-relevant military capabilities is mirrored in the NZDF's assessment of the changing strategic environment. The Strategic Defence Policy Statement 2018 recognizes that increased pressure on the rules-based order and resource competition will disrupt

New Zealand's neighbourhood (New Zealand Defence Force 2020, 7). The assessment states that it is New Zealand's "highest priority . . . to operate in New Zealand's territory, including its Exclusive Economic Zone, and neighbourhood from the South Pole to the Equator" (7). Supporting New Zealand's presence in the Ross Dependency and working with other agencies to respond to activity in the Southern Ocean is described as one of the NZDF's principal roles, and the need to monitor and protect the Ross Sea Marine Protected Area is referred to directly (8, 11).

The assessment notes that New Zealand has a direct interest in stability on the Antarctic continent, and that it has a responsibility to contribute to that stability. In examining the changing strategic environment, the assessment also notes that

> New Zealand's responsibilities in the Southern Ocean include coordination of search and rescue activities in the Ross Sea, as well as detecting and responding to illegal, unregulated and unreported fishing. The Defence Force maintains capabilities on behalf of the Government that are able to operate in these distant and harsh environments. The declaration of the Ross Sea Marine Protected Area highlights the importance of Defence Force activities—notably maritime surveillance and patrol—in support of agencies like the Ministry for Primary Industries and the Ministry of Foreign Affairs and Trade in meeting these responsibilities.

It is further stated that

> Interest by both state and non-state actors in Antarctica and its surrounding waters will likely grow over the coming years. This will lead to increased congestion and crowding, as well as pressure on key elements of the Antarctic Treaty System, such as the prohibition on mineral extraction. States are planning and building new facilities. The planned Italian runway in Terra Nova Bay could support broader activities by a range of states interested in the region. Chi-

na has begun work on its fifth base in Antarctica, on Inexpressible Island.

While an evolved treaty system is likely to remain the key framework for governing activities in Antarctica, difficulty in distinguishing between allowed and prohibited activities under the Antarctic Treaty system could be exploited by states seeking to carry out a range of military and other security-related activities. (New Zealand Defence Force 2020, 22)

This is the clearest statement of New Zealand's concerns and interests in Antarctica in recent policy pronouncements by the New Zealand government.

Mirroring the increased focus on Antarctica in New Zealand's defence and security policy making, there have been an increasing number of scholarly accounts by New Zealand academics noting increased concerns about the region. The most prominent polar scholar in New Zealand, Professor Anne-Marie Brady, has noted a variety of concerns in recent publications. First, the presence of the Russian Global Navigation Satellite System and China's installation of the BeiDou Navigation Satellite Station is described as a game changer for those countries' ability to project power in Antarctica. Brady (2019, 253) has also noted the pressure on Antarctic mineral resources, with Bulgaria, Belarus, China, India, Iran, South Korea, Turkey, and Russia all having expressed an interest in accessing them. Given the fundamental nature of these changes, Brady has argued that the New Zealand government's "piecemeal approach" may not be commensurate with the challenges ahead (253).

On China, Brady has stated that it is the only state that has "consistently failed to report the extent of its military activities in Antarctica and the military use of some of its facilities there" (2019, 258). The great powers more broadly, Brady has argued, are using their Antarctic bases "to control offensive weapons systems and relay signals intelligence," (258) which suggests that the very notion of what constitutes territory in the Antarctic may need to be reconsidered in light of emerging technologies. Brady also noted that research into the manipulation of polar magnetic fields (aurora, ionosphere) for information disruption and denial purposes is also a worrying trend (258). The dual-use satellite facilities already in the Antarctic allow for military functions (command, control, communication, and computers, and intelligence, surveillance, and reconnaissance) to be derived from civilian infrastructure.

Other scholars have taken a similar view. Patrick Flamm, for example, has noted that scientific projects in the Antarctic have always had a political element to them, arguing that the recent defence statement by New Zealand "is a clear act of Antarctic securitization," understood as "the manner in which invocations of danger, threat, and risk are used to appeal to the need for political and financial resources" (2018). Flamm also noted that New Zealand's approach to the Antarctic, including new defence investments, is one issue in New Zealand security that commands widespread and cross-party political support, not least because of the environmental activities that it facilitates, including monitoring climate change. Another key issue highlighted by Flamm is the negotiation of the marine protected area (MPA) in the Ross Sea, which is home to more than 30 per cent of the world's Adélie penguins, around one-quarter of all emperor penguins, around 30 per cent of Antarctic petrels, and around half of Ross Sea killer whales (New Zealand Foreign Affairs and Trade, n.d.). The MPA came into effect in 2017 as a result of a joint NZ–US proposal, but, as Flamm has noted, it will only last for thirty-five years before needing to be renewed, and it comes with a host of issues in relation to sovereignty, enforcement, and monitoring. According to Flamm, contentious relations with other powers in the Arctic can be transformed, as the relationships between South Korea and New Zealand in the region has shown: South Korea established a research station and icebreaker capabilities there in the 2000s, and similarly sees its role as a "small" state in normative terms and as a way to achieve wider international influence. As one scientist interviewed by Flamm said,

> We were a small country, but we developed quickly and now the Antarctic programme is a way of gaining a proper international status. It's also about contributing to the international community in a responsible way. They don't think about economic resources that can be gained from

Antarctica but about status and our national brand. A good
reputation will have economic effects as well. (2021, 3)

Scholarly opinion in New Zealand has also been brought to bear on
the economic challenges the country faces in maintaining a presence in
the Antarctic. This is a common theme across the small states literature:
small states have limited resources and therefore face more difficult choices
about how to use them. The reconstruction of Scott Base, New Zealand's
home in Antarctica, for example, is set to cost NZ$344 million. As Lars
Brabyn has argued, "the Scott Base rebuild is estimated to generate 45,564
tonnes of greenhouse gas emissions, which seems ill-advised given the
Government's declaration of a climate change emergency, a housing crisis,
and a public service wage freeze. Many sustainable homes and jobs could
be created back in New Zealand with $344 million" (2021). These types of
pressures are only likely to be accentuated by the challenges wrought by
the COVID-19 pandemic on New Zealand's economy.

New Zealand's Antarctic Interests

What are the key issues for New Zealand in Antarctica, and what are New
Zealand's key interests? As a small state with limited military power, and
one long committed to efforts toward disarmament and the shoring up
of international institutions, New Zealand's strong normative and institutional approach to the region appears to be of paramount importance.
New Zealand takes the view that many small states in the polar North
do: that it does not want the Antarctic (or the Arctic) to become a region
where "might is right." With this is mind, the division between military
and civilian activities appears to become blurred—both globally and also
increasingly in the polar regions. The fact that states can establish what are
ostensibly military camps in the region that are used for civilian purposes
is a difficult issue that will likely come under greater scrutiny.

New Zealand will need to monitor this consistently and effectively, but
it also has wider analytical significance for the shelter-seeking argument
advanced in this chapter. The norms that small states have sought to establish are being contested by hybrid activities that blur the lines between acceptable and unacceptable behaviour. Establishing and protecting norms
will be more difficult in this context. New Zealand maintains a strong

commitment to the Antarctic Treaty system, but as recent analyses suggest, the system may need to be updated or amended and strengthened to allow for greater accountability, transparency, and enforcement of the treaty's provisions. As the security environment changes, it should not be assumed that the treaty system will remain fit for purpose.

New Zealand's ability to protect its interests will depend on its partners (and indeed the strength of other alliance relationships, such as between the United States, the United Kingdom, and Australia). Although New Zealand has not formally been part of an alliance since 1984, its relationship with Australia and the United States will continue to be important. As a small state, New Zealand does not have the military capability or resources to hold or project power in the territory alone. Although New Zealand has invested in its Antarctic vessels and capabilities that will be able to be used to complement the work of other nations in protecting the region, working with Australia and the United States will continue to be a priority.

There is a growing awareness in New Zealand of China's increasingly assertive approach to international affairs. This is based to a significant degree on concerns about China's activities elsewhere, most prominently in the South and East China Seas, but also through its Belt and Road Initiative and its increased level of activity in the Arctic and other regions. China's engagement in Antarctica should be seen by New Zealand policy makers as part of these broader trends. As a small nation with a level of economic dependency on China, New Zealand will be walking a difficult diplomatic line if China's Antarctic activities continue to push the boundaries of acceptability. In this sense, New Zealand, and indeed small states in the Far North, face an increasing security dilemma that stems from their economic dependency on Chinese markets and goods and their desire to have the United States engaged in upholding norms and rules in the polar regions.

Maintaining the Ross Dependency claim and Scott Base will be financially challenging for New Zealand. Small states have small budgets and maintaining overseas commitments is more difficult to justify, especially in the context of the economic hit that the COVID-19 pandemic has wrought on New Zealand. The estimated cost of rebuilding the base, $250 million, is a tall order for New Zealand policy makers. At the same time, the economic benefits that New Zealand derives from Antarctica will need to be protected. This includes maintaining New Zealand's status as a gateway to the Antarctic and protecting fishing stocks, especially as depletion of these stocks in the Southern Ocean has a knock-on effect in New Zealand's exclusive economic zone. As Frame et al. have argued, however, while New Zealand's economic interests need to be protected, the gateway cities to the Antarctic (Christchurch, Hobart, Punta Arenas, and Cape Town) should "act [not] as a proxy for national interests" but as part a "connected Antarctic system of access" (2021, 6).

Finally, New Zealand's defence capability developments seem to be geared toward intelligence, reconnaissance, and maritime surveillance functions, allowing them to maintain an adequate situational awareness of the Southern Ocean, countering some of the technological advancements by potential adversaries in the region, but also—especially crucial to the focus on alliances in this chapter—making a contribution to collective efforts to guard against any revisionism or environmental exploitation in the region.

Beyond Seeking Shelter: A More Assertive Role for New Zealand in Antarctica?

This chapter has argued that New Zealand's approach to Antarctica has been integrally related to its smallness: it has sought shelter in alliances, international institutions, and security, maritime, and environmental norms to protect its interests and security in the region. New Zealand's policy has also closely followed the shifting and turbulent patterns of interaction within the international system and has been a response to geopolitical competition and the overarching dynamic of climate change too.

Shelter-seeking theory certainly implies vulnerabilities and risks in small states' foreign policies, and this is no doubt reflected in New Zealand's foreign policy. But New Zealand has also actively tried to shape regional dynamics and has been effective in doing so. Small states do have agency in international relations, as New Zealand's experiences in the Antarctic attest. The chapter has also suggested that although small states might depend on alliances (or at least strategic partnerships), they have a range of tools at their disposal to pursue their interests, which link security with non-security objectives, and involve asserting influence through a wide range of forums (Steff and Dodd-Parr 2019, 98).

There are opportunities for New Zealand to continue to exert influence. One way this might be achieved is to conduct a more forceful strategic narrative about Antarctica through its defence and security policy: Indigenous connections to the Antarctic could be further emphasized in New Zealand's foreign and security policy statements, and the emphasis should be human and environmental/ecological security concerns, rather than geopolitical ones. The narrative that large states are exploiting the polar regions for their own narrow strategic purposes is a powerful one, and if small states worked collectively across both polar regions, they could form a powerful global advocacy that is both in their interests and protects the regions for their own intrinsic values.

Of course, a different path is also possible, which demonstrates that shelter seeking can happen in multiple ways. This would involve more closely aligning with the United States, Australia, the United Kingdom, and other powers in the region to take a more alliance-led approach to Antarctic security. Doing so may have consequences for New Zealand's ability to promote normative, non-conflictual approaches to regional security dynamics. But in the environment created by the Russian invasion of Ukraine, small states will need to consider their choices and may decide (as Finland and Sweden have done in respect of their decision to join NATO, for example) that great powers do not pay much regard to laws and norms and that harder balancing options are preferable.

Finally, this chapter provides further evidence to suggest that what goes on in the polar regions does not and will not stay there. Antarctic politics have been closely related to the superpower confrontation of the Cold War, and future geopolitical confrontation between the United States, Russia, and China will have impacts in both polar regions. New Zealand's hardening position on the Antarctic and growing concerns about the region are related to events in Ukraine, the South China Sea, the South Pacific, and the Arctic, suggesting what is becoming a big problem for small states: the impact of increasingly globally connected security dynamics. It is not entirely clear how New Zealand can respond to these dynamics in a way that best advances its Antarctic interests. Emphasizing the issue of connectivity, both between world regions and security realms, could be one option—including more forcefully enunciating the idea of connectivity in New Zealand defence policy statements. In this way, a broader range of actors might find they have a stake in the future of Antarctic security and stability and lend weight to New Zealand's efforts to keep Antarctica peaceful and protected.

REFERENCES

Ayson, Robert. 2022. "New Zealand's Foreign Policy Turnaround." *Incline*, 20 May 2022. https://www.incline.org.nz/home/new-zealands-foreign-policy-turnaround.

Brabyn, Lars. 2021. "$344m Scott Base Rebuild Wasteful and Unnecessary." *Stuff*, 23 June 2021. https://www.stuff.co.nz/science/125524065/344m-scott-base-rebuild-wasteful-and-unnecessary.

Brady, Anne-Marie. 2019. "Climate Change: Antarctic Geopolitics and the Implications for New Zealand Foreign Policy." In *Small States and the Changing Global Order*, edited by Anne-Marie Brady, 253–70. Cham, CH: Springer International Publishing.

Burton, Joe. 2013. "Small States and Cyber Security: The Case of New Zealand." *Political Science* 65 (2): 216–38. https://doi.org/10.1177/0032318713508491.

Finnemore, Martha, and Kathryn Sikkink. 1998. "International Norm Dynamics and Political Change." *International Organization* 52 (4): 887–917. https://doi.org/10.1162/002081898550789.

Flamm, Patrick. 2018. "Geopolitics and New Zealand's Antarctic Presence: New Zealand Is Increasingly Mobilizing Resources to Secure a Share of the Southern Continent." *The Diplomat*, 25 July 2018. https://thediplomat.com/2018/07/geopolitics-and-new-zealands-antarctic-presence/.

———. 2021. "An Unlikely Partnership? New Zealand–South Korea Bilateral Cooperation and Antarctic Order." *Polar Record* 57 (E4). https://doi.org/10.1017/S0032247420000479.

Frame, Bob, Yelena Yermakova, Patrick Flamm, Germana Nicklin, Gabriel De Paula, Renuka Badhe, and Francisco Tuñez. 2021. "Antarctica's Gateways and Gatekeepers: Polar Scenarios in a Polarising Anthropocene." *Anthropocene Review*, 20 June 2021. https://doi.org/10.1177%2F20530196211026341.

Greener, Peter. 2022. "Will There Be a Labour Defence White Paper in 2023?" *Incline*, 28 May 2022. https://www.incline.org.nz/home/will-there-be-a-labour-defence-white-paper-in-2023.

McClure, Tess. 2022. "New Zealand and Allies Allowed 'Vacuum' to Develop in Pacific, Former Foreign Minister Says." *The Guardian*, 27 May 2022. https://www.theguardian.com/world/2022/may/27/new-zealand-and-allies-allowed-vacuum-to-develop-in-pacific-former-foreign-minister-says.

New Zealand Army. n.d. "Antarctica." New Zealand Ministry of Defence, accessed 22 August 2022. https://www.defence.govt.nz/what-we-do/diplomacy-and-deployments/deployment-map/antarctica.

New Zealand Defence Force. 2020. "Strategic Defence Policy Statement." http://www.nzdf.mil.nz/downloads/pdf/public-docs/2018/strategic-defence-policy-statement-2018.pdf.

New Zealand Foreign Affairs and Trade. n.d. "Ross Sea Region Marine Protected Area." New Zealand Foreign Affairs and Trade, accessed 10 August 2022. https://www.mfat.govt.nz/en/environment/antarctica-and-the-southern-ocean/ross-sea-region-marine-protected-area/.

New Zealand Government. 1998. "Ratification of Environmental Protocol to the Antarctic Treaty." New Zealand Government, 15 January 1998. https://www.beehive.govt.nz/release/ratification-environmental-protocol-antarctic-treaty.

———. 2019. *Defence Capability Plan 2019.* Wellington, NZ: Ministry of Defence. https://www.defence.govt.nz/assets/Uploads/03acb8c6aa/Defence-Capability-Plan-2019.pdf.

Roberts, Nigel. 2012. "Story: Antarctica and New Zealand." *Te Ara—the Encyclopaedia of New Zealand*, 20 June 2010. http://www.TeAra.govt.nz/en/antarctica-and-new-zealand.

Steff, Reuben, and Francesca Dodd-Parr. 2019. "Examining the Immanent Dilemma of Small States in the Asia-Pacific: The Strategic Triangle between New Zealand, the US and China." *Pacific Review* 32 (1): 90–112. https://doi.org/10.1080/09512748.2017.1417324.

Thorhallsson, Baldur. 2019. "Shelter Theory and Iceland: Options for a Small State." *Middle East Insights* 218:1–5. https://mei.nus.edu.sg/wp-content/uploads/2019/11/Insight-218-Baldur-Thorhalssen-final-online.pdf.

Wehi, Priscilla M., Nigel J. Scott, Jacinta Beckwith, Rata Pryor Rodgers, Tasman Gillies, Vincent Van Uitregt, and Krushil Watene. 2021. "A Short Scan of Māori Journeys to Antarctica." *Journal of the Royal Society of New Zealand* (6 June 2021): 1–12. https://doi.org/ 10.1080/03036758.2021.1917633.

PART III

Polar Coda

Heather Nicol, Timo Koivurova, and Douglas Causey

The chapters in this volume conceptualize the relationship between the polar regions and the challenges for their governance through several environmental, political, economic, historical, and geopolitical lenses. They propose we think of the Arctic and the Antarctic through comparable security frameworks that examine the nature of environment, human resilience, and defence-sovereignty in both contemporary and historical contexts. In some cases, the notion of comity among nations serves as a model for differential analysis. Kelman's analysis of disaster risk response, prevention, and enabling recovery, for example, shows that these are direct consequences of the mutual association among Arctic states and can possibly serve as a model to emulate for the southern polar region. The idea that governance of one region should be a "model" for the other has emerged in the twenty-first century as speculation differs about the consequences of climate change for the Arctic Ocean. Several of the authors in this volume observe that while the historical experience of Arctic and Antarctic polar regions has been shaped by similar geopolitical processes, the actions of the international community in the Arctic are predicated on a very different model of governance (i.e., co-operative post–Cold War processes) than for the Antarctic. Recent events involving the Russian invasion of Ukraine in 2022 may influence the extent of this co-operation going forward, but these have not negated the very real desire among Arctic nations for continuing circumpolar engagement. There are several

Arctic and international treaties that continue to hold the course toward international co-operation.

While the historical geopolitics of the polar regions reflect convergence in some areas—such as mapping and exploration, environmental destabilization, rapid climate change, and the rising importance of scientific polar research as a strategic interest—the differences are profound. Warner's analysis of key principles in global environmental law and their application to the southern polar region highlights the regional application of international law. Even laudatory factors used commonly in the Arctic, such as sustainable development, ecosystem-based management, the precautionary principle, and scientific environmental assessment may pose unique challenges when applied within the Antarctic. This conflict is echoed by Press, who reminds us that despite some obvious equivalencies, there are also considerable differences between the polar regions—not only in terms of their geography and history, but also because of the consequences of different governance structures. A system of layered governance prevails in the Antarctic whereby the Antarctic Treaty System (ATS) provides the common mechanism for national interests and aspirations through consensus.

Nonetheless, the ATS does not prevent geopolitical tensions and national interests from arising. Indeed, Vince explores some of the governance and sovereignty issues experienced by Australia regarding its Antarctic Territory and its adjacent exclusive economic zone. These have either directly or indirectly led to political tensions over maritime boundaries, the use of marine resources, and environmental protection. Similarly, Burton finds the current direction of New Zealand's Antarctic policy is fraught with risk and contention. Layton's analysis of geopolitical and environmental security in Australia's Antarctic underscores the uncertain consequences and realities based on today's observations.

Slightly more problematic in this framing of Arctic versus Antarctic regional governance is the positioning of Greenland. In exercising its powers, it remains a dependency of Denmark. Greenland's status is not so unusual in the context of the myriad Indigenous governance actors emerging within the northern polar region, yet it is not comparable to the types of territorial status ascribed to governments within the ATS. As Menezes notes, Greenland is growing in presence and importance in unprecedented ways, as evidenced by the significance of colonial geopolitics and international relations within the region.

Commonality and difference, comity, and treaty status are among the themes explored in this volume. In fact, there are three clear and definable cross-cutting themes that could stimulate further comparative work in the future. Common threads of analysis are nowhere better defined than in the chapter in which Causey, Kee, and Dunkle observe that the challenges, threats, and realities in the polar regions are best understood through multi-causal analysis that connects the complexity of environmental, human, and defence security. They capture the importance of understanding the interconnectivity inherent in a complex, multi-factorial framework. Driving this complexity is change at the macro and micro levels—from the ecology of the ice edge to the larger-scale transformation of polar ecosystems.

But the authors of this book also recognize a second cross-cutting theme: transformation has ecological spillover consequences, and these changes involve important multidirectional connections between human security and defence responses that require multi-track forms of diplomacy. For example, international agreements that provide the framework for governance through the ATS regulate activities for both the Antarctic continent and the surrounding seas. The division between environment, human security, and defence activity is increasingly nebulous as each of these factors are implicated in a relationship of mutual impact and response.

This notion of complexity resulting from the clear relationship between frameworks of changing regional environments, their governance, and emerging trends in diplomacy, is traced throughout the volume, and indeed leads to a third cross-cutting theme. As all contributors observe, the management of key issues emerging from transformative environmental features contribute to both the transient and complex nature of diplomacy and its successes. Small states may find themselves working toward larger co-operative arrangements, while large states find themselves engaged in more complex and potentially disruptive unilateral relationships triggered by conflicts arising from changing environments. As Kelman suggests, even in the polar regions, disaster diplomacy may be a fraught and unsuccessful strategy for furthering international co-operation. If environmental transformations prompt new understandings of human security and defence imperatives, there is no guarantee or empirical evidence that they will be either peaceful or co-operative, despite the "exceptionalism" narrative that has emerged around features of governance in the Arctic and Antarctic regions.

Is this truly the case? Is each region unique? Much as the Arctic Council has become a forum for promoting international stability through environmental co-operation in the northern polar region, this is also the case in the Antarctic region. As Vince observes, the ATS evolved from a response to potential conflict over territorial claims and superpower competition to a comprehensive regional governance regime. Many of the contributors to this volume thus reference the ATS and its importance in the stable environmental and geopolitical governance of the region, precisely because it includes agreements pertinent to oceans governance and the management of marine resources in the Southern Ocean. Similarly, the nature of intergovernmental co-operation for the circumpolar North has been forged by the Arctic Council.

The exceptional context of polar relations thus underpins the contributions in this volume, although not all contributors would agree on the nature of that exceptionalism. Geostrategic futures may not reflect the stable geopolitical past in either region. Although the Arctic and Antarctic have evolved as regions with relatively stable governance, managed through the Arctic Council or the Antarctic Treaty, the evidence discussed in this volume suggests that the road ahead is bumpy. There are choices fraught with security interests for near-Antarctic states, and choices regarding political alliance for ensuring strategic resources in the Arctic region. The collaborative resolution of intertwined economic and strategic interests among the Five Eyes countries (the United States, the United Kingdom, Australia, Canada, and New Zealand) might establish precedents for the circumpolar North, but it leaves open the question of the changing international relationship in the South. No choices about governance and policy can ignore environmental transformations, particularly because of their geostrategic implications. Layton suggests that there are various scenarios relating to environmental change and its consequences for governance within the Antarctic. Those range from states that wish to keep Antarctica a pristine wilderness for scientific research to those that wish to exploit its marine, genetic, and mineral resources. Warner reminds us that the threats posed by climate change, the associated impacts of ocean acidification, and increased human activities in Antarctica are daunting, given that ongoing implementation of international environmental law principles and approaches continue to present a challenge for the region. The management of the future within this region depends heavily on diplomatic and governance responses and the direction of international law in the future. The chapters in this volume suggest that much of the future depends on the management of geopolitical and geo-economic interests.

Nicol and Heininen argue that there has always been a global element to polar geopolitics and international relations. While rapid climate change and melting ice is opening the Arctic region to new environmental, geographical, and geopolitical realities, it would be wrong to think that both polar regions have not experienced transformative change in the past—or that previous transformations have followed directly comparable paths. Polar geopolitical processes are, and have always been, intimately tied to broader processes of international relations, global development, and geographical change. To this we can now add the global influence of climate change. The lesson here is that we should expect geopolitics to not merely drive regional security paradigms, but also to respond to them in ways that reflect broader international interests in different ways, given that national and regional/global circumstances intersect at different scales. Greenland is indeed an example of one response, as Menezes contends, while the responses of New Zealand and Australia to similar challenges reflect different regional conditions. Most of the chapters in this volume suggest that national contexts do matter, and they offer ways to understand and manage the political ramifications of complex environmental change through diplomacy, innovation in governance, and co-operation. At the same time, they must respond to new international trends, the most significant of which, for security purposes, is not climate change.

The question we are left with is whether there are lessons to be learned from understanding the polar regions in a comparative context. To some extent, the answer could go either way. Certainly, political co-operation as a strategy remains key in both regions. In the northern polar region, the Arctic Council has grown in importance with environmental change, current events notwithstanding. In the southern polar region, similar trends appear to be unfolding, yet in different ways and through different processes that are regionally specific and draw upon different governance structures. Nonetheless, there are concerns that future events and regional geopolitical tensions might also emerge. Will the tensions in the Arctic reproduce themselves in the South in similar ways, or might the governance structures of the Antarctic provide a road map that might eventually be applicable to the North? We may wish to circle back to the beginning of this volume for the answer. The potential for destabilizing change very much depends upon the nature and direction of change in the environment, human security needs, and defence imperatives, and the legal, diplomatic, and governance strategies they encounter. Stark geopolitical outcomes and a legacy of disaster and conflict are not the only options. Instead, they are the result of a failure to reconceptualize the new security environment.

This volume raises the possibility that the polar regions can be understood as comparative and comparable yet differing in detail. Their experience of transformative paradigms in environmental and defence security are comparable and include elements of global human security that are at risk from large-scale changes to sea levels, weather conditions, and the context for both human and traditional security. In the latter case, the dimensions of human security are different, but not incommensurate in their significance.

This volume has outlined some of the specific ways in which an argument can be made for comparative study. As we are writing at a time of political instability, it remains to be seen how events currently unfolding because of tensions elsewhere will affect the polar regions. The test will be whether Arctic international co-operation remains viable, or whether the Antarctic will stand alone as the only peaceful polar region. Regardless, considerable environmental challenges await.

Contributors

Roger Bradbury: Dr. Roger Bradbury is Emeritus Professor of Complex Systems Science in the National Security College, Australian National University. He worked for many years in the Australian intelligence community on the strategic analysis of international science and technology issues.

Joe Burton: Dr. Joe Burton is an Associate Lecturer in the School of International Relations at the University of St. Andrews in Scotland. Prior to that he was Marie Curie research fellow at the Université libre de Bruxelles working on the European Commission–funded project Strategic Cultures of Cyber Warfare (CYBERCULT). He was also a Senior Lecturer in the New Zealand Institute for Security and Crime Science at the University of Waikato. Joe is the author of *NATO's Durability in a Post-Cold War World* (SUNY Press, 2018), the editor of *Emerging Technologies and International Security: Machines, the State and War* (Routledge, 2020), and his work has been published in *International Affairs, Defence Studies, Journal of Cyber Policy, Asian Security,* and *Political Science.*

Douglas Causey: Dr. Douglas Causey is Professor of Biological Sciences at the University of Alaska Anchorage, Faculty Affiliate of the Harvard Kennedy School's Belfer Center Arctic Initiative, and a Global Fellow of the Wilson Center's Polar Institute. An ecologist and evolutionary biologist by training, he has authored more than two hundred publications on the environmental correlates of Arctic climate change, and he and his students are actively conducting research in Alaska, the Bering Sea, and in northwestern Greenland. He has published extensively on policy issues related to the Arctic environment, Arctic environmental security and bioterrorism, and public health.

Brenda Dunkle: Brenda Dunkle is a graduate student at the University of Alaska Anchorage and an affiliate at the Arctic Domain Awareness Center.

Lassi K. Heininen: Dr. Lassi Heininen is Professor (emeritus) of Arctic Politics at the University of Lapland (Finland), Professor of International Relations at the Northern (Arctic) Federal University (Russia), editor of *Arctic Yearbook*, and leader of UArctic's TN on Geopolitics and Security. His research fields include international relations, geopolitics, security studies, environmental politics, and Arctic studies. He lectures to, and supervises, PhD candidates from Finnish and foreign universities, speaks regularly at international conferences, and chairs the GlobalArctic Mission Council of the Arctic Circle. He publishes in, and acts as reviewer for, international academic journals and publications. Among his recent publications are "The Post-Cold War Arctic," in *Global Arctic: An Introduction to the Multifaceted Dynamics* (Springer, 2022); "Arctic Geopolitics from Classical to Critical Approach," in the journal *Geography, Environment, Sustainability*; *Arctic Policies and Strategies—Analysis, Synthesis, and Trends* (co-authored with Everett, Padrtova, and Reissell; International Institute for Applied Systems Analysis, 2020); and *Climate Change and Security: Searching for a Paradigm Shift* (co-edited with Exner-Pirot; Palgrave Pivot, 2020).

Randy "Church" Kee: Major General Randy "Church" Kee, United States Air Force (retired), serves as Senior Advisor, Arctic Security Affairs, responsible for establishing the Ted Stevens Center for Arctic Security Studies, the Department of Defense's sixth and newest regional center, which is being established in Anchorage Alaska. Formerly he was the Executive Director of the Arctic Domain Awareness Center at the University of Alaska, a Department of Homeland Security Center of Excellence. He has led at the Squadron, Group, Wing, and Air Ops Center levels. His staff assignments include US Transportation Command, Headquarters USAF, and the US Joint Staff in both Operations plus Strategic Plans and Policy Directorates. He has contributed to US Arctic strategy, supported domain awareness technology development, and provided defense support to Arctic crisis response. His military service culminated in his appointment as Director of Strategy, Policy, Planning and Capabilities for US European Command in Stuttgart, Germany. General Kee is a Global Fellow at the Woodrow Wilson Center Polar Institute and serves an important role for the International Cooperative Exchange for Polar Research.

Ilan Kelman: Dr. Ilan Kelman (http://www.ilankelman.org and Twitter/Instagram @ILANKELMAN) is Professor of Disasters and Health at University College London, England, and a Professor II at the University of Agder, Kristiansand, Norway. His overall research interest is linking disasters and health, integrating climate change into both. Two main areas are (i) disaster diplomacy and health diplomacy (http://www.disasterdiplomacy.org) and (ii) island sustainability involving safe and healthy communities in isolated locations (http://www.islandvulnerability.org).

Timo Koivurova: Dr. Timo Koivurova is a research professor at the Arctic Centre, University of Lapland, Finland.

Peter Layton: Dr. Peter Layton is a Visiting Fellow at the Griffith Asia Institute, Griffith University, a Royal United Services Institute Associate Fellow, and a Fellow of the Australian Security Leaders Climate Group. He has extensive aviation and defence experience, a doctorate on grand strategy, and, for his work at the Pentagon, the United Sates Secretary of Defense's Exceptional Public Service Medal. His posts, articles, and papers may be found at https://peterlayton.academia.edu/research.

Christian Leuprecht: Dr. Christian Leuprecht is Class of 1965 Distinguished Professor at the Royal Military College of Canada and Editor-in-Chief of the *Canadian Military Journal*. He also directs the Institute of Intergovernmental Relations in the School of Policy Studies and is an Adjunct Research Professor in the Australian Graduate School of Policing and Security at Charles Sturt University. A former Bicentennial Professor in Canadian Studies at Yale University, Eisenhower Fellow at the NATO Defence College, and Fulbright

Research Chair in Canada–US Relations at John Hopkins University's School for Advanced International Studies, he is an elected member of the College of New Scholars of the Royal Society of Canada and recipient of the Cowan Prize for Excellence in Research at the Royal Military College of Canada.

Dwayne Ryan Menezes: Dr. Dwayne Ryan Menezes is the Founder and Managing Director of Polar Research and Policy Initiative. He has long pursued a career at the intersection of academia, policy, social entrepreneurship, and the arts. In his academic career, he is a historian of the British Empire, the Commonwealth, and the polar regions. He read History at the London School of Economics and Political Science at the University of Cambridge, graduating from the latter with a PhD in History. At present, he serves as Associate Fellow at the Institute of Commonwealth Studies, University of London, and Honorary Fellow at the UCL Institute for Risk and Disaster Reduction, University College London.

Heather N. Nicol: Dr. Heather Nicol is the Director of the School for the Study of Canada, Director of the Frost Centre for Canadian Studies and Indigenous Studies, and a Professor of Geography in the School of the Environment at Trent University. Her research is focused on exploring the dynamics that structure the political geography of the circumpolar North, with a specific focus on the North American Arctic and Canada-US relations. Her recent work is focused on cross-border relations, tensions, geopolitical narratives, and mappings of power and sovereignty. She is currently exploring circumpolar geopolitics in relation to globalization, security, environment, and governance. Nicol is a Fulbright Scholar and was the 2015–16 Visiting Fulbright Chair at the University of Washington, at the Centre for Canadian Studies, and the Henry M. Jackson School of International Studies.

A. J. (Tony) Press: Dr. Tony Press is an Adjunct Professor at the Institute for Marine and Antarctic Studies at the University of Tasmania. He was the Director of the Australian Antarctic Division from 1998 to 2009 and has considerable experience in Antarctic governance and in climate science. He is has written extensively on Antarctic affairs.

Joanna Vince: Dr. Joanna Vince is an Associate Professor of Public Policy at the School of Social Sciences in the College of Arts, Law and Education at the University of Tasmania. She publishes extensively in international academic journals and publications across disciplinary areas on oceans governance issues. Her research focuses on international, domestic, and comparative oceans governance; marine resource management; marine plastic pollution and governance solutions; hybrid and non-state, market-driven governance in fisheries and aquaculture; and the effectiveness of governance arrangements in deterring illegal, unregulated, and unreported fishing. She is a recipient of the Harold D. Laswell Prize in 2016 for her contribution to theory and practice in the policy sciences.

Robin Warner: Dr. Robin Warner is an Emeritus Professor at the Australian National Centre for Ocean Resources and Security, University of Wollongong, Australia. Her research interests include law of the sea, oceans governance, international marine environmental law, and climate law. She is the author of more than a hundred publications on ocean law and policy, including *Protecting the Oceans beyond National Jurisdiction: Strengthening the International Law Framework* (Martinus Nijhoff, 2009).

Index

Antarctic Treaty System (ATS) (*continued*)
on the Conservation of Antarctic Marine
Living Resources (CCAMLR), 5; and Koreas,
96; and Scientific Committee on Antarctic
Research (SCAR), 147; stability of, 150; as
umbrella term, 78; and United Nations, 148;
and United Nations Convention on the Law
of the Sea (UNCLOS), 155. *See also* Antarctic
Treaty; Antarctic Treaty Consultative
Meetings (ATCMs); Antarctic Treaty parties
Antarctica: air operations in, 189–90; boundaries
in, 69; Chinese policy in, 7, 10; and
climate change, 1, 148–50, 192–93, 203,
250–51; defence security in, 38; discourse on
militarization in, 151; and East Antarctica,
184, 190–91, 193; environmental challenges
in, 10, 203; environmental protection in,
1, 10; exploration of, 69–70; exploitation of
resources in, 1, 5, 7, 170–71, 195–98; in the
future, 190–93; geopolitical challenges in, 2,
71, 148; and global environmental law, 10,
203; human activities in, 203, 217, 223, 251;
ice issues in, 148–49, 169, 193; international
security across, 1; invasive species in, 149;
New Zealand policy in, 10, 243; remoteness
of from human populations, 149, 203, 223;
science in, 149–51; security challenges in,
3–4; and similarities/differences with the
Arctic, 6, 31, 7–9, 145; sustainable resource
exploitation in, 196; tourism in, 95–96, 150,
162, 168–69; unique international legal status
of, 149. *See also* Antarctic Treaty; Antarctic
Treaty System (ATS)
ANZUS alliance, 152, 229, 232
Arctic: and Arctic governance, 9, 23, 77, 81,
145; and Arctic Council (AC), 3, 10–11;
and Asian Arctic, 17, 20; Canadian-US
(CANUS) co-operation in, 25–28;
Chinese activities in, 22–24, 110, 241;
defence security in, 38, 41, 45; defined,
1, 17; and economic development, 19, 77;
environmental challenges in, 32, 38, 48;
environmental change in, 1, 18–19, 49, 251;
environmental protection in, 1, 65, 74–75,
77, 79; environmental security in, 28, 45; and
European Arctic, 17, 68, 71; as "exceptional,"
8, 25, 47, 250; exploration of, 41, 59–60,
64–65, 67; fauna in, 18, 32; flora in, 18, 32;
in the future, 27–28, 49, 79, 252; geopolitical
challenges in, 2, 24, 46, 238; governance
challenges in, 1, 247; human activity across,
19, 20–21, 49; Indigenous communities in,
27, 31, 33, 43; inhabitants of, 18–20, 32–33,
35, 40–41, 46–48; and illicit activities, 19,
34–35, 46; and marine resources, 6, 10;
and maritime transportation, 5, 19, 33, 49;

and mediation of national interests, 24, 50,
100; military activities in, 28, 34, 45, 47, 62;
and North American Arctic, 17, 20, 25, 28;
reductions of sea ice in, 18–21, 32, 37, 110,
149; resource exploration in, 19, 23, 34, 72,
95; security challenges in, 3–4, 19, 25, 45,
102; security risks in, 19, 23, 25, 27, 46; and
similarities/differences with Antarctica,
6–9, 41, 61, 145, 149; thawing permafrost
in, 18–19, 32, 37, 48; tourism in, 19–20, 26,
34, 46; traditional lifestyles in, 19, 33, 37, 48.
See also Arctic Basin; Arctic Circle; Arctic
Council (AC)
Arctic Basin, 17, 23
Arctic Circle, 2, 17, 41, 90
Arctic Council (AC): agenda of, 47, 75, 80, 83; and
Arctic governance, 11, 25, 43, 46, 250; and
Arctic security, 4, 27, 38, 76; and China, 22,
77; and environmental co-operation, 78–81,
250–51; and multi-track diplomacy, 43, 51;
and non-Arctic observer states, 3–4, 100; and
prevention of pollution and disasters, 93–94,
96; and Russian invasion of Ukraine, 2, 4, 60;
history of, 3, 75; Indigenous groups as part
of, 27, 84; members of, 2–3, 27, 43, 83. *See also*
Arctic; Arctic Ocean
Arctic Ocean: and Arctic security, 26, 50, 52, 76
bordering states, 2, 83, 90, 98; climate change
in, 32, 247; commercial possibilities in, 19,
46; geopolitical tensions in, 47, 66, 76; and
governance, 146; and resource exploitation,
5, 19; and UN Convention on the Laws of
the Sea (UNCLOS), 4, 60; Russian claims in,
76–77; US and Canadian disputes in, 76. *See
also* Arctic; Arctic Council (AC)
areas beyond national jurisdiction (ABNJ),
158–59, 164, 166
Argentina: Antarctic airbase of, 190; Antarctic
claims of, 69, 72, 90, 99, 150; and Antarctic
Treaty, 147, 150, 158; and Commission on the
Limits of the Continental Shelf (CLCS), 161;
and disaster diplomacy, 100; and Falkland
Islands (Malvinas), 72; and Falklands War,
151–53; and UK, 94, 99, 151–52; and US
Energy Resource Governance Initiative, 128,
135
ASMAs. *See* Antarctic Specially Managed Areas
(ASMAs)
ASPAs. *See* Antarctic Specially Protected Areas
(ASPAs)
Asian Arctic, 17, 20
ATCMs. *See* Antarctic Treaty Consultative
Meetings (ATCMs)
Atlantic Charter, 134
Atlantic Ocean, 95, 149

L

Labrador, 89, 111, 129

LNS Greenland, 113

London Mining, 113

London Stock Exchange (LSE), 115–16, 118–19, 131

LOSC. *See* Law of the Sea Convention (LOSC); United Nations Convention on the Law of the Sea (UNCLOS)

Law of the Sea Convention (LOSC). *See* United Nations Convention on the Law of the Sea (UNCLOS)

LSE. *See* London Stock Exchange (LSE)

M

Madrid Protocol: area regulated by, 156; and Australia, 179; and China, 181; and comprehensive environmental evaluation (CEE), 218–20; consensus clause of, 78, 81; designation of Antarctica in, 179; environmental impact assessment (EIA) provision of, 217–18, 220–22; and initial environmental evaluation (IEE), 218, 220; and marine protected areas (MPAs), 168; and moratorium on resource exploitation, 60; parties of, 221; prohibition of mineral resource extraction, 161; and review of scheduled in future, 171; and specially designated areas (ASPAs, ASMAs), 166; and territorial claims in Southern Ocean, 159. *See also* Environmental Protocol (Antarctic Treaty); Protocol on Environmental Protection to the Antarctic Treaty

Malvinas, 151. *See also* Falkland Islands; Falklands War

Marine Protected Areas (MPAs): concerns about, 171; and Convention for the Conservation of Antarctic Marine Living Resources (CCAMLR), 166–68, 216–17; and Madrid Protocol, 168; and Marine Biodiversity Beyond National Jurisdiction (BBNJ) agreement, 164; proposals for, 167–68, 217; in Southern Ocean, 166, 168, 171, 194–95; and UN Convention on the Law of the Sea (UNCLOS), 216

MARPOL. *See* Convention for the Prevention of Pollution from Ships (MARPOL)

Mawson Station (Antarctica), 186, 189–90

Morrison, Scott, 130

MP Materials, 126–27

MPAs. *See* Marine Protected Areas (MPAs)

multi-track diplomacy, 42–43, 51–52. *See also* diplomacy

N

Nansen, Fridtjof, 95

NATO. *See* North Atlantic Treaty Organization (NATO)

Netherlands, 34, 160, 184; as Five Eyes (FVEY) third-party partner, 134; as sponsor of scientific research in Antarctica, 165

New Zealand: Antarctic bases of, 227, 241; and Antarctic security, 231; and Antarctic Treaty, 150, 158, 233, 239; and ANZUS alliance, 229; Antarctic claims of, 69, 90, 150, 181; engagement of in Antarctic, 227, 232–33; interests of in Antarctic, 228–39, 241–43; Antarctic policy of, 228, 242, 248; and Australian territorial claims in Antarctic, 158; and China, 241; and Commission on the Limits of the Continental Shelf (CLCS), 161; and critical mineral supply chain, 132; Defence Force (NZDF), 232–33, 235–36; and disaster diplomacy, 100; and Environmental Protocol (Antarctic Treaty), 233; exclusive economic zone (EEZ) of, 242; and Five Eyes (FVEY) alliance, 132, 134; foreign policy of in Antarctica, 231, 242–43; limited military capabilities of, 241–42; and marine protected areas (MPAs), 168; record of Antarctic engagement, 231; and Ross Dependency, 241; security policy of in Antarctica, 243, 245; security in Southern Ocean, 235; as sponsor of scientic research in Antarctica, 165; and US Energy Resource Governance Initiative, 135; and US National Technology and Industrial Base, 136

NORAD. *See* North American Aerospace Defense Command (NORAD)

North American Aerospace Defense Command (NORAD), 7, 26–27

North American Arctic, 20, 33, 48; Canadian-US (CANUS) co-operation in, 28; defined, 17; illicit activities in, 34; security in, 25, 30, 48, 50, 71

North Atlantic Treaty Organization (NATO), 24, 27, 92, 98, 229; and geopolitical tensions in the Arctic, 7, 98; and Norway, 92, 97; and Soviet Union, 71, 99; and Warsaw Pact, 74

North Korea, 94, 97, 130

North Pole, 41, 66, 68, 77, 93

North Warning System, 26

Northern Sea Route (NSR), 20–21, 49, 111; and changing Arctic sea ice, 110; and Russia, 5, 19, 21, 32

Northwest Territories, 17, 26, 128–29

Northwest Passage, 19–20, 32, 49, 82; dispute about between Canada and US, 20, 76, 77, 98

Norway: Antarctic claims of, 69, 90, 150; and
Antarctic Treaty, 95, 150, 158; Arctic claims
of, 68, 76; as Arctic Council (AC) member,
3, 43; and Arctic Military Environmental
Cooperation project, 2; and Arctic Ocean,
90; and Australian claims in the Antarctic,
158; and China, 97; and Commission on
the Limits of the Continental Shelf (CLCS),
161; and concerns about militarization of
Antarctica, 183; and disaster diplomacy, 9,
89–92, 96–98, 101; and Dronning Maud Land
Air Network (DROMLAN), 184; as Five Eyes
(FVEY) third-party partner, 134; and Koreas,
97; as NATO member, 92; as a neutral state,
92, 96; and New Zealand, 99; and Poland,
101; and Russia, 93–94, 97–98; and South
Pole expedition, 95; and Svalbard, 93
NSR. *See* Northern Sea Route (NSR)
Nunavut, 17, 26, 111

O

orcas, 90. *See also* killer whales

P

Panama Canal, 33
penguins, 41, 149, 156, 238
Peter I Island, 95
Poland, 91, 100
polar bears, 41, 90
Polar Silk Road, 34, 100, 111. *See also* China
Press, Anthony, 186
Protocol on Environmental Protection to the
Antarctic Treaty, 72, 146–48, 233. *See also*
Environmental Protocol (Antarctic Treaty);
Madrid Protocol

Q

Queen Maud Land, 95, 184

R

rare earths: and China, 124–27, 133; in defence
sector, 123, 126; defined, 122; demand for,
122–23; European dependence on Chinese
supply of, 124, 132; exploration of, 34; in
electric vehicles, 122; and green energy
transition, 122; importance of, 124; need
for among Five Eyes (FVEY) countries, 122;
processing and supply in Australia, 129–30;
processing and supply in Canada, 128–29;
processing in UK, 131; supply in Greenland,
116, 121, 132–33; projects in US, 126–27, 130;
supply restrictions by China, 125; in tech
sectors, 122, 124. *See also* critical minerals
Rio Tinto Group, 113, 118–19

Robinson, Jessica, 131
Romania, 185
Ross Dependency, 231–33, 236, 240
Ross Sea, 149, 167, 217, 223, 236, 238
Rothwell, Donald, 159
Russia: Antarctic airfields of, 182, 184; Antarctic
bases of, 185–86, 189; and Antarctic
exploration, 69; as Antarctic Treaty
Consultative Party, 145; and Antarctic
Treaty System (ATS), 10, 152–53; Antarctic
claims of, 5, 99–100; Antarctic interests
of, 4; Arctic bases of, 21, 180, 184; Arctic
claims of, 77, 90; as Arctic Council (AC)
member, 3, 43; Arctic interests of, 4; Arctic
residents in, 41; as Arctic maritime power,
21; and Arctic military activities, 21–22, 24;
and Arctic military infrastructure, 34; and
Arctic Military Environmental Cooperation
project, 2; and Arctic Ocean, 90; as chair of
Arctic Council (AC), 4; and Commission on
the Limits of the Continental Shelf (CLCS),
160; and competition with China and US in
the Antarctic, 243; competition with China
and US in the Arctic, 47; and Convention
for the Conservation of Antarctic Marine
Living Resources (CCAMLR), 5; and defence
security, 38, 47; and Dronning Maud Land
Air Network (DROMLAN), 184; exploitation
of Antarctic marine resources by, 6; in East
Antarctica, 184; interest in Antarctic mineral
resources by, 237; invasion of Ukraine by,
2, 4, 145, 152–53, 184, 242; and Finland,
99; and hostility in the Arctic, 98, 100; and
icebreaking ships, 22; and international
rules-based order, 4; and marine protected
areas (MPAs) in the Antarctic, 167–68; and
Northern Sea Route (NSR), 19–21, 32; and
Norway, 76, 92–94, 97–98; and resource
exploitation in the Arctic, 20; as sponsor of
scientific research in Antarctica, 165; and
Svalbard Treaty, 93; and tensions with fellow
Arctic nations, 24. *See also* Soviet Union;
Union of Soviet Socialist Republics (USSR)

S

Scientific Committee on Antarctic Research
(SCAR), 147, 161, 170
Scott, Robert, 95
sea levels, 148, 252
seals, 41, 156, 214
Second World War, 71, 92
Shenghe Resources Holding Company Ltd., 111,
127, 133
Singapore, 91, 134
South Africa: and Antarctic Treaty, 150